T0326339

MEDIEVAL AND RENAISSANCE CLOTHING AND TEXTILES

THE DUTCH HATMAKERS OF
LATE MEDIEVAL AND TUDOR LONDON

MEDIEVAL AND RENAISSANCE
CLOTHING AND TEXTILES

ISSN 2044–351X

Series Editors
Robin Netherton
Gale R. Owen-Crocker

This series focuses on the study and interpretation of dress and textiles throughout England and Europe, from the early medieval period to the sixteenth century. It seeks to bring together research from a wide variety of disciplines, including language, literature, art history, social history, economics, archaeology, and artifact studies. The editors welcome submissions that combine the expertise of academics working in this area with the more practically based experience of re-enactors and re-creators, offering fresh approaches to the subject.

The series is associated with the annual journal
Medieval Clothing and Textiles.

Proposals or queries should be sent in the first instance to the editors or to the publisher, at the addresses given below; all submissions will receive prompt and informed consideration.

Ms. Robin Netherton, robin@netherton.net

Professor Gale R. Owen-Crocker, gale.owencrocker@ntlworld.com

Boydell & Brewer Limited, PO Box 9, Woodbridge, Suffolk

Previous volumes in this series are listed at the back of this volume.

THE DUTCH HATMAKERS OF LATE MEDIEVAL AND TUDOR LONDON

WITH AN EDITION OF THEIR BILINGUAL GUILD ORDINANCES

SHANNON McSHEFFREY

and

AD PUTTER

THE BOYDELL PRESS

First published 2023
The Boydell Press, Woodbridge

ISBN 978-1-83765-080-4

The Boydell Press is an imprint of Boydell & Brewer Ltd
PO Box 9, Woodbridge, Suffolk IP12 3DF, UK
and of Boydell & Brewer Inc.
668 Mt Hope Avenue, Rochester, NY 14620–2731, USA
website: www.boydellandbrewer.com

A CIP catalogue record for this book is available
from the British Library

The publisher has no responsibility for the continued existence or accuracy of URLs for external
or third-party internet websites referred to in this book, and does not guarantee that any content
on such websites is, or will remain, accurate or appropriate

This publication is printed on acid-free paper

Contents

PART II: TEXTS

Illustrations

TABLES

The authors and publisher are grateful to all the institutions and individuals listed for permission to reproduce the materials in which they hold copyright. Every effort has been made to trace the copyright holders; apologies are offered for any omission, and the publisher will be pleased to add any necessary acknowledgement in subsequent editions.

Acknowledgements

This book would not have come into being without help and support from others. Many people went above and beyond in their assistance to our foray into the history of hatmaking. Harry Duckworth's research on the Hatmakers and Feltmakers of early modern London paved the way for us; he unstintingly shared materials with us and provided comments on our efforts to unravel the hatmakers' history. Charlotte Berry and Chanelle Delameillieure both leaped into answering our queries about their fields of expertise (London guilds in Charlie's case, the handling of wrongdoing in Dutch and Flemish cities in Chanelle's) with great generosity. Rachel Frost, John Lee, and Gale Owen-Crocker freely shared with us their impressive expertise in the field of historical costume. We also thank Rachel Frost for supplying us with an image of a reconstructed feltmaker's bow, reproduced in this book with her kind permission and that of her photographer, Laurence Winram. Many other colleagues kindly answered questions, read drafts, and/or gave us leads and support: Adrian Ailes, Caroline Barron, Stephanie Brown, Giles Darkes, Bart Lambert, Kate McClune, Milan Pajic, Eric Reiter, Remco Sleiderink, Myra Stokes, and Quentin Verreycken.

The language and the manuscript of our Dutch hatmakers presented us with all kinds of technical questions, on which we consulted with subject specialists. Chris de Wulf, Evert van den Berg, and Pieter van Reenen read the section on the scribal dialects and offered both insights and reassurance. We are also grateful to Pieter van Reenen for creating for us various as yet unpublished dialect maps and for his permission to reproduce these and a number of published dialect maps. On matters codicological and palaeographical, we count ourselves fortunate to have had guidance from Erik Kwakkel, Stephanie Lahey, and Daniel Wakelin. The Conservation Studio Manager at the London Metropolitan Archives, Caroline De Stefani, helped us to recover some badly faded text in the manuscript by sending us ultraviolet photographs of relevant pages from the manuscript.

For permission to produce an edition of London, Guildhall Library, MS 15838, and to reproduce images of it, we are obliged to its owners, the Haberdashers' Company, and in particular to David Bartle, the Company's archivist.

The anonymous reviewers for Boydell and Brewer gave us invaluable advice that has made this a better book. We thank Caroline Palmer and Elizabeth McDonald from Boydell and Brewer for guiding this book through the publication process.

Ad Putter's research towards this book was generously funded by the Leverhulme Trust and Shannon McSheffrey's by the Social Sciences and Humanities Research Council of Canada, which together with Concordia University and the University of Bristol also funded Open Access and other publication costs. A grant from the Arts Faculty Research Fund of the University of Bristol also enabled us to employ Gruff Kennedy to provide assistance with formatting and referencing and Tanya Izzard to help with the index. Their help and the financial support of our Universities and external funders are gratefully acknowledged.

Abbreviations

BHO   British History Online

CCR   A. E. Stamp, et al., eds, *Calendar of Close Rolls*, 47 vols (London: HMSO, 1900–63)

CPR   *Calendar of Patent Rolls, 1232-1509*, 53 vols (London, 1891–1961)

CP40   The National Archives, Common Plea Rolls

EETS   Early English Text Society

GL   Guildhall Library

HMSO   His Majesty's Stationery Office

L&P   J. S. Brewer, James Gairdner, and R. H. Brodie, eds, *Letters and Papers, Foreign and Domestic, of the Reign of Henry VIII*, 21 vols in 35 parts (London: HMSO, 1862–1932)

LCA   Stuart Jenks, *The London Customs Accounts*, Hansischer Geschichts-verein 74 (Cologne: Böhlau, 2018), <https://www.hansischerg-eschichtsverein.de/london-customs-accounts>

LMA   London Metropolitan Archives

MED   Middle English Dictionary <https://quod.lib.umich.edu/m/middle-english-dictionary/dictionary>

MNW   Middelnederlandsch Woordenboek

OED   Oxford English Dictionary <https://www.oed.com>

SR   *The Statutes of the Realm*, 11 vols (London: G. Eyre and A. Strahan, 1810–28)

TNA   The National Archives

WNT   Woordenboek der Nederlandsche Taal

Preface

This book is about a community of immigrant craftsmen who tried to make their living in London in the late fifteenth and early sixteenth century. The members of this little community were Dutch speakers, and hatmaking was their chosen craft. That we can tell their story so fully is due to some remarkable contemporary records and documents that have survived in London archives. The most interesting and important of these is a small parchment manuscript that is today preserved as part of the Haberdashers' archives in the Guildhall Library of London. The manuscript in question, Guildhall Library, MS 15838,[1] is barely known because it has never been edited; but it contains among other items the byelaws that were drawn up by this group of Dutch speaking hatmakers after they had organised themselves into a guild towards the end of the fifteenth century. They called themselves the Fraternity of St James in English and het Broederschap van Sint Jacob in Dutch.

Their guild Ordinances are fascinating and unique for reasons at once historical and linguistic. Historically, they are, to our knowledge, one of the few surviving statutes of an 'alien' fraternity in England that operated not just as a social and religious guild but as a craft association. The reasons why this is so unique are explained more fully below, but the long and the short of it is that legally and conceptually the existence of an alien craft association was an anomaly in this period. The guilds of London regulated the production and retail of artisanal produce: to engage in such business you needed to belong to a guild and, in the years around 1500, to be a guild member, be it apprentice or master, you were normally expected to be a native of England or the crown's other appurtenances (Wales, Ireland, Calais, and so on). Those born outside the realm – aliens or strangers in the English lexicon of the day – were thus usually excluded from guild membership, and if they founded fraternities of their own these fraternities were generally religious and social ones and not craft associations. The Dutch Hatmakers, however, broke this rule. The fraternity they founded was a craft guild (though like most other such guilds, they made ample provision for religious and

---

[1]   The full reference in the London Metropolitan Archives catalogue, GL CLC/L/HA/A/009/MS15838.

Fig. 1   Map of the Low Countries. © Jktu21/Dreamstime.com.

social observances too). How they managed this and how they were eventually brought into line are topics for a later chapter.

If the Ordinances of the Dutch Hatmakers are unique on historical grounds, they are also unparalleled for linguistic reasons, for the document was drawn up in 1501 in two languages, English and Dutch. By 'Dutch' here and in the rest of the book we refer to the West Germanic language spoken and written in the area approximately covered by the present-day Netherlands and the Flemish-speaking region of Belgium.

On the borders of the Netherlands and Germany, Dutch is hard to distinguish from varieties of Low German, and in medieval usage 'Dutch' in fact included speakers of both these languages. It is only in more modern parlance that 'Dutch' came to refer to a citizen of the Netherlands. To avoid confusion, we need to emphasize that when 'Dutch' is used of a person in this book it refers to a speaker of Dutch (including the dialect of Flemish and the Low Saxon dialects spoken in the borderlands of present-day Germany and the Netherlands). 'Dutch' or 'Belgian' in the modern sense is anachronistic for this period, since the modern nation states of The Netherlands and Belgium were yet to be born. The Hatmakers came from what was at the time a patchwork of principalities, including, among others, the counties of Flanders, Holland and Zeeland, the Duchy of Brabant (stretching roughly from the modern province of North Brabant to that of Flemish Brabant) and the Duchy of Gueldres, which at the time extended beyond present-day Gelderland into parts of Germany and Limburg. In the later fourteenth century, the Dukes of Burgundy began to bring many of these territories under their jurisdiction, but they continued as semi-autonomous lands with their own cultures, laws, and dialects. As we shall see, the Dutch Hatmakers, too, came from different regions in the Low Countries ranging from Zeeland in the west to Gelderland in the east.

There were, as is well known, many Dutch-speaking immigrants living in late medieval and Tudor England but of their language we possess very little evidence before the second half of the sixteenth century. A Dutch inscription on a tombstone on English soil, a promissory note written in Dutch for an English merchant, the odd code-switched word embedded in Latin or English texts: these are the kinds of scraps on which scholars interested in the social history of the Dutch language in England before 1550 have had to feed. The Ordinances offer something quite different. It is a substantial document that gives historical linguists and dialectologists plenty of material to work with, and it is also the earliest document to have been drawn up bilingually in English and Dutch.

For these historical and linguistic reasons, Guildhall Library, MS 15838 deserves to be much better known than it is. In addition to the bilingual Ordinances, which were copied down in 1501, the Guildhall manuscript contains the agreement, dated 1511, by which the Dutch Hatmakers joined the Haberdashers and so lost their independence as an alien craft guild. To put the manuscript and the Dutch Hatmakers back on the map, we have provided in the first part of this book (Part I: Study) a microhistory of the community whose language and practices are codified in the Ordinances, and in the second part (Part II: Texts) a complete edition of the Ordinances and of some other shorter texts contained in the manuscript.

However, the Guildhall manuscript is not the only source that can bring back to life the experiences of this migrant community. Some of the hatmakers who are named in the Ordinances and the 1511 agreement made wills which have survived, and some appear as signatories in various other archival documents, including, as we shall see, a petition to Parliament of 1531. They also left a paper trail in the London diocesan consistory court records. According to the Haberdasher wardens who brought a case against four hatmakers in 1514, the latter failed to observe the agreement that was signed by the Haberdashers and Hatmakers when the two merged in 1511. Careful study of all these archival remains has allowed us to piece together the story of the Dutch hatmakers in far greater detail than we had thought possible when we first became interested in them.

Their lives and the records they left behind raise a host of questions which we attempt to answer. First, since London evidently afforded these Dutch hatmakers opportunities for improving their lot, we need to ask what skills and techniques they could offer that London craftsmen did not already possess. What made hatmaking in particular an occupation that tempted craftsmen from the Low Countries to uproot themselves and their families to emigrate to London? Second, how did these new immigrants work around the exclusionary politics of the City of London? To what extent did they adapt to the practices and customs of their new working environment or continue to work as they had done in their home country? Third, what happened to the Dutch Hatmakers when the Fraternity of St James, which they founded, was taken over by the Haberdashers? Was this a happy union or a hostile take-over? What do we know about the fortunes of the Dutch Hatmakers after their merger?

In addition to these broader historical issues, there are codicological and philological questions which can, to some extent, be solved through close analysis of the manuscript and the language it contains. What kind of manuscript is this, and who wrote the bilingual Ordinances? As we shall see, two scribes worked on this bilingual text. Did an English scribe write the English text and a Dutchman the Dutch, or was the Dutch and English text copied by two bilingual scribes? If so, where were they from? What, if any dialect characteristics can we tease out of their Middle English and Middle Dutch writings, and do the language and the handwriting of the scribes mark them out in any way as foreigners? The remarkable fact that the Ordinances are bilingual also raises questions: how fluent and idiomatic is the Dutch and the English language of this document? If words and constructions are not typical of the language of the period, are they innovations or aberrations? Did these two languages influence each other, and, if there are signs of interference, can we tell which language was the dominant one? In the five chapters of our study (Part I) we address all these questions, more or less in the order we have put them here.

Chapter 1 considers the factors that made the Dutch hatmakers so competitive in the crowded English marketplace for headgear in this period. Most contemporary people – except for children and unmarried women – wore some kind of headcover, and London had its own guilds that sought to meet the intense demand. These guilds included the Cappers or Hurers, the Hatter-merchants and the Haberdashers, the latter intent on establishing a near-monopoly on the retail of fashion accessories, which hats had certainly become by the later medieval period. And yet despite this competition and the protectionist policies of the City of London, the Dutch Hatmakers managed to corner a lucrative area of the market. As we argue, their success depended on multiple factors. The demand for fashionable clothes and headgear rose steeply following the Black Death, because the resulting labour shortage drove up wages – which in turn fuelled the 'consumer economy' of the fifteenth century. Hatmaking was a good line of business to pursue in this economic climate, and all the more so because changes of fashion were driving prosperous English people away from close-fitting caps towards felt hats with high crowns and wide brims. Producing this newly fashionable headgear necessitated the use of different materials – the best being beaver fur – and different techniques and tools, most notably the feltmaker's bow. Hatmakers of the Low Countries had already by the late fourteenth century developed a special reputation for making fashionable hats. They were initially imported into England, but from about the second quarter of the fifteenth century it was not just hats that were making the North Sea crossing from Low Countries to England but also hatmakers. They settled in cities such as York and London, and it was in London that they set up their own trade association, the Fraternity of St James, in defiance of the rule that aliens could not run a craft guild.

The Fraternity met at Blackfriars, in the Dominican friary, and in Chapter 2 we consider the role that Blackfriars and the 'liberties' of London played in the lives of alien workers, and examine the extent to which they adapted their practices to fit their new working environment. Because the liberties lay outside of the jurisdiction of the city, they gave immigrant craftsmen the freedom to set up shops and workplaces. The friaries of late medieval and early Tudor London also catered for the spiritual needs of the immigrant community: many friars themselves were immigrants from the continent and so friaries could supply pastors and confessors that could communicate with aliens in their mother tongue. In other ways too, the brothers of the Fraternity of St James clung to their social identities as Dutchmen. The Ordinances, while comparable to those of other London guilds in some respects, also have some peculiarities that betray their Dutchness. They suggest, for example, a shorter apprenticeship period, a regionally and professionally mobile workforce, and they contain one of the earliest mentions in English of 'letters of attestation', which journeymen coming from abroad were expected to bring in order to prove that they had completed their training to their former masters' satisfaction. They further set forth measures for settling violent disputes between members of the Fraternity. These procedures for internal arbitration or expulsion and the finely graded system of fines (commensurate with the nature and severity of the injury and harm) were normal in the Low Countries but not in England.

The anomalous existence of the Fraternity of St James as an alien craft guild came to an end in 1511 when the Dutch Hatmakers were absorbed into the ever-expanding Company of the Haberdashers. In Chapter 3 we consider the market forces that explain this merger and follow the changing fortunes of the Dutch hatmakers after the merger. The text of the 1511 agreement, which directly follows the bilingual Ordinances in the Guildhall manuscript, may give the impression that the Hatmakers and the Haberdashers entered into this new arrangement as equal partners, but the reality seems to have been rather different. The register of enrolments into the Haberdashers' Company shows that the Dutch hatmakers never entered the Company as equal members. Cases brought by several haberdashers against particular Dutch hatmakers in the consistory court in the years following the merger lay bare the tensions that arose between the Hatmakers and the Haberdashers as the latter sought to extend their control from retail – their traditional sphere of operation – into matters of production, which the hatmakers, with good reason, regarded as their own area of expertise and jurisdiction.

Another commercial revolution to which the Hatmakers had to adapt was the gradual shift from traditional workshop production, where the master and his small household oversaw the entire manufacturing process, to proto-industrial production methods. The Ordinances already register this shift in modes of production in the form of an explicit prohibition against the outsourcing of piecework, but we can see the commercial revolution very clearly in the 1531 petition of the cappers and hatmakers to parliament. The petition records the numbers of workers employed by individual hatmakers, and these numbers suggest dramatic increases in scales of production. They further show that some of the Dutch Hatmakers of the former Fraternity of St James had thrived and had become 'industry leaders' of the hat business.

The historical changes that confronted the hatmakers are also evidenced in the physical manuscript. The codicological aspects and bilingual format of this manuscript are central in Chapter 4. Unlike printed books, which can be produced in multiple copies in a single day, handwritten manuscripts often took shape over a much longer period, and it was normal for them to acquire later additions and accretions. The Guildhall manuscript contains precisely this kind of historical layering, and the layers are closely intertwined with the changing fortunes of the Hatmakers. The bulk of the manuscript was written in 1501 by two scribes, but some ordinances were added later by the second scribe. Then in 1511 a third scribe added the agreement with the Haberdashers. At some later point, probably after the manuscript had come into the hands of the Haberdashers, yet another hand added the final item in the manuscript: the oath of office to be sworn by newly elected wardens of the Haberdashers. This item of business concerned the Haberdashers rather than the Hatmakers, and so the Hatmakers appear to have lost control over the contents of the manuscript, just as they had ceded control of their Fraternity to the Haberdashers. The bilingual layout of the Ordinances is also discussed in this chapter. The writing of guild records was often entrusted to local scribes. The Dutch Fraternity had a clerk who may have started off the writing, but the second hand was trained in the writing of English documents and was probably that of a local professional. However, it is very clear from the dialect features that both scribes were themselves Dutch speakers, the first probably originating from Gelderland, the second from the southwest, perhaps Flanders.

Both scribes were bilingual and in the last chapter, Chapter 5, we look at their linguistic competence and take a closer look at the relationship between the texts in the two languages: was one a translation from the other or were they, as we believe, more or less independent formulations of the same ideas? We also look at words and constructions that appear in this document for the first time. The evidence suggests that the English language of the Ordinances was not just competent but linguistically innovative.

Finally, a complete edition of the three texts in the Guildhall manuscript is given in Part II of this book. The edition has glosses and notes to explain Middle English and Middle Dutch words and constructions that might otherwise cause readers difficulty.

This book has been, from start to finish, a collaboration between a historian (Shannon McSheffrey) and a specialist in medieval languages and literature (Ad Putter), and there is a rough division of historical and philological matters between Chapters 1–3 and Chapters 4–5 plus Part II. We hope, however, that readers of this book will come away from reading this book, as we have come away from writing it, with an appreciation that these are not separate disciplines but ones that inform and need each other.

PART I

Study

CHAPTER 1

Citizen Guilds, Stranger Artisans, and the Hat Trade in London, circa 1500

MAKING HATS IN LATE MEDIEVAL LONDON

Virtually everyone in medieval Europe wore something on their heads much of the time. Hoods, coifs, veils, caps, bonnets, and hats were central to the market in accessories, an especially important sector of the consumer economy after the Black Death. Headgear also served a crucial social function, marking gender, status, occupation, and age.[1] Different craft workers and merchants had a stake in the various stages that took raw materials such as wool, animal pelts, and straw through processing and fabrication to the market stall: in London, wool carders, spinners, knitters, weavers, fullers, feltmakers, hatmakers, cappers, hurers, hatter-merchants, haberdashers, and other occupational groups were all involved in making and retailing headgear.

In English, the occupational terms capper, hurer, hatter, and hatmaker – four artisanal occupations centrally concerned with making headgear – were imprecisely distinguished from one another and shifted in meaning over the fourteenth and fifteenth centuries.[2] By the end of the fifteenth century, however, clearer distinctions between hurers-cappers, hatter-merchants, and hatmakers had developed.

Hurers-cappers controlled the piecework chain that culminated in knitted and felt caps, a ubiquitous head covering especially for men in late medieval England.[3] Caps

---

[1] Elizabeth Coatsworth and Gale Owen-Crocker, *Clothing the Past: Surviving Garments from Early Medieval to Early Modern Western Europe* (Leiden: Brill, 2018), p. 29.

[2] Harry Duckworth, *The Early History of Feltmaking in London 1250–1604*, Research Paper No. 1 (London: Worshipful Company of Feltmakers, 2013), p. 5.

[3] The term 'hurer-capper' combines the French and the English words that had been in use in the two vernaculars, Anglo-Norman and English, spoken in England in the centuries immediately following the Norman Conquest. Possibly 'hurers' originally worked with hair rather than wool. See Elizabeth Coatsworth, 'Hurers', in *Encyclopedia of Medieval Dress and Textiles*, ed. Gale Owen-Crocker, Elizabeth Coatsworth, and Maria Hayward (Leiden: Brill,

were made throughout Europe, including in England, which had developed a sub-stantial cap-making industry in the fifteenth century.[4] The multiple steps involved in fashioning caps (wool carding, spinning, knitting, fulling, felting, and so on) were car-ried out largely by low-status non-citizen English workers and by immigrants, known in the vernacular as aliens or strangers. A 1512 statute banning the importation of hats and caps to England claimed that 'thre score thowsand persones' were engaged in the many steps of cap- and hatmaking (carders, spinners, knitters, thickers, dyers, shearers, cappers, hatmakers); though 60,000 workers is almost certainly an exagger-ation for effect, there is no doubt this was an important economic sector.[5] In London, citizen cappers, members of the guild, fashioned the final product and either sold it wholesale to other merchants, such as hatter-merchants and haberdashers, or retailed the caps themselves. Hatter-merchants (also sometimes simply called 'hatters' in the late fifteenth century) sold rather than made hats and bonnets, most of which were imported from the Low Countries, France, and Italy.[6] Other merchants, especially haberdashers who sold accessories of all kinds, were also important retailers of hats and other headgear.

Hatmakers, of course, made hats – the term used in English to designate a head covering with a defined crown and a brim, which could be made of straw or of felt, or occasionally of other materials. Little is known of straw hats in this period, although it is clear they were very common, as customs accounts indicate that large numbers were

---

2016), p. 284. By the later fifteenth century, the English terms 'hurers' and 'cappers' were used interchangeably or in compounds.

4   Heather Swanson, *Medieval Artisans: An Urban Class in Late Medieval England* (Oxford: Basil Blackwell, 1989), pp. 50–52; Donald Leech, 'Stability and Change at the End of the Middle Ages: Coventry, 1450–1525', *Midland History* 34 (March 2009), 19–20; Duckworth, *Early History*, pp. 3–10; Kirstie Buckland, 'Cappers', in *Encyclopedia of Medieval Dress and Textiles*, pp. 110–12.

5   3 Hen. VIII, c.15, *The Statutes of the Realm*, 11 vols (London: G. Eyre and A. Strahan, 1810–28), III, 33–34. A group of parliamentary petitions brought by Haberdashers' and Cappers' guilds in eight English cities in 1531, discussed in chapter 3, adduced more specific numbers for each centre, which added up to about 13,000 workers, including more than 5,000 in London and its immediate environs. London, Archives of Parliament, HL/PO/JO/10/3/178/1 through 8.

6   Careful examination of various records (including wills and other personal documents) indicates that the term 'hatter', which appears attached to English men in records in this period (including as the name of a London guild), was synonymous with 'hatter-merchants' or 'hatter-sellers'; they were engaged in importing and selling hats, to be distinguished from hatmakers, who fabricated them. In considering the terminology, we looked at wills from 1374–1570 indexed in Marc Fitch, ed., *Index to Testamentary Records in the Commissary Court of London, 1374–1570*, Historical Manuscripts Commission, JP 12–13, 2 vols (London: HMSO, 1969, 1974); and in the Prerogative Court of Canterbury (National Archives, PROB 11, using 'hat*' as a search term in the occupation field), and at entries in *Calendar of the Patent Rolls Preserved in the Public Record Office, 1485–94* (Henry VII, Vol. 1) (London: HMSO, 1914) and *Calendar of the Patent Rolls Preserved in the Public Record Office, 1494–1509* (Henry VII, Vol. 2) (London: HMSO, 1916). This differs from the interpretation in Ian W. Archer, *The History of the Haberdashers' Company* (Chichester: Phillimore and Co., 1991), p. 61.

imported to England in the fifteenth and sixteenth centuries.[7] They may have primarily served a utilitarian purpose, as a sunshade for those who laboured outside, such as agricultural workers: peasants tilling the ground or harvesting are frequently depicted wearing them in late medieval art. Some images, however, also show wealthier people wearing straw hats for the same purpose of shading from the sun when travelling.[8] The famous Arnolfini portrait by Jan van Eyck (painted in Bruges, 1434) even shows Giovanni di Nicolao Arnolfini indoors with an impressive, black-dyed straw hat.[9] There is almost no evidence of straw hats being manufactured in medieval England;[10] perhaps it simply made more economic sense to import them.

Felting – the matting of animal fibres such as sheep's wool through wetting, heating, pressing, and rubbing – had long been known in England as in other parts of Europe, and hats as well as other pieces of clothing or accessories were certainly made in England from at least the fourteenth century and likely before, though not much is known about such manufacture.[11] Such felt was pliable: it could be moulded, though without support it would not keep its shape. By the fourteenth century, artisans in Germany and the Low Countries also began to use new techniques (described below) to make felt from the fine hairs of animal fur, which created a material that more effectively retained its shape once it had been moulded, allowing for new fashions of hats with defined brims and crowns. These were what late-medieval and early-modern

[7] See for instance, *LCA*, 2.12, pp. 222–23; *LCA*, 3.1, p. 281; *LCA*, 4.10, p. 275; *LCA*, 4.11, pp. 556–57; *LCA*, 4.13, p. 364; and Marie-Rose Thielemans, *Bourgogne et Angleterre: Relations politiques et économiques entre les Pays-Bas et l'Angleterre, 1435–1467* (Brussels: Presses Universitaires de Bruxelles, 1966), p. 243. Our thanks to Caroline Barron for discussing straw hats with us.

[8] Medieval depictions of straw hats – very handily gathered here: 'Straw Hats', *Medieval and Renaissance Material Culture: The Linkspages at Larsdatter.com* <http://www.larsdatter.com/strawhats.htm> – show them generally worn by peasants (e.g. in *Les très riches heures du duc de Bérry, June and July*) but by no means only by peasants (e.g. also *Les très riches heures, August*).

[9] Jan van Eyck, 'The Arnolfini Portrait', <https://www.nationalgallery.org.uk/paintings/jan-van-eyck-the-arnolfini-portrait>.

[10] The only straw hatmaker we have found for this period in England is Martin Johnson, Gelderlander, a 'strawen hatmaker alias spliter hatmaker', who appears among those granted letters of denization on 19 Aug 1530, *L&P*, IV, no. 6600(19). In the Low Countries, too, hatmakers from Gelderland are known to have migrated to urban centres to produce straw hats, which appears to have been a speciality of the Gelderland region. See Antoon Viaene, 'Hoedenvlechters uit Gelderland werkzaam in Brugge omstreeks 1440', *Biekorf* 70 (1969), 163–68.

[11] Elisabeth Crowfoot, Frances Pritchard, and Kay Staniland, *Textiles and Clothing c.1150–c.1450: Finds from Excavations in London, c.1150–c.1450*, Museum of London: Medieval Finds from Excavations in London (London: HMSO, 1992), pp. 75–76; Coatsworth and Owen-Crocker, *Clothing the Past*, pp. 50–52; Chris Heal, *Felt-Hatting in Bristol & South Gloucestershire. I: The Rise*, ALHA Books, 5 (Bristol: David Harrison Printing for Avon Local History & Archaeology, 2013), pp. 2–7.

English people called 'felt hats',[12] and in what follows we shall keep to that usage. The finest felt hats were made of beaver hair, and since beavers had become extinct in England by around 1300,[13] beaver hats were luxury items, and the Low Countries had developed a reputation for making the best. From the later fourteenth century onwards, the cloth-making industry that had fuelled the urban economy of the Low Countries went into decline, but the towns that had once depended on the cloth trade bounced back by supplying the demand for high-end luxury objects, tailoring, accessories, illuminated manuscripts, and also hats.[14] When the Cardinal of Aragon passed through the Low Countries in the early sixteenth century what impressed him particularly was the quality and variety of hats for sale in the city of Bruges.[15]

The first sign that the English customers with money to spare looked to the Low Countries for felt hats comes from 1384. In that year the customs accounts for the port of London list the import of two dozen 'capellis de bever' by merchant Richard Filby, on a ship that probably came from Flanders. By the 1390s, imports of *capelle de bever* were common in the customs records.[16] The felted beaver hats had become distinctly fashionable by the time Chaucer depicted his Merchant in the Prologue to the *Canterbury Tales* (c. 1390). Chaucer says that his Merchant does a lot of travelling 'Betwixe Middelburghe and Orwelle', that is, between Middelburg in Zeeland and Orwell Haven on the Suffolk coast, and he is very well turned out on the pilgrimage from Canterbury to London: 'Upon his heed a Flaundryssh bever hat, / His bootes clasped faire and fetisly' [elegantly] (lines 272–73).[17] Just how desirable a 'bever hat' was is apparent from the crimes of one John Cook, alias Lynton, who in 1390 was sentenced to death for stealing 'a baselard [short sword] mounted with silver, a beaver hat, a silk purse with five silver-gilt rings'.[18]

An illustration of a felt hat of the period can be found in another painting by the Bruges-based painter Jan van Eyck. His portrait of Baudouin de Lannoy, c.1439 (fig. 2), shows Baudouin, chamberlain to Philip the Good, Duke of Burgundy, and ambassador to Henry V of England, with the collar of the Golden Fleece and an

---

12   Christopher John Heal, 'The Felt Hat Industry of Bristol and South Gloucestershire, 1530–1909' (unpublished doctoral dissertation, University of Bristol, 2012), pp. 48–50.

13   Lee Raye, 'The Early Extinction Date of the Beaver (*Castor fiber*) in Britain', *Historical Biology* 27 (2015), 1029–41.

14   Andrew Brown and Jan Dumolyn, *Medieval Bruges, c. 850–1550* (Cambridge: Cambridge University Press, 2018), pp. 264–67, and on hatmakers, see p. 242.

15   Don Antonio de Beatis, *Voyage du Cardinal d'Aragon (1517–1518)*, ed. And trans. Madeleine Havard de la Montagne (Paris: Perrin, 1913), p. 110. For an English translation, see J. T. Hale and J. M. A. Lindon (trans.), *The Travel Journals of Antonio de Beatis* (London: Hakluyt Society, 1976), p. 97.

16   See *LCA*, 1.4, p. 111 for the 1384 record, and *LCA*, 1.5, pp. 265–66 for the index entry for many records in the 1390s.

17   Larry D. Benson, ed., *The Riverside Chaucer* (Boston: Houghton Mifflin, 1987).

18   He escaped execution by intercession of the queen: *CPR 1388–92*, p. 328. Our thanks to Adrian Ailes for this reference.

imposing fur hat that flaunts his high social status.[19] As Van Eyck's painting shows, felt hats created opportunities for displays of fashion, and the fashion in headgear, for those who could afford it, was away from tight-fitting caps to hats with wide brims and high tops. By the mid-fifteenth century such hats had become indispensable to the modish young gentleman. John Paston II wrote to his younger brother, John III, in 1469, directing him to send 'hastely' a hat from London, for he could not venture out of doors with those he had, as 'they be so lewde': so please, he reiterated, send 'a blak or tawny hat'.[20]

The skills and processes for making felt hats had developed in the Netherlands, Flanders, northern France, and Germany in the fourteenth century and remained the preserve of specialised artisans from those regions well into the sixteenth. These artisans refined the making of hats both by using high-quality fur from animal pelts to make the felt from which they were fabricated, and by developing the skill of 'bowing' the fibres to ready them for felting. The tool that had advanced that skill was the felt-maker's bow, shown below in a modern reconstruction (fig. 3) by the historical costume-maker Rachel Frost, who uses traditional techniques to make felt hats.

Kathleen Walker-Meikle who saw Rachel Frost in action describes the production process as follows:

> The beaver's guard hairs (which are long and wiry) were first plucked out by hand. Only the down hair, which would then be shaved from the pelt, can be used for felting. The cut fur is laid before the bow carder. The felter plucks the string with a wooden pin, which creates vibrations, and the fur is thus teased and 'mixed' up. Once carded in this way, the fur can be piled onto a surface ready for the next step.[21]

The next steps were steaming, compressing, shaping the matted felt around a hat block, and stiffening the interior with glue. The hat could then be lined and decorated with feathers.

According to Walker-Meikle, the feltmaker's bow which revolutionised the making of felt hats was not introduced into England until the second half of the sixteenth century by Huguenot refugees, but our evidence suggests that Dutch hatmakers may have brought them in earlier than that. The rise and spread of the technology can be traced

---

[19] Van Eyk's paintings are so detailed that the fabric of his painted hats can be determined on close inspection. The fur hairs of the hat are visible in the close-ups viewable at <https://www.smb.museum/en/museums-institutions/gemaeldegalerie/collection-research/conservation-care/jan-van-eycks-portrait-of-baudouin-de-lannoy/>. Similarly, the tall black hat in Van Eyck's Arnolfini portrait can be identified on close inspection as one made of straw, and not of beaver fur as is often claimed.

[20] Norman Davis, ed., *The Paston Letters and Papers of the Fifteenth Century*, 2 vols (Oxford: Clarendon Press, 1971), I, 540–41.

[21] Kathleen Walker-Meikle, 'Felt-and Hat-Making Workshop (School of Historical Dress)', *Renaissance Skin*, 2018 <https://renaissanceskin.ac.uk/news/felt-and-hat-making-workshop-school-historical-dress/>. We have emended 'wool' to 'fur'. See also John Thompson, *A Treatise on Hat-making and Felting* (Philadelphia: Henry Carey Baird, 1868), pp. 38–39.

Fig. 2   Jan van Eyck, Portrait of Baudouin de Lannoy, c. 1439. © BPK, Gemäldegalerie, Staatliche Museen, Berlin.

Fig. 3 The hatmaker Rachel Frost in journeyman's dress with a modern reconstruction of a feltmaker's bow. Photograph Laurence Winram. © Rachel Frost.

in the iconography of St James the Less. In later medieval iconography, he is typically represented with a fuller's club, used for beating and cleaning wool; but from the late fourteenth century onwards he is also depicted with a bow which probably represents the hatmaker's bow, for St James was the favourite patron saint of hatmakers. Perhaps the earliest depiction of St James with a feltmaker's bow, rather than a fuller's club, is a stone sculpture of the saint in the south portal of Augsburg Cathedral (c.1356).[22] About a century later, this iconography appears in England, the earliest example there being the statue of St James the Less on the upper tier of saints on the West Front of Exeter Cathedral, sculpted in the 1480s.[23] Carrying a spear in his left hand, he holds the feltmaker's bow in his right. From London itself, and from around the same time as the Dutch hat-making Fraternity of St James was active there, comes a gold figure of St James holding a feltmaker's bow (the string is now missing) (fig. 4).[24] This little statuette was probably imported into London from the Low Countries, for the saint is named 'Jacob', not 'James',[25] just as he is in the Dutch text of the Ordinances. Locally produced in London and dated 1536 is a set of apostle spoons including one with a decorative finial showing St James the Less, looking exactly as he does in the Flemish statuette.[26] The reason why the Dutch Hatmakers of London chose James (or 'Jacob') as their patron saint will now be clear: they made felt hats (see the references to 'feltes' in articles 18 and 23) and presumably wielded the feltmaker's bow for which St James had become known.

Before migrant hatmakers began plying their craft in England, perhaps as early as the 1420s, felt hats were imported into England, such imports being recorded from at least the fourteenth century onward.[27] The customs accounts of the late-medieval period show considerable fluctuations over the fifteenth and sixteenth centuries in imports of headgear of various kinds (caps, bonnets, hats). Documented hat imports began to expand in the later 1430s[28] and hit a peak in the customs records in 1449 and 1450, when more than 38,000 felt hats were imported, mostly by Dutch and German merchants.[29] This was clearly a significant consumer commodity in the mid-fifteenth century.

---

[22]   Richard P. Bedford, *St James the Less: A Study in Christian Iconography* (London: Quaritch, 1911), p. 26. Not much later (1377) is the Escutcheon of the Hatmakers' guild of Cracow, showing a beaver hat and a felt-maker's bow: J. F. Crean, 'Hats and the Fur Trade', *Canadian Journal of Economics and Political Science* 28 (1963), 373–86.

[23]   Bedford, *St James the Less*, p. 49. Bedford erroneously gives the date as fourteenth century.

[24]   Bedford, *St James the Less*, p. 27.

[25]   'The Apostle James the Younger', *Victoria and Albert Museum* <https://collections.vam. ac.uk/item/O91807/the-apostle-james-the-younger-figure-unknown/>.

[26]   Private collection; reproduced and discussed by J. W. Caldicott, *The Values of Old English Silver and Sheffield Plate from the XVth to the XIXth Centuries* (London: Bemrose, 1906), pp. 36–37.

[27]   *LCA*, 1.4, 206, 207; *LCA*, 1.5, 262, 265–66, 275.

[28]   *LCA*, 2.6, pp. 234–35; *LCA*, 2.7, pp. 159–60; *LCA*, 2.8, p. 189; *LCA*, 2.9, pp. 376–77.

[29]   *LCA*, 2.10, calculated from entries at p. 276. Marie-Rose Thielemans (*Bourgogne et Angleterre*, p. 243) calculated that 26,826 felt hats entered the city of London between 1 April and 25

Fig. 4   Small silver parcel-gilt figure of the Apostle James the Younger, 1500–19, of Dutch or German make. © Victoria and Albert Museum.

The lively London trade in hats does not need to be left to our imagination because it is evoked in the poem *London Lickpenny* (c. 1440), formerly attributed to John Lydgate. The poem relates the experiences of a countryman from Kent who goes to London to seek justice at the court of Westminster, only to discover that without money he is nothing. Once outside the doors of Westminster Hall, he hears the voices of Flemings:

> In all Westminstar Hall I could find nevar one
> That for me would do, thowghe I shuld dye.
> Without the dores were Flemings grete woon;
> Upon me fast they gan to cry
> And sayd, "Mastar, what will ye copen or by —
> Fine felt hatts, spectacles for to rede?"
> Of this gay gere, a great cause why
> For lake of money I might not spede. (49–56)[30]

The 'fine felt hatts' are here paired with 'spectacles' which were also imported in large numbers from the Low Countries until the first London spectacle makers, again immigrants from the Low Countries, started to make them on English soil in the 1440s.[31] The poet registers the Dutch connection of spectacles and beaver hats not only by naming the hawkers as 'Flemings' but also by imitating their language. *Copen*, conveniently glossed as 'by' (buy), was authentically Flemish, also as regards the spelling with <c> (<k> being the spelling found in northern Dutch dialects). It is tempting to imagine the Flemings here as peddlers selling their wares on the street,[32] but this may not be appropriate. The merchandise is costly and upmarket, 'gay gere' (finery), fit for 'masters', and beyond the means of the narrator. Such merchandise was in fact for sale in Westminster Hall. In this period, the hall was lined with shopkeepers' stalls, which were let out by the Warden of the Fleet as *ex officio* keeper of the palace. In 1489 he charged 6s. 8d. a year for every ten feet occupied,[33] a price a peddler could hardly afford. The vocal 'Flemings' in *London Lickpenny* were probably stationed 'without the dores' by the entrance to Westminster Hall to entice passers-by to visit the stall in the hall, where the latest fashion was on display. It was still so in the days of Samuel Pepys, who reports in his diary (20 January

---

September 1450. Numbers continued to remain high in the 1450s and 1460s: *LCA*, 2.12, pp. 222–23; *LCA*, 3.1, p. 281; *LCA*, 3.2, p. 300.

30 '*London Lickpenny*', in *Medieval English Political Writings*, ed. James M. Dean, TEAMS Middle English Texts (Kalamazoo, MI: Medieval Institute, 1996).

31 Joshua Ravenhill, 'The Earliest Recorded Spectacle Makers in Late Medieval England: Immigration and Foreign Expertise', *Notes and Queries* 65 (2018), 11–13, and Michael Rodes, 'A Pair of Fifteenth-Century Spectacles Frames from the City of London', *The Antiquaries Journal* 62 (1982), 57–73.

32 As does Jonathan Hsy, 'City', in *A Handbook of Middle English Studies*, ed. Marion Turner, (Hoboken: New Jersey: Wiley, 2013), pp. 315–29.

33 Sir John Baker, *Oxford History of the Laws of England*, VI, 1483–1558 (Oxford: Oxford University Press, 2003), p. 128.

1659/60), 'Thence to Westminster Hall where Mrs Lane and the rest of the maids had [bought] their white scarfs'.[34]

Around the time that *London Lickpenny* was written, 'Flemings' were beginning to make felt hats in London. Customs accounts from the 1420s show the import of 'hatte here' (hat hair) and 'hatte wolle'. This was presumably wool from sheep (especially merino wool) and hair from beavers, goats,[35] and other mammals suitable for the making of felt for hats.[36] The importers were almost invariably Dutch or German and their buyers in England seem to have been their hatmaker countrymen who had settled in England.[37] By the 1430s, we begin to see the names of those Dutch hatmakers who had migrated to England in government records. Below we list the names of the earliest Dutch hatmakers we have found in these records.[38]

Table 1: Early Evidence for Dutch Hatmakers in England, 1400–70

1436	Godfrey van Elest of Southwark, hatmaker, born in the bishopric of Liège, CPR 1429–36, 552
1436	John Sonne of London, hatmaker, born in Gelderland, CPR 1429–36, p. 551
1440	Arnold Arnoldesson, hatmaker, TNA, E179/184/21
1440	John Lyoner of Southwark, hatmaker, TNA, E179/184/211
1446	Clays Hattmaker, importer of 'hat wool' to London, LCA 2.9, p. 83
1457	Albright Sas of London, 'hattemaker', CCR 1454–61, p. 374
1458	John Derykson of Westminster, beerbrewer and hatmaker; CCR 1454–61, 279, p. 304
1459	John Gisbertson alias van Bevon of Southwark, 'hattemaker', CCR 1454–61, p. 438
1461	Nicholaus Wilde of York, 'felthatmaker', Register of the Freemen of York, I, p. 182
1462	John Mogan of York, 'felthatmaker', Register of the Freemen of York, I, p. 183

[34] https://www.pepysdiary.com/diary/1660/01/20/.

[35] For the use of goat hair in the manufacture of felt hats, see the bill obligatory of 1455 by the Antwerp hatmaker Cornelijs Laureyss, who owed the London haberdasher William Welbec 'vilten hoeye van boxhare gemaect' (felt hats made of goat hair): Antwerp, Municipal Archives, FelixArchief, Regesten van de schepenregisters, SR#50.

[36] Duckworth, *Early History*, 9–10; Rosemary Weinstein, *The History of the Worshipful Company of Feltmakers, 1604–2004* (Chichester: Phillimore, 2004), pp. 17–22.

[37] *LCA*, 2.4, p. 277; *LCA*, 2.6, pp. 234–35; *LCA*, 2.7, p. 106; *LCA*, 2.9, pp. 83, 376.

[38] We list all Dutch hatmakers before 1470, when references to Dutch hatmakers become more plentiful (non-Dutch hatmakers are rare in these records, some of which are of course skewed as they are alien tax lists). Our list builds on, but extends, the data available in J. L. Bolton, ed., *The Alien Communities of London in the Fifteenth Century: The Subsidy Rolls of 1440 & 1483–4* (Stamford: Paul Watkins, Richard III and Yorkist History Trust, 1998) (hatmakers at p. 122) and the England's Immigrants Database (<www.englanddsimmigrants.com>).

1462, 1467	Deryk de Wale (Dedericus de Vale) of Southwark, hatmaker, CCR 1461–68, pp. 145, 452
1463	Peter Knyfe of York, 'felthatmaker', Register of the Freemen of York, I, p. 183
1463	Godfrey Geldrope of London, hatmaker, CCR 1468–76, p. 409
1464	Peter Williamson of York, hatmaker, Register of the Freemen of York, I, p. 184
1464	John van Acon of York, hatmaker, Register of the Freemen of York, I, p. 185
1465	Nicholas Gilbert of York, hatmaker, Register of the Freemen of York, I, p. 186
1465	John Butwell of Surrey, hatmaker, TNA, E 179/236/94, m. 1
1465	John Holt of Surrey, hatmaker, TNA, E 179/236/94, m. 1
1465	Deryk Isbrand of Surrey, hatter, TNA, E 179/236/94, m. 1
1465	Herman Gerardson of Surrey, hatter, TNA, E 179/236/94, m. 1
1466	John van Beregyn of Southwark, hatmaker, CCR 1461–68, p. 331
1467	Adrian Ale of London, hatmaker, Mackman and Stevens, BHO CP 40 Calendar,* TNA, CP 40/823, rot. 322; CP 40/825, rot. 123d
1468	Peter van Cleve of Southwark, hatmaker, Mackman and Stevens, BHO CP 40 Calendar, TNA, CP 40/828, rot. 210d
1469	John Moens of York, hatmaker, Register of the Freemen of York, I, p. 190

* Jonathan Mackman and Matthew Stevens, 'Court of Common Pleas: The National Archives, CP40, 1399–1500', (*British History Online*, 2010) <http://www.british-history.ac.uk/no-series/common-pleas/1399-1500>; the cases may be accessed in this online resource by the National Archives references that follow.

A list of aliens in the kingdom in 1436 includes two hatmakers, Godfrey van Elest of Southwark, born in the bishopric of Liège, and John Sonne of London, born in Gelderland. The raw materials from which they made their hats could have been provided by fellow Dutchman Clays Hattmaker, who in the mid-1440s imported 400 lb of 'hat wool' through the port of London (and perhaps himself practised the trade his surname suggests). Though references to the trade of hatmaker of any nationality remain sparse in accessible English records through the first half of the fifteenth century, by the 1460s references begin to multiply, virtually always attached to men whose names were probably or certainly Dutch. In most cases the type of hat these men made is not specified, but in the case of three men admitted to the freedom of the city of York in the early 1460s (Petrus Knyfe, Johannes Mogan and Nicholaus Wilde), the trade was described as 'felthatmaker'.[39] All three were probably Dutch speakers. 'Knijf' is a very old Dutch surname;[40] Mogan is again found in the York House Books in 1484, in an entry certify-

---

[39] Heal, 'The Felt Hat Industry', p. 48; Swanson, *Medieval Artisans*, p. 50; Duckworth, *Early History*, pp. 9–10.

[40] See 'Knijf', *Nederlandse Familienamenbank* <https://www.cbgfamilienamen.nl/nfb/>.

ing that 'John Mogan, ducheman' is a freeman and denizen of the city;[41] and Nicholaus Wilde may be the same Nicholas Wilde who received letters of denization in 1470, where he is said to have been born in Kampen in the Bishopric of Utrecht. His profession is there described as skinner, but, of course, skinners, like felt hatmakers, worked with fur.[42] By the 1470s, the number of artisans designated as 'hatmaker' increases, almost all of them Dutch immigrants by the evidence of their names or by more explicit evidence.[43]

The Dutch hatmakers settled in various parts of the metropolitan region. In the 1483–84 Alien Subsidy roll, ten 'Teutonic' hatmakers, nine hatmaker servants, and three hatters were listed for London and Middlesex; about half lived in Portsoken ward on the east end outside the walls, and the others in the central or western wards in the City (Vintry, Candlewick Street, Castle Baynard).[44] Dutch hatmakers also made their homes in Southwark by the late fifteenth and sixteenth century and perhaps were more plentiful there than on the north side of the Thames: almost a third of hatmakers found in the records of the court of Common Pleas between 1460 and 1540 resided in Southwark and Bermondsey, significantly outnumbering those who gave London itself as their place of residence.[45] Southwark had evidently become an important centre for hatmaking by the time the Fraternity of St James had formed; Martha Carlin found from the archbishop's manor court rolls in Southwark between 1504 and 1511 that hatmaker was the second most common occupation after brewer, another Dutch-dominated industry.[46] Whether hatmakers working south of the Thames became members of the Blackfriars fraternity is unclear, but it is likely.

The beginnings of domestic production of felt hats by these Dutch migrants may correlate with a decline in the import of these products. According to customs records, the number of hats brought from overseas to the port of London fell precipitously in the later fifteenth century. To be sure, the figures from the customs records likely reflect more than raw imports: the last decades of the fifteenth century were marked by considerable controversy over customs collection. Nonetheless, it is significant that imports never again reached the level of the mid-fifteenth century, probably because domestic manufacture now served much of the market.[47] The customs accounts also

[41] Meg Twycross, 'Some Aliens in York and Their Overseas Connections: up to c.1470', *Leeds Studies in English* 29 (1998), 359–80.

[42] Bolton, *Alien Communities*, p. 56, n 49.

[43] As shown by a search for 'hatmaker' in the database of documented aliens: *England's Immigrants 1330–1550: Resident Aliens in the Late Middle Ages* <http://www.englandsimmigrants.com>.

[44] Following the index entries in Bolton, *Alien Communities* , p. 184.

[45] Searching 'hatmaker' in Mackman and Stevens, 'Court of Common Pleas', and in Rosemary Simons and Vance Mead, 'CP40 Indices', in *Anglo-American Legal Tradition*, ed. Robert C. Palmer <http://aalt.law.uh.edu/Indices/CP40Indices/CP40_Indices.html>.

[46] Martha Carlin, *Medieval Southwark* (London: Hambledon Press, 1996), pp. 280–84.

[47] *LCA*, 4.10, pp. 428, 430, 442; *LCA*, 4.11, pp. 538, 541, 556–57; *LCA*, 4.13, pp. 349, 352, 364. It should be noted that from the 1510s import numbers rose again, though not to mid-fifteenth-century heights: *LCA*, 4.11, pp. 556–57 for 1513–14 has entries which total about 16,000 hats,

shed some light – though there are still some large shadows – on how the form of hats and the terms used to identify them changed over the century and a half these customs accounts cover. The shifts in nomenclature of the headgear indeed make it difficult to determine when high-quality felted hats, as opposed to cheaper wares, are meant: the *capella de bever* in the late fourteenth-century accounts was presumably the same as Chaucer's 'Flaundrissh bever hat' and indeed in the 1390s the term *capella de bever* was shifting to *bever hatte*.[48] From the 1430s through to the 1450s, *bever hatte* disappeared from the records and instead *felt hatte* became the most common term. These were more or less the same item, although the use of beaver hair likely became less prominent as the fifteenth century went on.[49] In turn, both 'felt' and 'beaver' hats may have been similar at least in material if not in shape to two kinds of hats common in the records from the 1460s into the 1480s, *Sent Omers hattes* and *Copyn hattes*. 'Sent Omers hattes' were presumably made in the town of Saint Omer in the Burgundian Netherlands, but the way the term was used suggests a specific style (unfortunately unknown) as well as location of manufacture; whether they were made of felt is also unknown.[50] A 'Copyn hatte' (see fig. 5) was a half-translation of the Dutch *Jacobshoet*, Coppyn or Coppen being a Dutch diminutive for Jacob[51] – an interesting bilingual and bicultural coining. A *Jacobshoet* was a felt hat with a wide brim folded up at the front and a relatively shallow crown; its name came from its association with pilgrims to the shrine of St James (or Jacobus) of Compostela in Castile.

Both the terms 'Copyn hattes' and 'Sent Omers hattes' disappear from the records after the early 1480s, at the same time as imports of headgear in general fall off. In the 1510s when the import of headgear once again rose in volume, many customs entries simply

---

including 9,000 simply designated 'hats' and 7,000 straw hats. *LCA*, 4.13, p. 364 has entries for about 14,000 hats evenly split between 'hats' and 'straw hats'.

48   *LCA*, 1.6, pp. 288, 295; *LCA*, 2.1, p. 239.

49   Scholars have noted the extinction of beavers in Europe through over-hunting and thus the substitution of other fibres for beaver hair in the making of superior felt; note, however, that beaver pelts continued to be imported to England into the early sixteenth century (e.g. *LCA*, 4.11, p. 536; *LCA*, 4.15, p. 348; cf. Elspeth M. Veale, *The English Fur Trade in the Later Middle Ages*, London Record Society 38 (London: London Record Society, 2003) <https://www.british-history.ac.uk/london-record-soc/vol38>, pp. 158–59, 175–76). Whether these beaver pelts were destined for hatmakers' shops or used more generally as fur is hard to know, though certainly beaver was frequently used for garments – see Veale, *English Fur Trade*, pp. 148–49. In any case, it is likely that other kinds of animal fibres came to be used in felt making during most of the sixteenth century, until North American beaver pelts became available from about the 1570s.

50   *LCA*, 3.2, p. 300; *LCA*, 3.3, pp. 232–33; *LCA*, 3.4, p. 293; *LCA*, 3.5, p. 292.

51   *LCA*, 3.1, p. 281; *LCA*, 3.2, p. 300; *LCA*, 3.3, pp. 232–33; *LCA*, 3.4, p. 293; *LCA*, 3.5, p. 292. See 'jacobshoed', *Historische Woordenboeken* <https://gtb.ivdnt.org/search/>. Its only attestation there is eighteenth century, but the word is medieval. See the earlier fifteenth-century example in A. G. B. Schayes, ed., 'Inventaire des joyaux et curiosités du duc de Brabant, Jean IV, en 1419', *Annales de l'Académie royale d'archéologie de Belgique* 9 (1852), 156–58 (p. 157).

Fig. 5 Saint James the Great wearing a 'jacobshoet' or coppyn hat, the traditional
pilgrim's headgear. Lucas Cranach the Elder, "Saint James the Great." © Harvard Art
Museums collections online, R906, https://hvrd.art/o/242552.

recorded 'hattes', along with 'strawn hattes' and some other variations; presumably the unqualified term designated felt hats, a term otherwise unattested in the import records in this period. Though by the early sixteenth century felt hats were certainly being manufactured in England, they were not yet made by English craftsmen: hatmaking in England in the decades around 1500 was the preserve of immigrants. The craft of fabricating moulded hats from high-quality felt was evidently not known to English hatters or cappers in this period. The hatmakers in London and elsewhere in the kingdom we have identified were all, as far as we can tell, immigrants from the Low Countries and Normandy.

Given the other evidence for the dominance of Dutch immigrants in the craft of hatmaking in England in the later fifteenth century, it comes as no surprise that the four masters of the Fraternity of St James named in the 1501 Ordinances can also be identified as Dutchmen.[52] Their names, 'Andrewe Morter, James Lese, Bartylmewe Brynke, Herry Gram' (art. 25), are slightly anglicised, as was the way, but the surnames are recognisably Dutch and of long standing. The Database of Dutch family names records a 'Hinryck Brynck' in Drenthe (c.1450) and an 'Ameltinck Brinck' in Harderwijk (1461), a 'Joannem dictum Gram' in Simpelveld, Limburg (c.1330). English 'Lees' in surnames is derived from 'lee' (open place), but it is also a Dutch patronymic surname (Lees = Laurentius), first documented in Leeuwarden (1540). 'Andrewe Morter' sounds English, but behind the name lurks 'Mortier' (from French *mortier*, Latin *mortarium* 'boggy ground'), a common surname in the southern Low Countries from the thirteenth century onwards. We find the same individual named as executor in the will (TNA, PROB 11/8/311) of another Dutch-speaking hatmaker, Johannes Blankynk, dated 1488, where his name is Andreas Mortier. Interestingly, Blankynk's will includes a bequest of twelve pence, *ad sustentacioni luminis sancti Jacobi in ecclesiam fratrum predicatorium* ('for maintaining St James's light in the church of the Friars Preachers [the Dominicans]'). No mention is made of a Fraternity of St James, but the fines in wax repeatedly mentioned in the Ordinances of the Hatmakers had the same pious objective as Blankynk did: to keep the candle at the altar of St James burning bright.

Though many of the hats sold in England at the turn of the sixteenth century were likely still imported from France and the Low Countries (especially from Bruges and Brussels),[53] increasing numbers of immigrants practising this trade moved to London

---

52   In 1511, when the Dutch Hatmakers of the Fraternity of St James merged with the Haberdashers' Company, only James Lese was still a master; but the incoming masters were certainly or probably also Dutch. A later record for Anthony Levyson or Leveson indicates he was born in Zeeland (TNA, C 1/1021/44); his surname that may well have been Anglicised: cf. Dutch 'Lievens' and 'Jan Lievenszoon' (1420, Zierikzee), in *Nederlandse Familienamenbank*. Gerard Rowst's will indicates close social ties with Dutch speakers (LMA, DL/C/B/004/ MS09171/9, fol 94rv, will of Gerard Roest, 1518), and both he and the Anthony de Wyne had common medieval Dutch surnames ('Roest' and 'De Wijn').

53   Wim Blockmans, Bert De Munck, and Peter Stabel, 'Economic Vitality: Urbanisation, Regional Complementarity and European Interaction', in *City and Society in the Low Countries, 1100–1600*, ed. Bruno Blondé, Marc Boone, and Anne-Laure Van Bruaene (Cambridge: Cambridge University Press, 2020), pp. 49–50.

and other parts of the country in the decades around 1500, a time when migration from the Low Countries to England and especially to London was generally quickening. The hatmakers from the Low Countries joined other Dutch immigrants in London working in artisanal trades associated with the manufacture of garments and accessories, an expanding sector of the economy. As Katherine French, Christopher Dyer, and others have detailed, fifteenth-century England experienced a 'consumer revolution', driven by clothing and accessories within the financial reach of many in English society: kerchiefs, prayer beads, pins, buttons, ribbons, clothes – and caps and hats.[54] The domestic production of such items began to involve increasingly elaborated labour structures that moved beyond the household model of artisanal production into proto-industrial piece work. The guild master with apprentices and journeymen employed in a workshop in his own house did not by any means disappear – indeed that remained in guild and civic ordinances the assumed organisation of work for a long time to come – but, in addition, guild masters in some occupations became the heads of complex chains of production where most of the labour was performed by networks of pieceworkers (carders, spinners, weavers, knitters, stitchers, and so on) who worked in their own chambers rather than in the master's shop, what a later time would call a 'putting out' system. Few of those pieceworkers were guild members (in London idiom, they were not 'of the freedom') and many were immigrants.[55]

Headgear manufacturers and retailers were, along with tailors, early adopters of this new structure of labour, especially the flourishing cap-making sector, which began to expand significantly in England in the 1480s and 1490s.[56] The years around 1500 saw some clashes among London guilds for control over these chains of cap production, which resulted first in the amalgamation of the Capper-Hurers and the Hatter-merchants in 1501, and then in the absorption of that united guild by the more powerful Haberdashers' Company in 1502. This pattern of smaller guilds merging or being swallowed up by larger ones is seen in other crafts, too.[57] The Dutch hatmakers who migrated to London in this same period thus arrived to find a complicated situation, and the same market forces that led to the absorption of the Capper-Hurers and the Hatter-merchants affected their guild too, for in 1511 the Fraternity of St James was taken over by the Haberdashers.

The Dutch Hatmakers' market advantage, which no doubt brought them to the notice of the Haberdashers who retailed hats and other accessories, was that their own artisanal

---

[54] Katherine L. French, *Household Goods and Good Households in Late Medieval London: Consumption and Domesticity After the Plague* (Philadelphia: Pennsylvania University Press, 2021); Christopher Dyer, *An Age of Transition: Economy and Society in England in the Later Middle Ages* (Oxford: Oxford University Press, 2005), pp. 42, 128, 147–48.

[55] W. Mark Ormrod, Bart Lambert, and Jonathan Mackman, *Immigrant England, 1300–1550* (Manchester: Manchester University Press, 2019), pp. 127–28.

[56] Charles Phythian-Adams, *Desolation of a City: Coventry and the Urban Crisis of the Late Middle Ages* (Cambridge: Cambridge University Press, 1979), p. 44; Swanson, *Medieval Artisans*, pp. 50–52; Leech, 'Stability and Change', pp. 19–20.

[57] George Unwin, *The Gilds and Companies of London* (London: Methuen, 1908), pp. 166–69.

craft had little or no competition from native Londoners. Indeed, the Ordinances of the Fraternity of St James are to our knowledge the first solid evidence for the manufacture of felt hats in London, and the likelihood that they were pioneers of a new industry is confirmed by what historians close to the period said about the history of felt hat production in England. Edmund Howes in his early-seventeenth-century continuation of Stow's Chronicle recorded that 'About the beginning of Henry the 8. began the making of Spanish feltes[58] in England, by Spaniards and Dutchmen, before which time & long since, the English vsed to ride and goe winter and sommer in knit capys, cloth hoods, and the best sort in silke thromd hatts [shaggy felt caps made from woollen 'thrums', pieces of waste thread or yarn]'.[59] Howes records this in his account of the reign of James I because this is when the English Feltmakers were first incorporated (in 1604). The journeymen of the Worshipful Company of Feltmakers also kept in memory the year in which felt hats were first produced in London. A document from 1820 shows their device (a journeyman hatter) with various historic events and dates printed next to it, including: 'Hats first invented 1456. First made in London 1510'.[60] Presumably the hats referred to here are those that concerned them, that is, felt hats. The chronologies of these later memorials are inaccurate – manufacture in London of felt hats almost certainly dated from the mid-fifteenth century – but they correctly remind us that the making of felt hats was a late medieval innovation.

Unlike the poorly remunerated and low-skill tasks their countrymen and -women performed in the different stages of cap-making, felt hatmaking was a niche and high-skill occupation. The hatmakers, moreover, had another advantage that even other high-skill immigrants such as goldsmiths did not: there were no English guild members who knew the specific processes the hatmakers from the Netherlands used. This did not stop the Cappers-Hurers, Hatter-merchants, and Haberdashers, themselves intensely competing with one another in the years around 1500, from attempting to bring these immigrant hatmakers under their control, but the hatmakers themselves resisted. In answer to attempts by the London guilds to absorb the hatmakers as subordinate members, the hatmakers organised their own guild, the Hatmakers' Fraternity of St James at Blackfriars. This was, in effect, a rogue guild, at least from the perspective of the City of London, as strangers could not be full members of London craft guilds, much less form their own.

---

58   Spain had been the usual source of beaver furs after the animal had become extinct in England (by 1300), though in the sixteenth century it also became an endangered species in southern Europe. See Raye, 'Early Extinction' and Veale, *English Fur Trade*, pp. 101–32. However, there is no evidence of Spaniards working as hatmakers or feltmakers in early-sixteenth-century London.

59   Edmund Howes, *The Annales, or a generall chronicle of England, begun first by maister John Stow* (London, Thomas Dawson for Thomas Adams, 1615), p. 840. On thrummed hats, see John S. Lee, 'Thrums', in *Encyclopedia of Medieval Dress and Textiles*, online edition, ed. Gale Owen-Crocker, Elizabeth Coatsworth, and Maria Hayward (Leiden, 2021), <http://dx.doi.org/10.1163/2213–2139_emdt_SIM_001171>

60   George Unwin, *Industrial Organisation in the Sixteenth and Seventeenth Centuries* (Oxford: Clarendon Press, 1904), p. 215.

ALIENS AND GUILDS IN LONDON

Immigration to London, especially from the nearby regions across the North Sea and the Channel, had long been a feature of London life. It has been estimated that aliens made up about six to ten per cent of the population of London in the fifteenth century, some 3,500 or more people, the Dutch making up a significant proportion of the stranger population.[61] The number of newcomers from overseas possibly increased in the last decades of the fifteenth century, and certainly concern about them is more visible in the sources. In the years around 1500 the proportion of London residents born outside the realm was high in comparison to later centuries, contrary to the frequent assumption that immigration became more common in the late Tudor and Stuart eras.[62] The waning years of the century coincided with a general economic contraction in England, which made strangers searching for work in the metropolitan area a subject of concern and, sometimes, hostility from their English-born peers.[63] The years around 1500 were marked both by heightened friction between immigrant artisans and English workers, and by some creativity on the part of the aliens in working around the structures by which London citizens and their guilds tried to control strangers' labour.

The place of immigrants in artisanal production in London at the turn of the sixteenth century was various. In principle, strangers were either excluded from work over which the London guilds held a monopoly or subordinated to the governance of citizen guild masters. In practice, the independence and power of immigrant artisans reflected the nature of the work involved and the positions of the different craft associations in the intersecting hierarchies between and within London guilds.[64] Some immigrants to London – the representatives of the Italian mercantile firms, for example – flourished despite their exclusion from the guilds of their English peers; others, such as the stranger goldsmiths, were able to establish working relationships with citizen counterparts that benefited both, though usually the English more than the strangers.[65] Many – probably

---

[61] Ormrod et al., *Immigrant England*, pp. 102–10; W. Mark Ormrod and Jonathan Mackman, 'Resident Aliens in Later Medieval England: Sources, Contexts, Debates', in *Resident Aliens in Later Medieval England*, ed. Nicola McDonald, W. Mark Ormrod, and Craig Taylor (Turnhout: Brepols, 2017), pp. 1–32; Matthew Davies, 'Aliens, Crafts and Guilds in Late Medieval London', in *Medieval Londoners: Essays to Mark the Eightieth Birthday of Caroline M. Barron*, ed. Elizabeth A. New and Christian Steer (London: University of London Press, 2019), p. 119; W. Mark Ormrod, 'England's Immigrants, 1330–1550: Aliens in Later Medieval and Early Tudor England', *Journal of British Studies* 59 (2020), 245–63.

[62] Ormrod et al., *Immigrant England*; Lien Bich Luu, 'Alien Communities in Transition, 1570–1640', in *Immigrants in Tudor and Early Stuart England*, ed. Nigel Goose and Lien Bich Luu (Brighton: Sussex Academic Press, 2005), pp. 192–210.

[63] Ormrod and Mackman, 'Resident Aliens', pp. 26–27.

[64] Davies, 'Aliens', pp. 125–26.

[65] Francesco Guidi-Bruscoli and Jessica Lutkin, 'Perception, Identity and Culture: The Italian Communities in Fifteenth-Century London and Southampton Revisited', in *Resident Aliens in Later Medieval England*, ed. Nicola McDonald, W. Mark Ormrod, and Craig Taylor (Turnhout: Brepols, 2017), pp. 89–104, 96; M. E. Bratchel, 'Regulation and Group-

most – immigrant workers, however, found their stranger status put them at a disadvantage in comparison to London citizens.

A factor of principal importance in understanding the labour situation and the place of immigrants in London in the decades around 1500 is that gender and birthplace were matters of the highest legal and political significance in defining how a worker could practise a trade. London citizenship and guild membership were co-dependent: one became a full member of one's guild and entered the freedom of the City by the same process. Participation in civic politics and selling goods at retail within City jurisdiction were restricted to citizen guild members.[66] Only men could fully inhabit the roles of London citizen and guild member, though sometimes widows of freemen could take over some aspects of their late husbands' status. And as of 1427, no one alien-born was to be admitted to London citizenship, and the full membership in a London guild on which entrance to the freedom depended, unless he were 'of the king's allegiance'; in this London differed from other English towns and cities, which tended to be less strictly exclusivist as regards place of birth, though not gender.[67] And if Englishness and male identity were necessary for London citizenship they were not in themselves sufficient: most English-born men in the London area were also non-citizens, termed 'forens' (now spelled 'foreigns'), from the Latin adjective 'forinsecus', outside. Forens were, like aliens, outside the freedom, not barred by virtue of their birthplace but by socio-economic status

---

Consciousness in the Later History of London's Italian Merchant Colonies', *Journal of European Economic History* 9 (1980), 585–610, 593; Charlotte Berry, 'Guilds, Immigration, and Immigrant Economic Organization: Alien Goldsmiths in London, 1480–1540', *Journal of British Studies* 60 (2021), 534–62.

66   Caroline M. Barron, *London in the Later Middle Ages: Government and People 1200–1500* (Oxford: Oxford University Press, 2004), pp. 204–16; Christian D. Liddy, *Contesting the City: The Politics of Citizenship in English Towns, 1250–1530* (Oxford: Oxford University Press, 2017); Maarten Prak, *Citizens without Nations: Urban Citizenship in Europe and the World, c.1000–1789* (Cambridge, Cambridge University Press, 2018), pp. 83–115.

67   See LMA, COL/CC/01/01/002, Journal 2, fol. 90r ('Concessum est quod nullus alienigenus admittatur in libertatem Ciuitatis nisi de ligencia domini Regis'); see also COL/CC/01/01/004, Journal 4, fol. 19v (3 March 1446); Ormrod, Lambert, and Mackman, *Immigrant England*, p. 40; Bart Lambert, 'Citizenry and Nationality: The Participation of Immigrants in Urban Politics in Later Medieval England', *History Workshop Journal* 90 (2020), 52–73; Miri Rubin, *Cities of Strangers: Making Lives in Medieval Europe* (Cambridge: Cambridge University Press, 2020), pp. 16–18, 46–49; Stephanie R. Hovland, 'Apprenticeship in Later Medieval London (c.1300–c.1530)' (unpublished doctoral dissertation, University of London, 2006), pp. 63–71; Matthew P. Davies, 'The Tailors of London and Their Guild, c.1300–1500' (unpublished doctoral dissertation, University of Oxford, 1994), pp. 183–84. Ki'chang Kim notes that the importance of being born under the king's dominion as the basis of subjecthood (rather than, for instance, oath-taking) was shifting in this period: Ki-ch'ang Kim, *Aliens in Medieval Law: The Origins of Modern Citizenship* (Cambridge: Cambridge University Press, 2000), esp. pp. 4–5, 57–59, 103–25, 147–75.

and life chances, as they had not completed an apprenticeship and thereafter entered the freedom through a guild.[68]

The fifteenth-century ordinances barring aliens from citizenship were not always observed in the decades following their promulgation, but at various times in the fifteenth century it was considered that immigrants who became 'denizens' (that is, those who renounced their allegiance to the land of their birth and instead swore obedience to the English king) had thereby become a subject and so could be admitted as citizens if sponsored by a London guild.[69] From about the 1480s onwards the exclusion of those born outside the realm – denizen or not – was more consistently enforced. Some London guilds were especially vigilant in their barring of the stranger-born: the Tailors' guild stripped an apprentice of his status in 1493 when it emerged that he had been born in Berwick-on-Tweed, just over the border in Scotland.[70] To verify the Englishness of their trainees, the London Skinners' and Tailors' apprentice binding books for the late fifteenth and early sixteenth centuries listed the birthplaces of those they enrolled. In both cases, totalling some five hundred apprentices, everyone was born in the king's dominions, the vast majority in England and a few in Wales, Ireland, and Calais.[71] By the second half of the sixteenth century, the very antiquity of the ordinances was invoked as critical precedents for even more exclusionary regulations.[72] The patchily surviving London Freemen's Register for the middle years of the sixteenth century shows the same consistency of birth under the king's dominion, with no exceptions, for the more than one thousand men admitted to citizenship.[73] The naming of fathers as well as the recording of birthplaces in the Skinners', Tailors', and civic freedom registers suggests that

---

[68] Matthew Davies, 'Citizens and "Foreyns": Crafts, Guilds and Regulation in Late Medieval London', in *Between Regulation and Freedom: Work and Manufactures in European Cities, 14th–18th Centuries*, ed. A. Caracausi, Matthew Davies, and L. Mocarelli (Newcastle: Cambridge Scholars, 2018), pp. 1–21. Many others who lived in the City and its environs were also non-citizens, including aristocrats, gentlemen, clergy, lawyers, and crown functionaries; the status of citizen was fully identified with guild membership and so normally available only to the merchants and artisans who comprised those guilds.

[69] On denizen status, see Ormrod et al., *Immigrant England*, pp. 24–29; Andrew Pettegree, *Foreign Protestant Communities in Sixteenth-Century London* (Oxford: Clarendon Press, 1986), pp. 15–16. For admissions, see a streak of grants of the freedom to strangers in 1473: LMA, COL/CC/01/01/008, Journal 8, folios 56r–66r. An example of denizen status as an apparent prerequisite for the grant of citizenship is the tailor John Bettes, who was granted denizen status in April 1493 and was then made free of the city through the Tailors' guild in July 1493. *CPR 1485–94*, 490; Matthew P. Davies, ed., *The Merchant Taylors' Company of London: Court Minutes 1486–1493* (Stamford: Richard III and Yorkist History Trust in assoc. with Paul Watkins, 2000), pp. 256–57, 261.

[70] Davies, 'Tailors of London', pp. 183–84.

[71] GL, CLC/L/SE/C/005/MS 30719/001; Hovland, 'Apprenticeship', pp. 63–71.

[72] Laura Hunt Yungblut, *Strangers Settled Here amongst Us: Policies, Perceptions, and the Presence of Aliens in Elizabethan England* (London: Routledge, 1996), pp. 36–37.

[73] Charles Welch, ed., *Register of Freemen of the City of London in the Reigns of Henry VIII and Edward VI* (London: London and Middlesex Archaeological Society, 1908); Steve Rappaport,

English paternity as well as birth may have been an informal or implicit condition for London citizenship from the later fifteenth century. This criterion would become explicit in London in 1574 when the Common Council issued an injunction forbidding citizens from taking on apprentices whose fathers had been born outside the realm, a restriction extended in 1625 to grandfathers.[74]

At the beginning of the sixteenth century, a few guilds were more friendly to strangers but the City government tended to keep a harder line. For instance, when the Goldsmiths' Company enquired with the City chamberlain in 1511 whether stranger goldsmith John de Loren could be made free of the City upon payment of a £20 redemption, the chamberlain replied he could not, 'that no straunger born sholde be made free'.[75] Exceptions continued to be made – other alien goldsmiths were granted the freedom in 1491 and 1514, for example[76] – but the conferral of London citizenship on an artisan or merchant born outside the realm was a rare event in the later fifteenth and early sixteenth centuries.[77] For some migrants to London, the exclusion from guilds was largely irrelevant – this was true for international merchants, who flourished in any case, and for the pieceworkers in the proto-industries of cloth- and garment-making, whose English-born peers were not guild members either. But most alien craft workers both able and desirous of operating their own workshops and selling their wares at retail – that is, those who would have been guild members had they been English – could not do so within London jurisdiction.

The interests of London citizen guild members as regards the labour of stranger artisans in the years around 1500 differed, depending on various factors: whether immigrant labour directly competed with citizens' ability to practise their trade or whether, conversely, the strangers' work benefited citizens (providing skilled or cheap

Worlds Within Worlds: Structures of Life in Sixteenth-Century London (Cambridge: Cambridge University Press, 1989), pp. 77–81.

74   Pettegree, *Foreign Protestant Communities*, 288–93; Yungblut, *Strangers*, pp. 76, 105; Lien Bich Luu, 'Natural-Born versus Stranger-Born Subjects: Aliens and Their Status in Elizabethan London', in *Immigrants in Tudor and Early Stuart England*, ed. Nigel Goose and Lien Bich Luu (Brighton: Sussex Academic Press, 2005), pp. 58–60; Jacob Selwood, *Diversity and Difference in Early Modern London* (Farnham: Ashgate, 2010), pp. 1, 15–18, 87–127.

75   London, Goldsmiths' Hall, Wardens Accounts and Court Minutes [WACM], Book 4C, pp. 71–72; see also p. 41 for a similar bid the year before though less clarity that it had been supported by the guild.

76   London, Goldsmiths' Hall, WACM A2, p. 491; Berry, 'Guilds'. See also below regarding the stranger weavers in 1497.

77   Davies, 'Aliens', pp. 137–38; Berry, 'Guilds'. An example of confusion caused by changing customs regarding the admission of immigrants to the freedom can be seen in the case of James Van Zant, alias James Bracy, a tailor born in Utrecht, who was granted London citizenship in 1473 and died by 1506; in 1517 the court of the mayor and alderman were evidently confused that his orphan daughter could be a ward of the City (a privilege of citizens) as both he and she seemed to them to be Dutch. LMA, COL/CC/01/01/008, Journal 8, fol. 66r; COL/CC/01/01/010, Journal 10, folios 360v–361r; COL/CC/01/01/011, Journal 11, fol. 36r; COL/AD/01/012, Letter Book M, fol. 144r; COL/AD/01/013, Letter Book N, fol. 35v; LMA, COL/CA/01/01/003, Repertory 3, fol. 134r; Bolton, *Alien Communities*, p. 64.

labour, sometimes necessary to the proto-industrial networks in the metropolitan area). The entirely mercantile guilds – for instance, the Drapers, Grocers, and Mercers[78] – did not admit strangers in any fashion in this period. The lower-ranked artisan guilds also tended to exclude or tightly restrict stranger labour when they could; from the fifteenth century, Londoners repeatedly attempted, with some success, to obtain parliamentary legislation disallowing strangers from working outside guild supervision in certain artisanal trades in the larger metropolitan area surrounding London.[79] Those statutes, however, exempted the liberties, independent economic zones in and around London (on which more below) that fell outside the jurisdiction of the City of London, with the resulting development of a thriving manufacture and retail of shoes and other leather goods in these liberties.[80] A more fruitful strategy that worked in certain economic sectors was the incorporation of immigrant labour in an inferior position, in those complex networks of production for the different stages of rendering raw materials into finished clothes and accessories, where citizen guild members were able to maintain their dominant status.[81] And in some high-skill artisanal trades, especially those producing luxury goods, it was profitable for guildsmen to incorporate aliens in a manner that brought mutual benefit to the Londoners and the stranger artisans. As Charlotte Berry's analysis of the Goldsmiths' company shows, partnerships between citizen and alien goldsmiths gave London guildsmen access to high-quality wares they could purvey to the luxury consumer and the stranger artisans a trouble-free retail pipeline for the goods they produced, without the worry of harassment for illegal sales. Strangers were even integrated, in a limited fashion, into the official structures of the guild, participating in searches of stranger goldsmiths' shops and participating in the nomination of wardens.[82]

---

[78] A. H. Johnson, *The History of the Worshipful Company of the Drapers of London*, 5 vols (Oxford: Clarendon Press, 1914), I, 275–76; Pamela Nightingale, *A Medieval Mercantile Community: The Grocers' Company and the Politics and Trade of London, 1000–1485* (New Haven, CT: Yale University Press, 1995), pp. 359–63, 392–95, 504–5; Anne F. Sutton, *The Mercery of London: Trade, Goods and People, 1130–1578* (Aldershot: Ashgate, 2005), pp. 114–18.

[79] Relatively few of these guilds have records surviving from the early sixteenth century; for those with surviving records we have found nothing about strangers as members of any kind in the Brewers' Company (GL, MS 5442/2); the Skinners' Company (GL, MSS 30727/2; 30719/1); the Coopers' Company (GL, MS 5614A). The Coopers did record quarterage they collected from 'forens', non-citizen English workers.

[80] 3 Edw. IV c. 4, 5; 17 Edw. IV c. 1; *SR*, II, 396–402, 452–61; similar exemptions were made in the labour statutes of the 1520s (14 and 15 Hen. VIII c. 2; 21 Hen. VIII c. 16; *SR*, III, 208–9, 297–98). The only statute governing alien labour in this period that does not exempt the precinct of St Martin le Grand, a significant centre for alien shoemaking and other leather work, is 1 Ric. III c. 9, *SR*, II, 489–93. See Shannon McSheffrey, *Seeking Sanctuary: Crime, Mercy, and Politics in English Courts, 1400–1550* (Oxford: Oxford University Press, 2017), pp. 112–39; Lien Bich Luu, 'Aliens and Their Impact on the Goldsmiths' Craft in London in the Sixteenth Century', in *Goldsmiths, Silversmiths, and Bankers: Innovation and the Transfer of Skill, 1550 to 1750*, ed. David Mitchell (Stroud: Alan Sutton, 1995), pp. 44–49; Rappaport, *Worlds*, pp. 45–47.

[81] Davies, 'Tailors of London', esp. pp. 99–102, 167–71, 187, 208–9.

[82] Berry, 'Guilds'.

The place of aliens in the Goldsmiths' Company, however, was not typical; from the 1490s into the seventeenth century other crafts saw hostility and rivalry, in some cases fierce, between stranger and English practitioners of artisanal crafts. As Jasmine Kilburn-Toppin has noted, the London guilds shaped a specifically English artisanal identity in response to the presence of skilled alien workers in the metropolis.[83]

The stranger-born were thus, with a few exceptions, barred from full membership in London craft guilds. In forming the Fraternity of St James in the Blackfriars convent, the late fifteenth-century Dutch Hatmakers attempted to create an alternative form of association outside the framework of the London civic guilds. Their fraternity was not, however, the first craft guild of strangers in London: the fellowship of Stranger Weavers in London flourished from the 1350s up to the 1490s as a guild distinct from the English Weavers' guild. That separate existence of the Stranger Weavers came to an end in the 1490s, when they were forced to come under the rule of the English Weavers. The suppression of the Stranger Weavers occurred at the same time as the Hatmakers organised their guild, so it is worth a closer look.

Clothmakers from the Low Countries had been offered the freedom to live and work in England by Edward III, and in 1352 they established a guild in London which was recognised by the Crown and soon after, with some reluctance, by the City. English and stranger weavers occupied different niches in the weaving industry, the English producing cheaper cloth and the strangers more fashionable coloured and rayed (striped) fabrics. In the post-Black Death economic readjustment, the English weavers fell on hard times while the demand for the more expensive cloth the stranger weavers made remained relatively robust. Their English counterparts resented the protection of the royal government under which the Dutch weavers flourished, that resentment likely spilling over into outright violence during the Great Rising of 1381, when perhaps forty Dutch weavers were massacred on the streets of London.[84] In the fifteenth century, the separate existence of the English Weavers and Stranger Weavers was maintained, though how the alien guild fitted into the urban governing structure is somewhat unclear. On the one hand, the guild's ordinances were approved by the mayor, aldermen, and common council in 1441, but on the other, it seems that the members of the Stranger Weavers were not citizens.[85] In the meantime, the weaving sector of London's cloth-making industry continued to collapse, for the English Weavers more precipitously than for the smaller number of Stranger Weavers, who still specialised in more expensive fabrics. It seems likely that their small size and insignificance allowed the survival of the Stranger

[83] Jasmine Kilburn-Toppin, *Crafting Identities: Artisan Culture in London, c.1550–1640* (Manchester: Manchester University Press, 2021), pp. 8–19; see also Lien Bich Luu, *Immigrants and the Industries of London, 1500–1700* (Aldershot: Ashgate, 2005), pp. 226–27.

[84] Bart Lambert and Milan Pajic, 'Immigration and the Common Profit: Native Cloth Workers, Flemish Exiles, and Royal Policy in Fourteenth-Century London', *Journal of British Studies* 55 (2016), 633–57; Frances Consitt, *The London Weavers' Company*, 2 vols (Oxford: Clarendon Press, 1933), I, 33–60, 180–91.

[85] LMA, COL/AD/01/010, Letter Book K, fol. 193v; Consitt, *London Weavers' Company*, I, 198–200.

Weavers into the last years of the fifteenth century despite more insistent exclusion of the alien-born from London guilds in the second half of that century; perhaps, also, they had a good relationship with prominent citizen merchants who handled the marketing of their luxury cloth.

Such tolerance for an anomalous alien guild would not outlast the 1490s. Open conflict between the two weavers' guilds flared up from time to time; one such episode fell in September 1497, prompting the mayor and aldermen to summon representatives of the *societates* or guilds of 'Englisshwevers' and 'Wevers Strangers' to address the issues on which they were at variance: the record of this summons in the City's Journal of the Court of Common Council put both brotherhoods on a par, each labelled a *societas*. At the end of November, the mayor and aldermen decreed a settlement, also entered into the Journal, which had a significantly different tone. The separate Stranger Weavers' guild had rhetorically simply vanished, replaced by twenty-five individually named alien weavers who agreed to join the 'Felaship' of English Weavers.[86] On the face of it, this agreement conferred considerable benefit on the twenty-five named stranger weavers even if it erased their collective identity: henceforth, they were to become full members of the 'Gilde of [Citizen] Weuers'. Moreover, in order to solve the category confusion of strangers as full guild members, a status normally reserved for citizens, twelve were granted the freedom of the City with the promise of more to come – a significant concession given the alien-unfriendly climate of the 1490s. The strangers were, in addition, to be integrated into the governing structure of the English Weavers' Company with reserved bailiff and warden positions for alien members. In return, the aliens were not henceforth to meet separately or in any other way to cultivate an independent existence. They could take apprentices, but only boys born in the realm.

All in all, then, the 1497 amalgamation of the English and Stranger Weavers appears to have offered the strangers a more-or-less equal place in a new larger guild. The twentieth-century historian of the craft, Frances Consitt, saw it generally as a peaceable union that allowed for power-sharing between the English and stranger weavers. Possibly that was indeed the general spirit in 1497, but any equitable arrangement was short-lived. Consitt reports that the bailiffs for 1498 duly included two English men and one 'freeman stranger', for instance, but the appointment of the stranger bailiff soon fell into disuse.[87] Moreover, the grant of citizenship that had been made to twelve alien-born weavers under the 1497 agreement was – as the City was to make clear – a one-time-only offer. Despite assurances to the contrary in the agreement, stranger weavers were to be refused the freedom (and, in 1503, several wardens of the guild were thrown into prison for daring to present an alien for citizenship).[88] In the sixteenth century the Weavers'

---

[86] LMA, COL/CC/01/01/010, Journal 10, folios 105v, 113r–115r; COL/CA/01/01/001, Repertory 1, fol. 29v; Consitt, *London Weavers' Company*, I, 33–60; 130; 223–26.

[87] Consitt, *London Weavers' Company*, I, 91.

[88] They were found guilty of having 'falsly and subtilly presentid' the stranger-born weaver to the chamberlain for admission to citizenship, 'expresly contrary' to the oaths they had sworn as citizens themselves. LMA, COL/CA/01/01/001, Repertory 1, fol. 128v.

Company settled into the same kind of relationship with its alien members as pertained in other guilds that incorporated (as opposed to outright excluded) strangers: the strangers were of a secondary status, working under the supervision of the guild, paying higher rates of admission to the craft, but without being considered full members eligible for governance positions.[89]

Other immigrant craftsmen sought another route: working outside the physical boundaries of the City of London and the jurisdiction of its guilds. For the purposes of guild jurisdiction, London's boundaries extended some three miles beyond the walls, but those seeking independent zones closer to or even within the City walls could find them in the many liberties in the metropolitan region. In liberties such as the precincts of the collegiate church of St Martin le Grand, the hospital of St Katherine by the Tower, or the Blackfriars convent, strangers could both produce and retail their wares outside the reach of the London guilds' monopolies. In the precinct of St Martin le Grand, within the London walls just north of St Paul's Cathedral, for instance, lived a dense population of stranger artisans, mostly from the Low Countries, who made and sold artisanal goods, especially shoes and pouches, much to the chagrin of the Cordwainers' and Pouchmakers' guilds.[90]

There is, however, no evidence that any hatmakers were among the hundreds of Dutch strangers who lived in St Martin le Grand,[91] a fact which points up some of the differences between the hatmakers and their countrymen who made shoes and pouches. For the latter, the ability to operate shops in which their wares could be sold directly to consumers was paramount, and the liberty privileges of the precinct of St Martin le Grand allowed them to do so outside the structure of the London guilds. Evidently the hatmakers, however, were not especially interested in retailing their products – or perhaps it was simply impracticable for them to sell directly to the more select market for finely-produced hats among courtiers and other elites. There were some hatmakers who lived in the precinct of the Hospital of St Katherine by the Tower, another liberty just outside the City walls on the east end, but complaints about them focused on London merchants buying wholesale from them rather than on their illicit retailing.[92] It seems that the craft of hatmaking in London focused on manufacture rather than retail, providing the hats wholesale to merchants, usually London citizen hatter merchants and haberdashers, who would take on the business of selling to the consumer.

---

[89] This is what Consitt implies, though she does not state this explicitly. *London Weavers' Company*, I, 130.

[90] Shannon McSheffrey, 'Stranger Artisans and the London Sanctuary of St Martin Le Grand in the Reign of Henry VIII', *Journal of Medieval and Early Modern Studies* 43 (2013), 545–71.

[91] Of the more than 500 residents of the precinct of St Martin le Grand traced for the period 1500–1550, none were hatmakers or cappers. Spreadsheet available here: Shannon McSheffrey, 'Research: Residents of St Martin Le Grand' <https://shannonmcsheffrey.wordpress.com/research/>.

[92] TNA, C 1/462/38.

Although in some crafts, such as shoe- and pouch-making, stranger artisans were able to work outside the guild structure through the whole process from manufacture to retail, the hatmakers appear to have wanted or needed to deal with London mercantile guilds to get their product to the consumer. Yet the stranger hatmakers were evidently unwilling to subordinate themselves to the guilds with whose members they would normally deal and tried instead to establish their own governance through the Fraternity of St James in Blackfriars. Though they did not use the jurisdictional freedom of liberties in the same way as the shoemakers and pouchmakers did, to both make and sell their wares, they did take advantage of the liberty privileges of Blackfriars in another way, forming their fraternity there outside the City's boundaries. Thus, the establishment of a formal guild for Hatmakers in the years around 1500 was likely an attempt to resist incorporation into one of these London guilds striving for control of both the headgear market and the craft workers, citizen, foren, and stranger, who produced caps and hats.

THE STRUGGLE FOR CONTROL OF THE HEADGEAR SECTOR

There was a good deal of aggressive manoeuvring among the different occupational groups in London involved in making and selling headgear in the years immediately around 1500. In 1501, the year in which the bulk of the bilingual ordinances of the Fraternity of St James were written down, the London guild of Hatters or Hatter-merchants – who sold, but did not themselves make, hats – amalgamated with (or perhaps took over) the London guild of Hurers-Cappers, who both made and sold caps.[93] The establishment of the united guild of the Cappers and Hatter-merchants seems to have been a bid by the wholesalers and retailers to control the production line and sale of headgear in the London market, likely in rivalry with other more powerful guilds. Particularly threatening to the headgear specialists were the Haberdashers, who sold accessories of all kinds, including hats and caps. The fifteenth-century consumer revolution had brought both significant growth in the haberdashery trade and a concomitant increase in stature for the London Haberdashers' guild, which moved from decidedly junior status in the London craft hierarchy in 1400 to a secure place among the Great Twelve Companies by the 1510s.[94]

If this union of the Cappers and Hatter-merchants was indeed an attempt to stave off the Haberdashers, it failed, for the following year, in 1502, the Haberdashers in turn absorbed the amalgamated guild, bringing the Hatter-merchants and Cappers under their aegis. The politics of these mergers and acquisitions are obscure and likely complex; possibly some citizen hatter-merchants and cappers were keen to join the more

---

93 *CPR 1494–1509*, p. 243; the incorporation of the new amalgamated guild of 'Hurers alias cappers and hatter-merchants' was dated 27 Apr. 1501; as the new year was reckoned from 25 March, this was only one month into 1501, so the Hatmakers' ordinances probably dated from after this move.

94 Archer, *Haberdashers' Company*, pp. 11–18.

powerful Haberdashers' Company while others may have lost independence and authority by the merger. Among the issues at stake in any case were the stranger artisans working both as cappers and as hatmakers in the London area: in 1500, before any of the mergers had taken place, the Cappers' and the Haberdashers' guilds clashed over which had the right to 'search' the shops (that is, assess the quality of goods and the number and training of servants) of stranger cappers.[95] In these years some guilds, notably the Haberdashers and the Tailors (in 1503 re-branded as 'Merchant Tailors'), found advantage both in subduing and absorbing lower-ranked citizen guilds and in more firmly establishing supervision over non-citizen pieceworkers who contributed to the making of accessories and garments.[96]

Haberdashers sold both imported and domestically produced goods. There was no strong reason for haberdashers to prefer to sell goods made by London artisan guild members rather than by strangers, or English non-citizens, or workers overseas; their interests lay in finding the most profit for themselves as importers and retailers, not in fostering domestic industry for its own sake.[97] Their focus was on cornering the supply of goods and controlling retail in the face of competition from other merchant guilds, especially the Tailors and the Mercers. In the very early years of the sixteenth century, haberdashers established more clearly their ownership of the retail sector in accessories; the political writer Clement Armstrong in the 1530s looked back on this decade as the point at which haberdashery shops began to proliferate in the City.[98] A major part of that move was first their amalgamation with the Capper and Hatter-merchant guilds, bringing both cap production and headgear retail more clearly under their control. The next step would be the incorporation of the Hatmakers' guild, which the Haberdashers were able to bring about in 1511, as we will see in more detail in chapter 3.

Before that happened, however, the hatmakers resisted. Though some citizen hatter-merchants and cappers may have benefited from their guilds' absorption into the more powerful Haberdashers' company, the stakes were different for the hatmakers: as strangers, their status in any London guild would have been inevitably subordinate. The disputes between the pre-amalgamation Haberdashers' and Cappers' guilds over who would govern alien cappers would have signalled to the stranger hatmakers their need to join forces to resist a similar imposition. The hatmakers had much more leverage than the stranger cappers, due to their unique skills and luxury product and (probably

95   LMA, COL/CA/01/01/001, Repertory 1, fol. 75rv.

96   Matthew Davies, 'Crown, City and Guild in Late Medieval London', in *London and Beyond: Essays in Honour of Derek Keene*, ed. Matthew Davies and James A. Galloway (London: Institute of Historical Research, 2012), pp. 247–68 (at 265–66).

97   Archer, *Haberdashers' Company*, pp. 8, 21–22; Davies, 'Tailors of London', pp. 114–32; and for near-contemporary commentary, Clement Armstrong, 'A Treatise Concerning the Staple and the Commodities of This Realme', in *Tudor Economic Documents, Being Select Documents Illustrating the Economic History of Tudor England*, ed. R. H. Tawney and Eileen Edna Power, 3 vols (New York: Barnes & Noble, 1965), III, pp. 109–10.

98   Armstrong, 'Treatise', p. 111; Archer, *Haberdashers' Company*, p. 21.

not incidentally) their aristocratic clientele. Possibly borrowing from the example of the Stranger Weavers, they created their own guild. They could not form a *citizen* guild, because as strangers they were ineligible for the freedom of London; they nonetheless decided in the late fifteenth century to form a craft association in the form of a religious fraternity dedicated to St James, outside London civic jurisdiction in the Dominican convent, Blackfriars, at the western end of the city.

CHAPTER 2

The Formation of the Hatmakers' Fraternity

Amid the manoeuvres and mergers among London craft associations at the turn of the sixteenth century, a group of stranger hatmakers formed a guild. Given the labour circumstances of late fifteenth-century London, they presumably hoped thereby to gain a more secure position through collective representation to avoid the fate of other stranger artisans in the metropolitan region, unable to operate their own shops or hire servants according to the needs of their business. As non-citizens, the hatmakers could not form a guild through the usual structure of London civic authority (the mayor, aldermen, chamberlain, and Common Council), so instead they placed their association at least nominally under the authority of the bishop. The Fraternity's home – the Dominican priory of the Blackfriars – may well also have been chosen specifically because Blackfriars was a liberty, a territory within London's walls but outside the purview of the civic government.

The first part of this chapter will examine the early sixteenth-century Blackfriars precinct and the role it played as a space 'in and yet not of the City', as contemporaries put it,[1] allowing for exceptions to London's restrictions on alien labour and retail. The second section will consider what the ordinances drawn up by the hatmakers tell us about the different practices of craft work and labour organisation in the Low Countries and England: when the Dutch hatmakers came to London, they brought with them assumptions about training, master-servant relations, and guild governance that diverged substantially from those held by their London counterparts.[2]

---

[1] Shannon McSheffrey, *Seeking Sanctuary: Crime, Mercy, and Politics in English Courts, 1400–1550* (Oxford: Oxford University Press, 2017), p. 61.

[2] It should be noted that guild cultures were not homogenous in the Low Countries. On some distinctions between the southern and northern Low Countries in this period, see Wim Blockmans, Bert De Munck, and Peter Stabel, 'Economic Vitality: Urbanisation, Regional Complementarity and European Interaction', in *City and Society in the Low Countries, 1100–1600*, ed. Bruno Blondé, Marc Boone, and Anne-Laure Van Bruaene (Cambridge: Cambridge University Press, 2020), p. 51.

THE BLACKFRIARS' PRIORY AND THE
STRANGER HATMAKERS

By 1500, the most prominent London guilds had their own company halls, but lesser guilds did not – and those without halls often used parish churches and the London friaries as their headquarters.[3] The Upholders (who bought and sold second-hand goods), for instance, were in Austin Friars; the Cobblers (who mended shoes) were in Crossed Friars (also known as Crutched Friars).[4] Thus, there was nothing unusual about the stranger hatmakers creating their craft fraternity in the Blackfriars' priory precinct. London's mendicant houses also catered to the religious and linguistic needs of the stranger communities in the City. The friars had themselves arrived as immigrants in thirteenth-century England and in the later medieval period friars continued to come from abroad.[5] More than the secular clergy, they understood the need to know the vernacular languages of the city-dwellers whom they served and who in turn served the interests of the friars. When interpreters or confessors who could speak languages other than English were needed, a friary was the place you went to find them.[6] It is thus no coincidence that other alien religious fraternities whose statutes survive also met in friaries.[7] The Austin Friars and Crossed Friars welcomed German, Dutch, and French-speaking religious fraternities in the later fifteenth and early sixteenth centuries, and Austin Friars in addition had Italian- and Spanish-speaking confessors with whom migrants might feel more comfortable.[8] In 1550 the former priory of the Austin Friars officially became the home of the Dutch Church (with services given in Dutch).

Blackfriars, too, had at least four fraternities associated with aliens in the early sixteenth century. One was a francophone fraternity of the Immaculate Conception, strictly religious and social in nature, which included as members court historian Bernard André, high-status merchants, and skilled artisans such as goldsmiths and printers.[9] An elaborate book survives of ordinances of the fraternity, founded in 1503, with an opulent full-page illumination as a frontispiece.[10] Two other confraternities were associated with Dutch

---

3   On the London mendicant houses, see Nick Holder, *The Friaries of Medieval London: From Foundation to Dissolution* (Woodbridge: Boydell, 2017).

4   LMA, COL/AD/01/012, Letter Book M, folios 5v, 32v.

5   Proportions and countries of origin are given in Jens Röhrkasten, *The Mendicant Houses of Medieval London, 1221–1539* (Münster: LIT, 2004), p. 536.

6   Michael Richter, *Sprache und Gesellschaft im Mittelalter* (Stuttgart: Hiersemann, 1979), pp. 177–79, and Röhrkasten, *Mendicant Houses*, p. 133, and, with specific reference to Dutch-speaking friars, p. 458.

7   Justin Colson, 'Alien Communities and Alien Fraternities in Later Medieval London', *London Journal* 35 (2010), 111–43; and W. Mark Ormrod, Bart Lambert, and Jonathan Mackman, *Immigrant England, 1300–1550* (Manchester: Manchester University Press, 2019), pp. 232–33.

8   LMA, DL/C/0206, folios 47rv; Colson, 'Alien Communities'; Holder, *Friaries*, p. 143.

9   Colson, 'Alien Communities', pp. 121–24.

10   See below, chapter 4. The manuscript, now Oxford, Christ Church, MS 179, is digitised here: <https://digital.bodleian.ox.ac.uk/inquire/p/e68477c0-ac65-4c5c-bac8-ceoc01a65202>.

migrants. One was dedicated to St Barbara, the patron saint of strangers, and approved by the bishop of London in 1511.[11] It was made up of men of diverse artisanal trades living in different parts of the City; the common thread was evidently their ethnic and linguistic identity, as the members who testified in a 1523–24 lawsuit involving one of their own were from Brabant (Leuven and Brussels) and the duchy of Cleves, now in Germany, but historically Dutch-speaking.[12] Like the other alien fraternities described by Colson, it appears to have been strictly religious and social. The third was the Fraternity of the Holy Trinity, commemorated in the bequest of Godfrey Spering, a beer brewer, who left money in his will (1489) to the fraternity 'kept by Dutchmen (*teuthonicos*) at the Friars Preacher (i.e. Blackfriars) in London'.[13]

The fourth brotherhood in Blackfriars, the Fraternity of St James of the Hatmakers, was different from these other alien fraternities in that it was clearly a craft association rather than a solely religious organisation. In contrast to the ordinances of the French Immaculate Conception fraternity, with which they were roughly contemporaneous, the purpose of the St James' ordinances was primarily to regulate the training, supervision, and accreditation of hatmakers in London. Nonetheless, the Fraternity of St James also had religious functions (fraternity masses, funeral observances for brothers and their wives, charity towards indigent members). The dedication to St James the Less – the patron saint of hatmakers[14] – epitomised the thorough intertwining of occupational and spiritual purposes of the guild; the amalgamated London guild of the Hurer [Capper]-Hatter-merchants, whose 1501 union lasted only for a year before their absorption by the Haberdashers' Company in 1502, also had a fraternity dedicated to St James.[15] Though not all religious fraternities were associated with a particular craft, before the Reformation almost all craft organisations in England, the Low Countries, and elsewhere in Europe were in some ways religious. They were usually associated with a particular church, dedicated to a particular saint, held special masses associated with that saint's feast day. This coupling of religious and economic functions became, if anything, stronger in the later fifteenth century.[16]

See an English translation of the ordinances in Colson, 'Alien Communities', pp. 136–41.

[11] LMA, DL/A/A/005/MS09531/009, Register of R. Fitzjames, Bishop of London, folios 29r–30v; Minnie Reddan and Jens Röhrkasten, 'The Black Friars', in *The Religious Houses of London and Middlesex*, ed. Caroline M. Barron and Matthew Davies (London: Institute of Historical Research, 2007), p. 119. St Barbara was a common dedicatee of Dutch migrant fraternities: the church of St Martin le Grand, ministering to the many Netherlanders living in the liberty precinct, had one attested in 1525, as did the Dutch-speaking community in Florence. See TNA, PROB 11/21/620, Will of Henry Stale, London, 1525; Mario Battistini, ed., *La Confrérie de Sainte-Barbe des Flamands à Florence. Documents relatifs aux tisserands et aux tapissiers* (Brussels: Commission royale d'histoire, 1931). The records edited by Battistini show that this, too, was a religious guild, which brought together members of various crafts.

[12] LMA, DL/C/0207, folios 198v–99r, 218r, 251v–252v, 253v–255v.

[13] TNA, PROB 11/11/708.

[14] David Gowler, *James through the Centuries* (Chichester: Wiley, 2014), p. 58.

[15] LMA, COL/AD/01/012, Letter Book M, folios 28r–29r.

[16] Matthew P. Davies, 'The Tailors of London and Their Guild, c.1300–1500' (unpublished doctoral dissertation, University of Oxford, 1994), pp. 1–43; Guido Marnef and Anne-Laure

If the location of the hatmakers' fraternity in Blackfriars and its mixed economic and religious functions were in no way unusual, their guild was different from both other London citizen craft associations and alien religious guilds. The location in the liberty of the Blackfriars precinct facilitated the alternative structures that the hatmakers who formed it envisaged. London craft guilds were usually subject to the authority of the mayor and aldermen and of the crown, not to ecclesiastical authorities.[17] As the example of the Stranger Weavers discussed in chapter 1 indicates, in earlier decades it had seemed possible for aliens to have a craft association integrated to some extent into the London civic environment; in 1441, the Mayor and Aldermen approved and registered the Stranger Weavers' ordinances. But the Stranger Weavers' separate existence was extinguished in 1497.[18] When the Dutch hatmakers were considering the formation of their fraternity in these same years, they would have needed both to locate their guild outside the jurisdiction of the City of London and to place their organisation into a line of authority other than the London civic hierarchy.

This need for an alternative political and legal structure was yet another reason why the hatmakers established their organisation in Blackfriars, which was not only a religious house suitable for a fraternity, but a liberty, a territory independent in a political, legal, and economic sense from the City of London's jurisdiction.[19] They were, in fact, not the only rogue craft association to do so: in 1503, the journeymen (or 'yeomanry') of the London Fullers' Company, in defiance of the senior members of their guild, also established an unauthorised guild at Blackfriars. All we know about it is that it had elements of a religious fraternity – it had a funeral cloth and a common box – but its suppression by the mayor and aldermen indicates clearly that it was seen as an attempt to develop a craft organisation separate from the main Fullers' guild. One important aspect of the suppression of the Fullers' yeomanry was that henceforth they were never to meet as a group outside the Fullers' Hall in the City.[20]

The Blackfriars' convent had from the late thirteenth century occupied a large precinct at the southwest corner of the City, south of Ludgate and bounded by the wall and the Fleet and Thames Rivers (see fig. 6). As in most ecclesiastical precincts in London by

---

Van Bruaene, 'Civic Religion: Community, Identity, and Religious Transformation', in *City and Society in the Low Countries, 1100–1600*, ed. Bruno Blondé, Marc Boone, and Anne-Laure Van Bruaene (Cambridge: Cambridge University Press, 2020), p. 144; Gervase Rosser, 'Crafts, Guilds and the Negotiation of Work in the Medieval Town', *Past & Present* 154 (1997), 21.

[17] Caroline M. Barron, *London in the Later Middle Ages: Government and People 1200–1500* (Oxford: Oxford University Press, 2004), ch. 9; Matthew Davies, 'Crown, City and Guild in Late Medieval London', in *London and Beyond: Essays in Honour of Derek Keene*, ed. Matthew Davies and James A. Galloway (London: Institute of Historical Research, 2012), pp. 247–68.

[18] See pp. 26–28 above.

[19] On the Blackfriars Liberty especially after the dissolution, see Anthony Paul House, 'The City of London and the Problem of the Liberties, c1540-c1640' (unpublished doctoral dissertation., Oxford University, 2006), pp. 115–52; and Christopher Highley, *Blackfriars in Early Modern London: Theater, Church, and Neighborhood* (Oxford: Oxford University Press, 2022), pp. 35–55. For more generally on the medieval convent and its precinct, see Holder, *Friaries*, pp. 27–56.

[20] LMA, COL/CA/01/01/001, Repertory 1, fol. 136r.

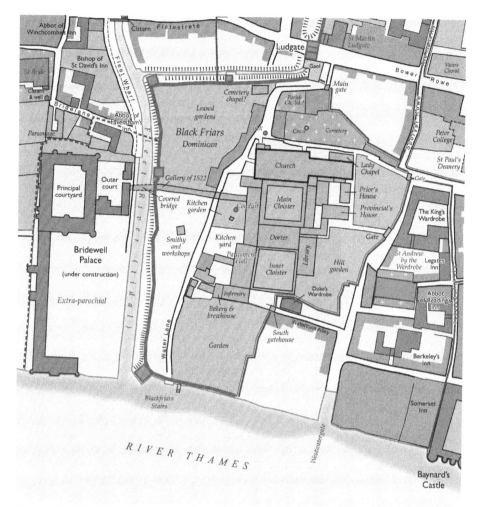

Fig. 6   The Blackfriars' Precinct in 1520 – Extract from *A Map of Tudor London*, 2nd edition, 2022, ed. C. Barron and V. Harding. © Historic Towns Trust, UK.

1500, there were tenements and shops leased to laypeople, though the character of the precinct in the decades around 1500 is surprisingly hard to determine. Because of its separateness, little is known about the scope of the Blackfriars' liberty privileges in practical terms: by analogy with other ecclesiastical liberties it would likely have had its own courts, both secular and ecclesiastical, but no records have survived and only a few administrative records from before the dissolution are extant, mostly in later copies.[21] In the later fifteenth century the heads of religious houses with liberty jurisdictions and

---

[21]   See the Loseley manuscripts, MSS L.b.185, 361, 384, 385, 402, 468, 470, now held at the Folger Shakespeare Library, Washington, DC <https://findingaids.folger.edu/dfoloseley.xml>.

substantial precincts experimented with different constellations of their privileges: both Westminster Abbey and the collegiate church of St Martin le Grand, just to the northeast of Blackfriars, had through the fifteenth century emphasised their privileges as sanctuaries. The Abbey hosted a substantial population of sanctuary-seeking felons and debtors, while in the later fifteenth century St Martin's began to turn more towards leasing shops and houses to alien artisans to work outside London guild regulation, attracting a dense population of stranger craft workers. Another London-area liberty, the hospital of St Katherine by the Tower, was a messy combination of charitable foundation, sanctuary for debt, haven for immigrant artisans, and semi-tolerated prostitution zone.[22] It is not clear where Blackfriars stood around the year 1500 in this universe of experimentation with liberty jurisdictions. It made no claim to sanctuary privileges (a lucrative but potentially troublesome sideline some religious houses, notably Westminster Abbey, claimed). There are some hints that the Dominican prior had farmed out the administration of some of its privileges to the prior of the Hospitaller order of the Knights of St John. The Hospitallers themselves vigorously explored various income-producing franchises and perquisites throughout their properties in the kingdom in these decades, including at the Hospitaller priory at Clerkenwell.[23]

The friars rented out tenements in the precinct from the fourteenth century,[24] though how many residents lived in the Blackfriars precinct around 1500, and who they were, is unclear. Fifteen years later, the picture is somewhat less fuzzy: the Blackfriars liberty, or at least sections of it, had become a pleasant and upscale neighbourhood, something like a gated community at the edge of the City, attractive in particular to elite non-citizens.[25] Emperor Charles V stayed in Blackfriars 'in great royaltie' when he visited London in

[22]   See Shannon McSheffrey, 'Liberties of London: Social Networks, Sexual Disorder, and Peculiar Jurisdictions in the Late Medieval English Metropolis', in *Crossing Borders: Boundaries and Margins in Medieval and Early Modern Britain*, ed. Krista J. Kesselring and Sara M. Butler (Leiden: Brill, 2018), pp. 216–36; also *Seeking Sanctuary*, esp. chapters 4, 5, 6.

[23]   Folger MS L.b.468; Godfrey Anstruther, 'The Last Days of the London Blackfriars', *Archivum Fratrum Praedicatorum* 45 (1975), 214. On the Hospitallers and jurisdiction, see McSheffrey, *Seeking Sanctuary*, ch. 4.

[24]   Holder, *Friaries*, p. 55.

[25]   See most recently, Highley, *Blackfriars*, pp. 14–34. Along with the non-citizens, Anthony House counted as a resident one prominent citizen – indeed, alderman, sheriff, and (in 1532–33) mayor – the haberdasher Stephen Pecocke, potentially significant for this study because of his involvement in Consistory court litigation against the hat makers in 1514 (House, 'City of London', p. 115; on the Consistory suit, see below chapter 3.) Pecocke leased a tenement from the prior from 1510; the terms of his lease and evidence that he paid for special permission for his property to have a door opening into the precinct suggest, however, that the property on which his dwelling house stood adjoined, but was not seen to comprise part of, the liberty. TNA, PROB 11/25/516, Will of Stephen Pecocke, 1536; TNA, PROB 11/32/637, Will of Dame Margaret Pecocke (1549); *Medieval Londoners Database* (New York: Fordham University, 2020) <https://mld.ace.fordham.edu/s/mld/person?id=539>; Raymund Palmer, 'The Black Friars of London', *Merry England* 13 (1889), 279; Anstruther, 'Last Days', 217; Folger, MS L.b.366 <https://luna.folger.edu/luna/servlet/s/pu735u>.

1522; Parliament was held there a number of times between the fourteenth and sixteenth centuries, including in 1514 and 1523; and the 1529 papal legates' inquiry regarding the marriage of Henry VIII and Queen Katherine of Aragon took place there.[26] A 1522 record lists as residents of the precinct Lord Zouche, Lord Cobham, Sir William Kingston, Sir Henry Wyatt, Sir William Parr, and other court notables.[27]

By the later sixteenth century, the precinct had also become one of the more notable enclaves of stranger artisans, similar to St Martin le Grand and St Katherine by the Tower. Our question is whether that population of stranger artisans went back to the beginning of the century. Scholarship on the London liberties after the dissolutions has argued that this immigrant population post-dated the mid-sixteenth century.[28] This is probably, but not certainly, correct: there is relatively little evidence for stranger artisans in the precinct before the 1560s. But there is *some* evidence, and it hints at the possibility of archival lacunae rather than absence of a community of alien residents. In 1562 John Vandart,[29] a seventy-five-year-old stranger hatmaker who testified regarding his knowledge of the precinct, gave an interesting formulation to describe his residence: he said that he had lived in the parish of St Andrew by the Wardrobe 'within the liberty of the Blackfriars' for over forty years, from the 1510s.[30] In a technical sense, the precinct was outside the diocese of London's parochial system, but those technicalities were not wholly observed. Some inhabitants of the precinct – the elite residents – did use one of the chapels of the priory as a parish church, labelled in some records as St Ann Blackfriars or St Ann Ludgate,[31] but Vandart's example indicates that not all did: the most extensive listing of London residents of the first half of the sixteenth century, the 1541 subsidy returns, registered Vandart in St Andrew's parish rather than in the parish of St Ann. This raises the possibility that others besides Vandart, listed as parishioners of St Andrew's, were actually resident in the liberty precinct rather than within the City proper. Though we

[26] Edward Hall, *Hall's Chronicle*, ed. Henry Ellis (London: J. Johnson, 1809), p. 640; William Dugdale, *Monasticon Anglicanum: A History of the Abbies and Other Monasteries, Hospitals, Frieries, and Cathedral and Collegiate Churches, with Their Dependencies, in England and Wales*, ed. Henry Ellis, 6 vols (London: Longman, Hurst, Rees, Orme & Brown, 1817), VI, 1487.

[27] *L&P*, III, no. 1053.

[28] House, 'City of London', pp. 146–47; Highley, *Blackfriars*, pp. 20–21, 47–49. Holder similarly does not mention aliens as residents in his discussion of the pre-Reformation Blackfriars precinct, *Friaries*, 52–55.

[29] The name is an anglicisation of the common Dutch surname 'Van den Aerde' (first documented in 1392). See *Nederlandse Familienamenbank*, s.v. 'Aart, van').

[30] Anstruther, 'Last Days', 224; he specified he was living there in 1517.

[31] *L&P*, III, no. 1053, XIX, no. 37; R. G. Lang, ed., *Two Tudor Subsidy Rolls for the City of London, 1541 and 1582* (London: London Record Society, 1993), pp. 37–42; John Stow, *A Survey of London*, ed. Charles Lethbridge Kingsford, 2 vols (Oxford: Clarendon Press, 1908), I, 341; Joseph Quincy Adams, 'The Conventual Buildings of Blackfriars, London, and the Playhouses Constructed Therein', *Studies in Philology* 14 (1917), 64–87. A 1502 will of a citizen founder in the City, John Bailles, asked for burial in St Anne's chapel in Blackfriars, but he lived in a City parish, St Benet Gracechurch. LMA, DL/C/B/004/MS09717/08, fol. 251v.

know little about Vandart, his name does appear on a 1531 list of hatmakers (see chapter 3); in that year he was a master of a hatmaker shop and had in his employ twenty people who worked at various stages of the hatmaking process.[32]

Vandart was not the only hatmaker parishioner of St Andrew's: for instance, Anthony Leveson, who (as 'Antony Levyson') was a signatory of the 1511 merger agreement to be examined in chapter 3, also lived in that parish. If he did not live in the Blackfriars precinct, he certainly lived near it. Neither St Ann Ludgate nor St Andrew by the Wardrobe had an extraordinary number of strangers, though, even in mid century; in 1541 nearby St Martin le Grand, though rather smaller in area than the Blackfriars precinct, had nearly seven times as many strangers as St Ann's and St Andrew's combined.[33] At mid century, St Martin's clearly had a much denser concentration of alien artisans and it is highly likely that would also have been true in 1500.

Yet in 1500 when the hatmakers were seeking to maintain independence from the supervision of London guilds, it made sense to settle and open workshops inside liberty jurisdictions like Blackfriars and St Katherine by the Tower to avoid searches by the various guilds wishing to establish dominance over them: the Cappers, the Hatter-merchants, and the Haberdashers. Blackfriars also had the attraction of aristocratic customers in the neighbourhood and the king's wardrobe, another important client, right next door. Following the agreement of 1511 by which the hatmakers came under the broad aegis of the Haberdashers' Company, however, living in the liberty to escape London jurisdiction and the supervision of its guilds became largely a moot point. Evidently men like John Vandart continued to live there, presumably for its other attractions. In any case, there is no need to assume that the Dutchmen who created the Fraternity of St James lived within the Blackfriars' precinct: other fraternities in the friaries attracted members from all over the City and beyond, and the Hatmakers' organisation likely did also.

THE HATMAKERS' GUILD: BETWEEN LONDON AND
THE LOW COUNTRIES

Precisely when our group of Dutch-speaking hatmakers came together to create the Fraternity of St James in Blackfriars is unknown. Almost all we know about the formation of the fraternity comes from the ordinances recorded in Guildhall Library, MS 15838. As we show in detail in chapter 4, palaeographical and dialectal evidence indicates that the articles themselves were written down at different times by two different scribes; the content of the articles, sometimes internally contradictory and with no obvious organisational principle, suggests that the collection of ordinances had accreted over some years rather than being devised at one or two sittings. Two dates are given in the

---

[32]   London, Archives of Parliament, MS HL/PO/JO/10/3/178/4.

[33]   Lang, *Two Tudor Subsidy Rolls*, pp. 5–9, 39–40, 74–75.

manuscript: the year 1501, in article 25, and the year 1511, the date of the agreement and union with the haberdashers. It seems likely, however, that the initial organisation pre-dated the writing of these ordinances; article 2, for instance, indicated that the quarterly fees, or quarterage, members were to pay should be 'such a summe as of olde tyme haue byn vsed and obserued'. This suggests some antiquity, though 'olde tyme' could be ten years or a century and may indeed refer even more vaguely to the general custom of quarterage. And while the members of this Fraternity of St James likely came from all over the City and from Southwark, too, whether the fraternity encompassed all the Dutch hatmakers working in the London area or only a subset of them is unknown. Unlike London citizen guilds, this fraternity had no mechanisms to enforce jurisdiction over all who practised the craft but, rather, could be only a voluntary association.

In many of the provisions, these ordinances closely resemble the regulations of both English and Low Countries guilds. Quarterly assemblies at which fees (quarterage) were paid (art. 14), fraternity feast days with a mass and penalties for non-attendance (art. 15), regulations regarding livery and mandating when it was to be worn (art. 15), payment of fees to move from trainee to member of the guild (art. 21), provision of alms to long-time members of guilds who had fallen on hard times or were elderly and infirm (art. 13, 17), compulsory attendance at funeral observances of brothers and sisters of the fraternity (art. 16): all were usual on both sides of the North Sea. The fees and the fines for breaking rules that are stipulated in the ordinances – e.g. 6s 8d (art. 3, 6, 7, 8, 11 etc.), 20s (art. 5, 9) – were standard amounts in English money (6s 8d was half a mark, 20s was £1). Article 4 forbidding brethren, including journeymen servants, from teaching the secrets of the craft to outsiders fits into the general tenor of guild ordinances through-out Europe. Guilds generally were attentive to confining the particular knowledge or skill of an artisan to members of the craft, the more so when the skill was particular; for instance, the London Pouchmakers in 1501 forbade members from teaching the craft of pouchmaking to those outside the guild.[34] There is more emphasis on secrecy, however, in the hatmakers' ordinances than in comparable English ordinances, likely reflecting the importance of controlling the specialised knowledge that allowed the hatmakers to monopolise felt hat manufacture in England.

TRAINING AND THE ORGANISATION OF WORK

Though in some ways the ordinances of the Fraternity of St James in Blackfriars resem-ble those of English guilds, in other ways they reflect the Dutch origins of the hatmakers and the substantially different structures of training and admission to guild membership prevailing in the cities of the Low Countries. In general, the labour conditions and organisation of work of Dutch and Flemish artisans were more flexible and less strictly regulated than in London.

---

[34] LMA, COL/AD/01/012, Letter Book M, fol. 39r.

Apprenticeships, for instance, were very different. The hatmakers designated (art. 3) a minimum of two years of training for 'learners', a period significantly shorter than London apprenticeships, which were both by custom and in practice at least seven years and sometimes as long as twelve.[35] A two-year training was, however, entirely consistent with practice in the Low Countries. Unlike the English system, where young adolescents entered apprenticeships in their early to mid teens, the training in the Low Countries was begun when the candidate was more mature (from late teens to as late as thirties) and had already had some general schooling and perhaps even years of work experience. The extent to which apprenticeships were regulated varied by craft, by city, and over time but, in general, in the later fifteenth century it was much less formalised than in London.[36] It is perhaps because the training practice among the Dutch hatmakers was quite different from English customs that the English-language ordinances and the 1511 agreement avoided the use of the word 'apprentice', instead using 'lerner', presumably as an English equivalent of the Dutch *leerknecht* or *leerling*. As far as we can determine, this is a unique use of this word in English in the context of craft training rather than book learning.[37] It is notable that the 1511 merger agreement with the Haberdashers also made no provision for the hatmakers taking apprentices in the English manner: reference is made to 'servants allowes' (hired servants), covenant servants, servingmen, journeymen, and learners. Though the hatmakers in London seem to have trained successors, these documents do not envisage the adoption of the long English apprenticeship. Too little is known about how hatmakers worked in the first half of the sixteenth century in London to clarify the terms on which training was accomplished. In the second half of the sixteenth century, the Haberdashers, aided by a 1563 Statute of Artificers and a 1566 act regulating the making of caps and hats, made largely successful efforts to regularise hatmakers' training along the same lines as English customs with minimum seven-year apprenticeships, supervised by the Haberdashers' guild.[38]

---

35 Stephanie R. Hovland, 'Apprenticeship in Later Medieval London (c.1300–c.1530)' (unpublished doctoral dissertation, University of London, 2006), pp. 87–92; Rhiannon Sandy, 'Apprenticeship Indentures and Apprentices in Medieval England, 1250–1500' (unpublished doctoral dissertation, University of Swansea, 2021), pp. 81–92.

36 Bert De Munck, *Technologies of Learning: Apprenticeship in Antwerp Guilds from the 15th Century to the End of the Ancien Régime* (Turnhout: Brepols, 2007), pp. 59–65; Karel Davids, 'Apprenticeship and Guild Control in the Netherlands, c.1450–1800', in *Learning on the Shop Floor: Historical Perspectives on Apprenticeship*, ed. Bert De Munck, Steven L. Kaplan, and Hugo Soly, (New York: Berghahn, 2007), pp. 65–84; Bert De Munck and Hilde de Ridder-Symoens, 'Education and Knowledge: Theory and Practice in an Urban Context', in *City and Society in the Low Countries, 1100–1600*, ed. Bruno Blondé, Marc Boone, and Anne-Laure Van Bruaene (Cambridge: Cambridge University Press, 2020), pp. 229–30.

37 'Lērner', *Middle English Compendium* <https://quod.lib.umich.edu/m/middle-english-dictionary/dictionary/MED25192/track?counter=1&search_id=7946638>, and OED, s.v. lerner, and see pp. 112–13, 125 below.

38 Duckworth, *Early History*, pp. 24–27; see also below ch. 3.

These differences in apprenticeship practice reflect the fundamentally different cultures of artisanal labour in the Low Countries and London. In London the apprenticeship system was an important means of controlling entry into craft occupations: by 1500 almost all those who became full members of London guilds were admitted after completing an apprenticeship they had begun in early adolescence. This served an important gatekeeping function, excluding any without parents or guardians who could or would arrange for and fund an apprenticeship contract for the adolescent boy in question.[39] By his mid teens, whether a boy would have the opportunity to become a master craftsman in London working within the guild environment was determined; only men with wealth and connections could bypass the apprenticeship system to enter a craft by redemption (paying a fee), while beginning an apprenticeship in one's twenties was rare.[40] The ordinances of the hatmakers, on the other hand, reflected the more open environment of craft work in the Low Countries. An apprenticeship, often of one or two years' duration,[41] was usually necessary to work as a 'free journeyman' and then a master in a craft. One might work as an 'unfree' journeyman, however, without an apprenticeship; undertaking formal training was only necessary if one wanted to be a master. An artisan could pursue such an ambition post-adolescence: it was not uncommon for a man to enter into an apprenticeship contract after having worked as an unfree journeyman for some years, having accumulated some capital and wishing to achieve the credentials to set up a shop of his own. In many cities in the Low Countries immigrants were tolerated or even welcomed, and if they had been trained elsewhere many craft guilds had measures that allowed them to demonstrate their skill for entry to the membership in place of an apprenticeship. Similarly, movement between allied crafts was fairly common.[42]

The hatmakers' ordinances reflect this more informal and less structured world of artisanal affiliation than pertained in London. Article 4, for instance, allowed fullers, weavers, tailors, and others to be accepted as brethren of the hatmakers' fraternity after they had been 'lafulli chosin' by demonstrating that they were 'instructe and lernid before in the seid craft of hatmakynge'. In the London guild system, it was possible for a member of one guild to transfer to another should he prefer to practise another craft, but it was

---

39 S. H. Rigby, *English Society in the Later Middle Ages: Class, Status, and Gender* (New York: St Martin's Press, 1995), pp. 158–59; Hovland, 'Apprenticeship', pp. 151–62; Sandy, 'Apprenticeship', pp. 95–101.

40 Sandy, 'Apprenticeship', pp. 78–81, 86.

41 This is the duration specified, for instance, in Guillame Des Marez, *Le Compagnonnage des chapelliers Bruxellois* (Brussels: Lamertin, 1909), p. 9.

42 De Munck, *Technologies of Learning*, pp. 59–65; Bert De Munck, 'One Counter and Your Own Account: Redefining Illicit Labour in Early Modern Antwerp', *Urban History* 37 (2010), 26–44; Reinhold Reith, 'Circulation of Skilled Labour in Late Medieval and Early Modern Central Europe', in *Guilds, Innovation, and the European Economy, 1400–1800*, ed. Stephan R. Epstein and Maarten Roy Prak (Cambridge: Cambridge University Press, 2008), pp. 114–42; Peter Stabel, 'Social Mobility and Apprenticeship in Late Medieval Flanders', in *Learning on the Shop Floor: Historical Perspectives on Apprenticeship*, ed. Bert De Munck, Steven L. Kaplan, and Hugo Soly (New York: Berghahn, 2007), pp. 158–78.

sometimes difficult or inconvenient. This meant in some cases that a citizen's nominal guild affiliation and his actual occupation were at odds. A trained skinner who entered the freedom through the Skinners' Company, for instance, could become a waxchandler by trade but might remain a member of the Skinners through his life.[43] As article 4 of the hatmakers' ordinances suggests, however, alien and foren artisans in the London area could be more adaptable and fungible in their craft identities and affiliations, and the many who came from the Low Countries would have seen this as normal. Work life was likely more flexible for the immigrants, who were both excluded from the London guilds but also freed from them.

Though Londoners likely would have bristled at the suggestion, this less- or at least differently-structured training and craft organisation neither caused nor resulted in poor training. It did mean, however, that workers' credentials sometimes needed establishing in ways other than completion of a guild-enrolled apprenticeship. Article 24 mandated letters of attestation from former masters for servants coming from overseas. This is one of the earliest signs of such testimonial letters for migrant craft workers in England, but it was a well-established practice in the Empire, France, and elsewhere on the continent, where a higher degree of labour mobility was both an assumption and a reality. Such letters were associated with the practice of the *Wanderjahr* for skilled trades such as goldsmithing: artisans migrated to different centres and presented testimonial letters stating their training and skills, often issued by civic or guild authorities in their previous place of residence.[44] The Goldsmiths and the Weavers, both trades for whom alien skills were indispensable, similarly asked for such testimonial letters from immigrants trained overseas,[45] but most other London guilds would have

---

43 See for instance William Colte, a skinner by guild affiliation and waxchandler by trade; John Knyll, who became his apprentice through the Skinners' guild in 1509, learned the craft of waxchandler from him rather than skinner. Both worked as waxchandlers and yet remained members of the Skinners; his actual work did not prevent Colte from serving as warden of the Skinners' guild in 1523–24. GL, MS 30719/1, fol. 41r; 30727/2, 60r, 211v; LMA, COL/CA/01/01/003, Repertory 3, fol. 174v. Though transferring from one craft to another had been more common earlier in the fifteenth century, and even around 1500 it was still possible to change affiliations, by that later date it could be difficult. The Waxchandlers refused to take Colte and Knyll as members, for instance (as above, Repertory 3, fol. 174v), and the Upholders fined members £20 if they sought to leave and join another guild (LMA, COL/AD/01/012, Letter Book M, 6v).

44 For examples of testimonial letters on the continent as far back as the late fourteenth century, see Knut Schulz, 'Handwerkerwanderungen und Neuburger im Spätmittelalter', in *Neuburger im Späten Mittelalter: Migration und Austausch in der Städtelandschaft des Alten Reiches (1250–1550)*, ed. Rainer Christoph Schwinges (Berlin: Duncker & Humblot, 2002), pp. 445–78 (448–54). On labour mobility more generally, see Stephan R. Epstein, 'Labour Mobility, Journeymen Organisations and Markets in Skilled Labour in Europe, 14th–18th Centuries', in *Le Technicien dans la cité en Europe occidentale, 1250–1650*, ed. Mathieu Arnoux and Piere Monnet, Collection de l'Ecole française de Rome, 325 (Rome: Ecole française de Rome, 2004), pp. 251–69; Reith, 'Circulation of Skilled Labour', pp. 114–42.

45 Lisa Jefferson, ed., *Wardens' Accounts and Court Minute Books of the Goldsmiths' Mistery of London, 1334–1446* (Woodbridge: Boydell, 2003), pp. 242–43; Consitt, *London Weavers'*

had no need for letters of attestation from overseas as, generally, aliens were simply not admitted. Indeed, in most cases craftsmen trained elsewhere in England were also excluded. The London guild system was predicated on a stationary work life from entry into apprenticeships in early adolescence until the end of one's career; though reality was certainly less simple (and exceptions could be made for those with connections and cash), almost all London guild members followed this path. Alien craftsmen in London, on the other hand, often – indeed probably usually – had migrated at an older age than early adolescence (though some had come as children with their families). For those from the Low Countries and likely elsewhere in Europe, too, this movement in one's twenties or later was normal and the organisation of craft work in cities accommodated migrants at different career stages.[46] Although the London guild system was much less adaptable, migrants were forced to work outside those structures anyway.

A potential disadvantage of this more flexible labour practice was instability for employers: servants with hatmaking skills were evidently in demand in London and thus it was a challenge to retain them for the length of their contract or covenant judging by the number of articles in the ordinances of the Fraternity of St James dedicated to that issue. In article 1, only those who had fulfilled their previous covenants with masters both in London and overseas were to be admitted; articles 6, 7, 11, 20, and 25 address the problem of servants departing from their masters without permission and the related problem of servants' being lured away by other employers. This was a concern also for London's citizen guilds,[47] but the hatmakers' ordinances place far more emphasis on illicit servant mobility than was usual in England. Such emphasis was common, however, in Dutch guild ordinances.[48] The repeated return to this issue from different angles in these ordinances suggests that hatmakers found it difficult to keep servants and to force them to fulfil the contracts or covenants that bound servant to employer. This reflected the more fluid structures of work among the hatmakers in particular and the artisans who worked outside the guilds in general; as foren and alien artisan shopholders worked outside the guilds and of civic authority, they also had fewer mechanisms to enforce covenants and contracts. This likely also speaks to the attractiveness of hatmaker servants: they had options. Indeed, provisions for servants who had broken their covenants to be

---

Company, p. 213; Berry, 'Guilds', pp. 545–49.

[46] Bruno Blondé, Frederik Buylaert, Jan Dumolyn, and Peter Stabel, 'Living Together in the City: Social Relationships Between Norm and Practice', in *City and Society in the Low Countries, 1100–1600*, ed. Bruno Blondé, Marc Boone, and Anne-Laure Van Bruaene (Cambridge: Cambridge University Press, 2020), pp. 81–82; Marc Boone and Peter Stabel, 'New Burghers in the Late Medieval Towns of Flanders and Brabant: Conditions of Entry, Rules and Reality', in *Neubürger im späten Mittelalter: Migration und Austausch in der Städtelandschaft des Alten Reiches (1250–1550)*, ed. Rainer Christoph Schwinges and Roland Gerber (Berlin: Duncker & Humblot, 2002), pp. 317–32; Stabel, 'Social Mobility', p. 159.

[47] Indeed, luring away ('withdrawing') another man's servant was an actionable trespass under English law. Morris S. Arnold, ed., *Select Cases of Trespass from the King's Courts, 1307–1399*, 2 vols, Selden Society 100 (London: Quaritch, 1985), I, xliv.

[48] De Munck and De Ridder-Symoens, 'Education', p. 230.

welcomed back to a master's employ suggests they were in such demand that they had to be forgiven their trespasses.

Like the ordinances of London citizen guilds, the hatmakers' ordinances assumed a workshop model of craft production, with a master, several journeymen servants, and perhaps a trainee working in the master's shop on the ground floor of his own house. Article 23, however, hints towards a different form of labour organisation, dependent on networks of pieceworkers, that had become evident in garment manufacture in London by the end of the fifteenth century, as described in chapter 1. The hatmakers were resistant to such changes, as indeed were other guilds, both in London and in the Low Countries. Article 23 mandated that craft work be confined to the shops of the brethren in the guild, that they must 'put no hattes forto be flosshede, nor cause no hattes to be flosshede, nor put no feltes to be made withoute his house'. What 'put' here means is presumably the practice that a century later became routinely designated by the verb phrase 'put out', namely 'to arrange for (work) to be done off the premises or "out of house" (by contractors, freelancers, etc.)'.[49] As with many other sectors of the garment industry, this was unsuccessful: by the early 1530s, as we shall see in the next chapter, the London hatmakers were operating large-scale piecework operations employing as many as one hundred workers.

CONFLICT AND THE POLITICO-LEGAL CONTEXT OF CRAFT ASSOCIATIONS

Though late medieval English and Dutch people shared many assumptions about social, economic, and political structures, immigrants from the Low Countries would have found that Londoners did some things differently. One difference was the management of interpersonal conflicts. In the Low Countries, violent quarrels and even homicides were often handled through compensation; in England, homicides in particular were under the sole purview of the royal courts and assaults were normally also dealt with through local or royal courts. One of the remarkable aspects of the hatmakers' ordinances is that they were written as if the members of the guild still lived under the broader political and legal conditions that applied in Dutch cities, especially those in the southern Low Countries, such as Brussels, Bruges, Antwerp, and Ghent. It is impossible to know whether this was intentional maintenance of home country practices or unconscious assumption that their customs were simply the way things were done everywhere.

It was common for guild ordinances in both England and the Low Countries to specify ways that conflicts between guild brethren were to be solved: as articles 8 and 9 reflect, disputes were usually to be handled in-house rather than taking them to outside

---

49   See OED, s.v. put, 10(c).

authorities or formal court proceedings.[50] If this preference for internal settlements would have seemed normal to an English observer, in other ways the hatmakers' ordinances proceeded from assumptions that would have been surprising to their English counterparts. Some lip service was paid to the different context: Article 8 stated that its provisions were not to meddle with matters that touched the king's highness or the liberty and right of the church. Nonetheless the ordinances that followed simply ignored the king's jurisdiction over criminal matters, with provisions that were premised instead on the substantially different legal system in the cities of the Low Countries.

Article 10's forbidding of 'maliciouse, iniurose, or words of dispite' is similar to language in English ordinances about verbal altercations,[51] but both the range of disputes and the language employed in article 12 fall outside what guilds in England normally regulated:

> Item, it is established and ordeyned that if any broder of the same fraternitte maliciousli drawe owt his daggar, sword, or knyf, or any other instrument defensive to hurt or wronge any man of the same fraternite, that he shall pay to the masturs and wardene at euery suche defaut ii s. iiij d. And he that drawith or castith hurt or wronge any man of the same fraternite with stonys, lovis, pottis, dishis, candilstickis, or any other thing [aboue rehersed [...]. And it be a mayme, he shall pay x s. ouyer and byside that he so hurtith and wrongyth shall compownde with hym that is so hurte and wronged and recompense and satisfy him for his hurtis and wrongis aftur the discrecion of the maisturs and wardens of the same fraternite or any other iuge before whome it shall fortune hym to be callid for the same trespasse. And if any broder of the seid fraternite wilfully sle any man of the same fraternite, that thenne he shal be put owt and vtturly excludet from the seid fraternite to be.

English guild ordinances did not legislate for such violent encounters between fraternity brothers, not because they never happened, but because homicide as a felony belonged to the king and assaults were normally heard at first instance in local courts (in London, wardmote inquests or, for more serious cases, the sheriffs' court).[52] Article 12, however, blithely ignores the English way of doing things. Even the language of article 12 – especially the list

---

[50] A couple of examples: the Upholders (1498), LMA, COL/AD/01/012, Letter Book M, fol. 7r; the English Weavers (1492), Frances Consitt, *The London Weavers' Company*, 2 vols (Oxford: Clarendon Press, 1933), I, 222.

[51] E.g. Upholders (1498), Stringers (1499), and Cobblers (1501), LMA, COL/AD/01/012, Letter Book M, folios 6v, 17v, 32v–33r; English Weavers (1492), Consitt, *London Weavers' Company*, I, 218.

[52] For England, see for instance Charles Gross, 'Modes of Trial in the Mediæval Boroughs of England', *Harvard Law Review* 15 (1902), 705; Miriam Müller, 'Social Control and the Hue and Cry in Two Fourteenth-Century Villages', *Journal of Medieval History* 31 (2005), 29–53. For the Low Countries, see Joost de Damhouder, *La pratique et enchiridion des causes criminelles* (Louvain: Jehan Bathen, 1555), pp. 139–40. Our thanks to Stephanie Brown and Quentin Verreycken for these references.

of items with which one might injure a person, 'stonys, lovis,[53] pottis, dishis, candilstickis' – resonated with Dutch-language formulas used in civic ordinances from the southern Low Countries, which carefully delineated different fines or compensations for different weapons, including stones, pots, and chairs.[54]

Even more strikingly assumptive of a Low Countries context is Article 12's prescription that any guild brother who maimed another 'shall compownde with' and 'recompense and satisfy' the person whom he hurt. Composition or settlement of interpersonal wrongs by money compensation, rather than state prosecution, was common in much of Europe, including in Netherlandish cities.[55] Arbitrated settlements did exist in England but were ad hoc and unlikely to be assumed as conventional in regulations.[56] In Dutch and Flemish cities composition was available for homicide as well as for less serious crimes and the hatmakers' ordinances presumed this was also true in London. The last clause in article 12, 'if any broder of the seid fraternite wilfully sle any man of the same fraternite, that thenne he shal be put owt and vtturly excludet from the seid fraternite', imagined a scenario where a member had killed one of his brethren and then carried on with his trade after settling with the victim's family. In England, guilds did not deal with such matters, as convicted slayers were executed, solving that delicate problem.

Article 12 operates with assumptions about the workings of courts and the law that are not only different from the English context but outright incompatible with English law.

---

53   To modern readers, loaves of bread may not seem an obvious offensive weapon, but hardened loaves were used as plates. In the Middle English romance *Sir Tristrem*, Morgan assails the hero with a 'lof' (871). See Neil Cartlidge, 'Medieval Romance Mischief', in *Romance Rewritten: The Evolution of Middle English Romance*, ed. Elizabeth Archibald, Megan G. Leitch, and Corinne J. Saunders (Cambridge: D. S. Brewer, 2018), pp. 27–48. See also a late 14th-century London homicide involving two Dutch men, an Italian man, and a Dutch 'frowe', instigated by the throwing of a crust of bread. Shannon McSheffrey, 'Quarrel over a "frowe"', *Sanctuary Seekers in England, 1394–1557* (2020) <https://sanctuaryseekers.ca/2020/07/06/frowe/>.

54   Louis Maes, *Vijf Eeuwen Stedelijk Strafrecht. Bijdragen tot de Rechts- en Cultuurgeschiedenis der Nederlanden* (Antwerp: De Sikkel, 1974), pp. 270–71, 274–76; Fernand Vanhemelryck, *De Criminaliteit in de Ammanie van Brussel van de Late Middeleeuwen Tot Het Einde van Het Ancien Regime (1404–1798)* (Brussels: Koninklijke Academie voor Wetenschappen, Letteren en Schone Kunsten van België, 1961), pp. 124–26. Our thanks to Chanelle Delameillieure for these references. English formulas in criminal indictments, by contrast, focused on purpose-made weapons ('swords, staves, knives, and daggers') rather than domestic implements. Such phrases are simply not to be found in guild records, as far as we know.

55   Bernard Dauven, 'Composition et rémission au XVe siècle: Confusion, concurrence ou complémentarité? Le cas du Brabant', and Guy Dupont, 'Le temps des compositions: Pratiques judiciaires à Bruges et à Gand du XIVe au XVIe siècle', in *Préférant miséricorde à rigueur de justice: pratiques de la grâce (XIIIe-XVIIe siècles)*, ed. Bernard Dauven and Xavier Rousseaux (Louvain-la-Neuve: Presses Universitaires de Louvain, 2017), pp. 31–52, 55–61. For English practice, see John G. Bellamy, *The Criminal Trial in Later Medieval England: Felony Before the Courts from Edward I to the Sixteenth Century* (Toronto: University of Toronto Press, 1998).

56   Edward Powell, 'Settlement of Disputes by Arbitration in Fifteenth-Century England', *Law and History Review* 2 (1984), 21–43.

It is not clear whether those who drew up the ordinances were oblivious or lazy (relying, for instance, on a model set of ordinances from a Low Countries guild that was simply copied), or deliberately stuck to a legal system that seemed more 'right' to them than English crown prosecution. Article 12 does suggest that those who drew it up had not long been resident in London and in this, as in the general structures of artisan workshops and labour, had not fully assimilated to the host culture.

GUILD GOVERNANCE

The hatmakers' ordinances leave the governance structure of the fraternity mostly implicit, though the basic outline is clear. 'Maisters', 'kepers', and 'wardens' ('meysters' and 'ouersienders' in Dutch) are mentioned in various articles; though in many London guilds, masters and wardens were two separate offices, for the hatmakers they were synonyms (see art. 2, 3, 9, 25).[57] There were four masters or wardens. The 1511 agreement mandated – and this was consonant with practice in London guilds – that on or near the guild's feast day, the feast of St James the Less (1 May),[58] the wardens were 'elected and chosen' from amongst the members of the craft. The vagueness of language – leaving unstated how such elections were conducted and who made the choices – was typical of London craft ordinances as well as these ones. The office of guild warden was in general both prestigious and burdensome in England in the years around 1500; many guilds mandated fines for those who refused to take on the office of warden, a problem the hatmakers also legislated for, as indicated by article 26.

Unlike the governors of most London guilds, however, the hatmakers' wardens were not responsible to the City Chamberlain and the Mayor and Aldermen. Instead, in articles 5, 26, and 27, reference is made to 'the bishop or ordinary [bishop's delegate]' as the next-level authority beyond the guild officials themselves. Placing a craft association under episcopal authority was unusual in the English context which, in general, saw such supervision as one of the basic functions of city and town governments, but there were precedents. A few London guilds – the Blacksmiths in 1434 and the Shearmen in 1452, for instance[59] – had registered their ordinances with both City and bishop. In the Shearmen's case, the duality of authority – 'the law spirituall and temporalle' – that the religious and

---

57 Somewhat confusingly, the word 'maister' was also used to mean a brother of the guild who operated a shop and employed servants, though as art. 3 and 5 suggest, it may not have been confusing in context.

58 In England, St James the Less was celebrated together with St Philip on 1 May. C. R Cheney, *A Handbook of Dates for Students of British History* (Cambridge: Cambridge University Press, 1997), p. 89.

59 Henry Charles Coote and John Robert Daniel-Tyssen, ed., *Ordinances of Some Secular Guilds of London, from 1354 to 1496* (London: Nichols, 1871), pp. 41–44, 47–56; Marc Fitch, ed., *Index to Testamentary Records in the Commissary Court of London, 1374–1570*, Historical Manuscripts Commission, JP 12–13, 2 vols (London: HMSO, 1969, 1974), I, 208; II, 302; originals, LMA, MS DL/C/B/004/MS09171/003, fol. 455r; MS DL/C/B/004/MS09171/005, folios 101v–107v.

civic functions of the guild entailed was acknowledged in some clauses by recourse both to the 'officers of the Bisshope of London' and to the City's chamberlain when internal measures did not suffice.[60] Though London citizen guilds invariably also had religious functions, there is little evidence that others submitted their ordinances to the bishop or his delegates. An exception that may prove the rule is the Fraternity of St Christopher of the Water Bearers, the ordinances of which were registered in the bishop's records in 1496;[61] the water bearers, sometimes called holy water clerks, were laymen who assisted in parish upkeep and administration. Though the ordinances did address occupational regulation, the Water Bearers were not a recognised guild in the civic sense and members of the fraternity were not citizens; moreover, their parochial function may have made it natural to ask for ratification of their regulations in the bishop's court. The ordinances of London citizen craft guilds registered in the civic records around 1500, on the other hand, do not mention diocesan officials alongside the chamberlain, mayor, and aldermen in the line of authority, as the Shearmen had in 1452.

The hatmakers, like the Water Bearers, were not freemen of London. They were aliens, and so had good reason around 1500 to think the civic hierarchy unlikely to welcome a stranger guild. The obvious alternative was to put the Fraternity of St James under the bishop's aegis. There is nothing in the ordinances themselves that indicate, however, that they were submitted to the bishop or his ordinary for approval, as the Water Bearers had done or as London citizen guilds did to the mayor and aldermen. There is, moreover, nothing about the formation of the Fraternity of St James in the surviving diocesan records, though the London bishop's registers for this period survive only in part.[62] It is notable that though the articles indicate generically the 'bishop or ordinary' as the ultimate authority, they do not specify which diocese they mean. As the fraternity was located in his diocese it would presumably be the bishop of London; perhaps it was left unspecified as some brothers of the fraternity likely lived across the Thames in Southwark, which was in the diocese of Winchester. But possibly those who founded the Fraternity of St James conceptualised their organisation as more or less independent of external authorities of any kind.

The ordinances written into Guildhall Library, MS 15838 show how a group of stranger artisans negotiated the significant differences between London and their cities of origin in the Low Countries. Both the structures and customs of artisan labour and the legal and political environment in which guilds operated were significantly different in late medieval Netherlandish cities than they were in London. Whether the hatmakers purposely

---

60   Coote and Daniel-Tyssen, ed., *Ordinances*, p. 54; the Blacksmiths' ordinances, by contrast, do not refer to any authority, civic or ecclesiastical, superior to the guild (*ibid.*, pp. 41–44).

61   Coote and Daniel-Tyssen, ed., *Ordinances*, pp. 79–81.

62   The ordinances of some other fraternities are in the records of the Commissary Court that mostly probated wills. There were also some in the main bishop's register, though the register for the years around 1500 is missing. Bishop Richard Fitzjames's register, 1506–22 (LMA, DL/A/A/005/MS09531/009), does not have any entries relating to the hatmakers but does record ordinances for two religious fraternities (folios 12v–13r and 29r–30v), including the Dutch fraternity dedicated to St Barbara at Blackfriars, discussed above, p. 35.

maintained or simply unconsciously assumed their home country practices is impossible to know. Nor, unfortunately, do we have any evidence about how the newly organised hatmakers used their ordinances or conducted their guild in the decade or so the Fraternity of St James operated as an independent craft organisation. In 1511, the hatmakers' guild was brought under the governance of the Haberdashers' Company.

CHAPTER 3

The Hatmakers and the 1511 Agreement

Around the year 1500 in the precinct of the London Blackfriars priory, the Dutch hatmakers in the metropolis created a rogue craft guild – rogue from the perspective of the London authorities, that is. This allowed them to remain independent from the English citizen craft guilds in London who claimed that stranger artisans could work only under their supervision. The hatmakers took their stand of independence in the context of a series of amalgamations and take-overs among the citizen guilds most centrally involved in the making and selling of headgear. In 1501 the Hatter-merchants and Hurers-Cappers amalgamated, perhaps to resist absorption by the Haberdashers; in 1502, however, this united company of the Hurers-Hatter-merchants was indeed brought under the authority of the Haberdashers. The Haberdashers' Company could now lay claim to control the headgear market in all its aspects: domestic production, import, and retail. Such monopolies were always aspirational in fifteenth- and sixteenth-century London: in practice, haberdashers could never corner all headgear imports (which continued to enter the country in large quantities through both English and stranger merchants),[1] but the Haberdashers' consolidation of power in the first decade of the sixteenth century was impressive. The Dutch hatmakers' fraternity nonetheless were able to continue their stubborn independence through the first decade of the sixteenth century.

The hatmakers could not hold out long, however, especially when the regime of the new king Henry VIII (r.1509–47) proved friendly to the Haberdashers' Company: the guild received a royal charter in 1510 and, as Ian Archer notes, by 1515 it had solidified its place at eighth among the Great Twelve Companies in the City.[2] In 1511, soon after receiving their charter, the Haberdashers convinced the royal council to order the hatmakers' fraternity to come under the rule of the Haberdashers.[3] This was the last piece of the puzzle, in a sense, for the Haberdashers' control of the headgear market from production

---

[1] See *LCA*, part 4, vols 1–15.

[2] Ian W. Archer, *The History of the Haberdashers' Company* (Chichester: Phillimore and Co., 1991), pp. 57–62.

[3] LMA, DL/C/0206, fol. 319r.

to retail. This was not simply about curbing the independence of the stranger hatmakers but also involved rivalry with other London citizen guilds, especially the Mercers and the Merchant Tailors, who also imported and sold hats and caps (and would continue to do so).[4] The Haberdashers nonetheless presumably henceforth largely controlled the sourcing of domestically-produced hats by controlling the London hatmakers, especially in tandem with a 1512 Act forbidding the import of hats from overseas.[5]

The absorption of the stranger hatmakers into the Haberdashers' Company was not without parallel: the stranger goldsmiths worked under the umbrella of the Goldsmiths' Company as skilled practitioners of a luxury craft, while the Stranger Weavers had experienced amalgamation with their London citizen counterparts. There were also, of course, differences. English and stranger goldsmiths and weavers practised the same craft, but the stranger hatmakers had no English peers. The Haberdashers' Company, with which the hatmakers were merged, were primarily merchants, not artisans; the citizen cappers who had become part of the company in 1502 also fabricated headgear, but by different processes and skills. Haberdashers sold goods that artisans in a broad spectrum of trades produced: caps, hats, purses, pouches, pins, ribbons, girdles, points, and so on. It was crucial for their business model to control access to the goods those artisans produced: as Archer notes, the rise of the Haberdashers was predicated on their ability to annex the artisanal crafts whose wares they sold.[6]

Caps and hats were central to haberdashery; as we have seen, hats especially were a high-end luxury commodity attractive to the desirable aristocratic market. Taking over the Dutch hatmakers would have been strategically useful to the Haberdashers, though the advantage it brought to the hatmakers, beyond the promise of enhanced retail opportunities, is less clear. Nevertheless, by 1511 the hatmakers could no longer hold out and were taken over by the Haberdashers. Historians of the Haberdashers' Company have presented the 1511 agreement between the Haberdashers and the hatmakers as a mutually advantageous deal, suggesting that it gave the latter the status of full and equal membership of the Company,[7] but that could not have been the case as the hatmakers were strangers and thus ineligible to become citizen guild members.

It is true that the 1511 document reads as a merger between two equal groups (and that itself is important, as discussed below). Later evidence shows, however, that the union was forced: multiple lawsuits between the Haberdashers' Company and hatmakers in

---

4   See for instance merchant tailor William Bonyvaunt who in 1550 had a large array of headgear (caps, hats, night-caps) in his shop. Matthew P. Davies, 'The Tailors of London and Their Guild, c.1300–1500' (unpublished doctoral dissertation, University of Oxford, 1994), p. 237.

5   The legislation was re-enacted in 1529: 3 Hen. VIII, c.15; 21 Hen. VIII, c. 9; SR, III, 33–34, 290. On this and other protectionist legislation, see Christopher John Heal, 'The Felt Hat Industry of Bristol and South Gloucestershire, 1530–1909' (unpublished doctoral dissertation, University of Bristol, 2012), pp. 49–51.

6   Archer, Haberdashers' Company, pp. 12–13, 29.

7   Rosemary Weinstein, The History of the Worshipful Company of Feltmakers, 1604–2004 (Chichester: Phillimore, 2004), pp. 5–6; Archer, Haberdashers' Company, p. 61.

the years that followed indicate that the relationship was not a happy one. In a 1514 lawsuit brought to the bishop's Consistory court by the Haberdashers' Company against four hatmakers over quarterage fees,[8] one of the Haberdashers' wardens, future Lord Mayor Stephen Pecocke, testified about the circumstances that led to the amalgamation: he and several other leading Haberdashers had presented their grievances about the alien hatmakers and cappers to the king's council. As a result, he said, 'the strangers were enjoined and mandated [by the council] to adhere and conform to the statutes and ordinances of the Haberdashers'.[9] In other words, a royal order was issued that stranger hatmakers would have to comply with the labour statutes that forbade their work outside guild structures and to place themselves under the Haberdashers' supervision. There is also evidence in that same 1514 lawsuit that further coercion was necessary in 1511 to enforce adherence to this order of the king's council: hatmaker John Pawpe testified that 'before he was sworn, his goods were seized and distrained by the wardens of the [Haberdashers'] guild and officers of the lord mayor for the payment of the quarterage', and that in order to have his goods back again he had had to swear an oath to the Haberdashers.[10]

This oath did not make those hatmakers members of the Haberdashers' guild, however, either in their own estimation or that of the Company itself. Anthony Leveson, one of the signatories of the 1511 agreement, testified in the 1514 lawsuit that he was 'not a brother or member of that fraternity or society [the Haberdashers' Company]', but rather an *artifex extraneus*, a stranger artisan. He was bound to pay quarterage fees to the Master and Wardens of the Haberdashers, but in his view that was as far as the relationship went.[11] Henry Hill, one of the Haberdasher wardens, concurred in his testimony, saying that the stranger artisans paid only quarterage, bearing none of the other 'burdens [*onera*]' of membership, and thus did not have full status in the guild as London

8   Master and Wardens of the Haberdashers *contra* Everard Presson, Anthony Leveson, John Pawpe, and John Nicoll, 1514–1515, LMA, DL/C/0206, folios 293r–294r, 301r–302r, 317r–321v.

9   'Interfuit quando ex parte Magistri et Gardianorum dicte fraternitatis proposita erat querela contra diversos extraneos et alienigenas hatmakers et capmakers coram quibusdam consilariis domini nostri regis, et tunc injunctum et mandatum fuit eisdem extraneos quod adhererent et conformarent se statutis et ordinacionibus illius artis seu fraternitatis anglice le haberdasshers'. LMA, DL/C/0206, fol. 319r. Records of the king's council in this period survive only in partial later copies at the Henry E. Huntington Library; unfortunately, this matter between the Haberdashers and the Hatmakers was evidently not of interest to the later copyists and does not appear in those records. See San Marino, CA, Henry E. Huntington Library, MSS EL 2652, 2654, 2655, 2768.

10   'Antequam sic juratus fuit, bona sua erant capta et districta per gardianos ipsius artis et officiarios domini maioris pro huiusmodi le quarterage videlicet iiii d pro singulis anni terminis solvendos et ut rehaberet illa bona sua juramentum predictum prestitit'. LMA, DL/C/0206, fol. 301r.

11   'Iste juratus non sit frater sive socius illius fraternitatis sive societatis ut dicit, tamen ipse pro seipso solvit eisdem Magistro et Guardianis iiii d singulis anni terminis tanquam artifex extraneus'. LMA, DL/C/0206, folios 293v–294r; see also Everard Presson's testimony (fol. 293r).

citizens did.[12] This was normal for strangers associated with London citizen guilds. Even in what appears to have been a friendly relationship between stranger goldsmiths and the London Goldsmiths' Company, the alien artisans were not included in the memorial masses and other collective observances that fostered the solidarity and conviviality historians have associated with guild life.[13] And in the case of the hatmakers and the Haberdashers, it does not appear that relations were friendly at all.

It is, of course, possible that some hatmakers were more inclined than others to enter into the 1511 agreement: perhaps Pawpe had had to be dragged kicking and screaming, while other hatmakers thought that alliance with this powerful guild would be of benefit to both parties. In fact, when Stephen Pecocke described the union as being 'for the public good of both crafts', he characterised the alliance in these positive terms.[14] Both the tone and the terms of the 1511 agreement have an *appearance* of equality and mutual respect. The hatmakers, by the terms of this agreement, were to retain considerable independence: the agreement refers to their continuing to have their own 'masters and wardens', for instance, who were to keep 'good order and rule'. Although the wardens were reduced in number from four to two, this was nonetheless a significant concession for stranger artisans in London in the 1510s. And the hatmakers were – as the witnesses in the 1514 suit put it – still to be considered a separate *ars* or *societas*. The 1511 agreement indeed bears out the interpretation that the hatmakers advanced in their defence of the 1514 Consistory suit, that the main relationship henceforth between the hatmakers and the Haberdashers' company would be pecuniary: most of the clauses in that agreement dealt with the fees hatmakers would pay on establishing their workshops or entering into service, to be split equally between the Hatmakers' Fraternity and the Haberdashers' Company. Though one clause limited to four the number of servants a hatmaker could employ at any one time, no other parts of the agreement referred to other common aspects of guild authority, such as the right of the Haberdasher wardens to inspect shops or wares.

So, for the master hatmakers at least, this might have seemed like an agreement they could live with. It may have had advantages: hatmakers could live and operate their workshops in City jurisdiction, rather than being confined to the liberties. Just possibly they also received a *quid pro quo* in the 1512 statute, 'An Act concerning Hattis and Cappis', which forbade the importation of hats and caps to England.[15] Though ostensibly the

12   LMA, DL/C/0206, fol. 318r.

13   See the lists of those who attended obits of guild members in London, Goldsmiths' Hall, WACM, Books 4C and 4D, passim (e.g. 4C, 122, 124, 132, 133, 135, 149, etc.). On guild solidarities, see Gervase Rosser, 'Going to the Fraternity Feast: Commensality and Social Relations in Late Medieval England', *Journal of British Studies* 33 (1994), 430–46. See also Gervase Rosser, *The Art of Solidarity in the Middle Ages: Guilds in England 1250–1550* (Oxford: Oxford University Press, 2015).

14   'pro bono publico utriusque artis videlicet tam haberdasshers quam hatmakers'. LMA, DL/C/0206, fol. 320v.

15   3 Hen. VIII, c.15, *SR*, III, 33–34.

statute addressed the labour problems of English workers in the capping industry, it also had the function of forbidding the import of ready-made hats as well as caps. As there was as yet no significant production of felt hats by English artisans, one important effect of the statute was to give a monopoly to the stranger hatmakers in London and elsewhere in England, who henceforth were in theory to provide all the hats for the domestic English market. Although the importation of headgear by no means stopped – merchants were granted special licences to import hats and caps[16] and there were complaints from cappers and hatmakers in the 1520s and 1530s that this and a subsequent 1529 statute reiterating the ban on imports were being ignored[17] – nonetheless there are indications that the 1512 statute did indeed stimulate a domestic industry in the production of both caps and, perhaps especially, hats.

THE HATMAKERS AND HABERDASHERS AFTER 1511

The Haberdashers themselves may not have envisaged the relative independence of the hatmakers that the wording of the 1511 agreement allowed for, expecting, perhaps, the establishment of a more conventionally subordinate relationship between the guild's masters and these stranger artisans. Certainly, within two or three years the Haberdashers had begun to take a hard line stance. It is important to note that the terms of the relationship between the hatmakers and the Haberdashers' Company were not dependent solely on the 1511 agreement; the 1514 Consistory suit refers also to an oath the hatmakers swore to the Haberdashers' Company upon their initial registration in the guild, a mass swearing-in of the hatmakers that presumably occurred shortly after the 1511 agreement.[18] The swearing of such an oath was a standard procedure for guild members throughout Europe.

The terms of the Hatmakers' oath were the subject of the 1514 suit in the Consistory court, The Haberdasher wardens contended that some of the hatmakers had violated the oath (that is, committed perjury, bringing it under the jurisdiction of the church court) because they were not paying the quarterage fees of 4d for each of their servants, which the haberdashers claimed they had sworn to do. The hatmakers, in their own defence, claimed that the oath they swore referred only to their duty to pay quarterage

---

[16] E.g. L&P, I, nos 821, 841, 947; II, nos 18, 419; LCA, 4.10, 442; LCA, 4.11, 556–57; LCA, 4.13, 364.

[17] London, Archives of Parliament, HL/PO/JO/10/3/178/1–8; the subsequent statute was 21 Hen. VIII, c. 9 (SR, III, 290). Revealing evidence for the continuing import of hats from the Low Countries comes from the testimony of the Antwerp-based merchant Bernart Tymbert, who (he says) had spent many years in England. When asked 'what merchandise the English need from this land' ('Gevraecht wat coopmanschap den Inghels behoeven van dese lande'), he listed merchandise including 'hats and bonnets, sculptures and paintings' ('hoyen ende bonetten, beelden, scilderien'). See H. J. Smit, Bronnen tot de geschiedenis van den handel met Engeland, Schotland en Ierland 1150–1585 (The Hague: Nijhoff, 1942), p. 417, no. 534.

[18] The testimony in the Consistory court case does not reference the 1511 agreement explicitly; rather the witnesses refer in 1514 to oaths having been sworn three years before.

for themselves, not for anyone else, and that they had faithfully done so. As the text of the oaths they swore no longer survives,[19] we cannot be certain whose characterisation is more accurate. Two clauses added to the merger agreement sometime after the initial 1511 text was written – perhaps occasioned by this 1514 suit – suggest, however, that the hatmakers won the case. Articles 5 and 6, written in a different hand and ink than the main body of that document,[20] lay out the individual responsibilities of hatmakers' servants; if such a servant 'shal be wilfull or obstinat, and pay not his duties accordyng as other of his saide brotherne done', they are to be fined by the Haberdashers' wardens.[21] No mention is made of masters being responsible for those servants' quarterage.

This deceptively minor matter, worth a few shillings in revenue for the Haberdashers' Company, was a stand-in for the extent to which the Haberdashers had the authority to supervise and regulate the hatmakers and their workshops. Though this Consistory court suit is the most detailed evidence we have found for the relations between the hatmakers and the Haberdashers' guild in the years following the 1511 agreement, other records survive indicating that in the 1510s the Haberdashers pursued, through a range of legal mechanisms, perceived violations of their authority over hatmakers and the buying and selling of their wares. There is an echo in a Chancery bill from around this same time of an apparently similar perjury suit in the London Consistory against three other hatmakers,[22] and in addition the Haberdasher wardens employed the might of the civic government to shut down shops, seize goods, and arrest and imprison both hatmakers and haberdashers who refused to subordinate themselves to the Company's authority.

The hatmaker Anthony Leveson both signed the 1511 agreement as one of the four wardens of the hatmakers that year and then appeared in 1514 as one of the defendants in the Consistory lawsuit refusing to pay quarterage for his servants. Possibly Leveson had initially agreed to the merger with the Haberdashers but then changed his mind when

---

19   Though the Haberdashers' oath for its stranger artisans has not survived, the oath for stranger goldsmiths has: London, Goldsmiths' Hall, WACM, Book B, pp. 237–43 (thanks to Charlotte Berry for providing photographs).

20   See below, pp. 72, 130.

21   Similarly, the Goldsmiths' 'othe of the Aliaunt Straungers' specified only that the oath-taker was to pay his own quarterage. London, Goldsmiths' Hall, WACM, Book B, pp. 237–43.

22   TNA, C 1/302/25. The hatmakers involved in this altercation were named John Vyllers, Adryan van Doyt, and William Norwiche. The surname of the latter interestingly suggests an English origin, but perhaps William had lived in Norwich before, and simply adopted the town's name as his cognomen. Dutch immigrants evidently accommodated their names to suit Anglophones. A colourful case (recorded in the Eyre of London, 1321) is that of Manneken Brummen (a common Dutch surname derived from a placename in Gelderland) who assumed the name 'John the Fleming'. Indicted of homicide, 'Mannekin le Brumman' had to persuade a jury that he had been acquitted, even though the record of that acquittal carried his English name 'John le Fleming': 'Mannekin himself said that Mannekin is a Flemish name, and he was a Fleming, and John was (his) English name and they are both one name. And the jurors say that he is the same person and therefore he goes quit': Helen M. Cam, ed., *The Eyre of London, Pt. 2: 14 Edward II (1321)*, Selden Society 85 (London: Quaritz, 1968), p. 80. Our thanks to Sir John Baker for this reference.

he saw the practical effects of the subordination. The testimony in the Consistory case where he appeared as defendant suggests that the hatmakers had begun to 'work to rule': though they had paid the relatively small quarterage payments for their servants in the first year or so following the merger, they had begun by 1513 or 1514 to follow the letter of their oath (at least as they characterised it) by paying only for themselves. Though they believed that the agreement had given them effective self-governance as regards the work of their craft and that it was no business of the Haberdashers whom they hired as servants, the Haberdashers wanted to be able to regulate the hatmakers' hiring and at least formally to administer the process of establishing credentials and supervising the quality of wares.

These were indeed two key areas of authority London guilds usually did control as regards their members and their stranger associates, so the Haberdashers may well have assumed that this was part of the deal when the hatmakers came under their governance. The text of the oath of the stranger goldsmiths, for instance, which, unlike that of the Dutch hatmakers' oath, does survive, clearly indicates both that the stranger artisans were to submit themselves wholly to the authority of the wardens and that all alien servants were to be presented to, and approved by, the wardens.[23] But the hatmakers rejected the Haberdashers' authority over them in these areas: as hatmaker John Pawpe said in the 1514 Consistory suit, in his judgment the Haberdashers did not have the 'authority and power' to regulate or approve his hiring of servants, because the 'master and wardens do not have skills in the craft of hat making'.[24] One can imagine that these craftsmen with specialist knowledge disdained the claims of the English haberdashers whose training and expertise were in an entirely different realm of import and retail. The Haberdashers, by contrast, may have found the different training practices and more fluid artisanal labour culture the hatmakers brought with them from the Low Countries strange and unrigorous. A mutual contempt pervades the witnesses' testimony in the Consistory suit.

The hatmakers' attitude, while understandable in one sense, was arguably unrealistic. Their counterparts in the Goldsmiths' Company had for some decades been subject to supervision and search by the guild's wardens; indeed right around this same time in the mid-1510s, the Goldsmiths successfully implemented procedures by which newly arrived stranger goldsmiths could demonstrate their skills to the guild through testimonial letters from guild or town officials of their place of origin overseas.[25] As discussed in chapter 2, the hatmakers had previously instituted a similar system of letters attesting to migrants' training and skills, but the 1511 agreement with the Haberdashers does not

---

[23] London, Goldsmiths' Hall, WACM, Book B, pp. 237–43.

[24] 'Habuit et habet quatuor servientes occupantes artem hatmakyng non admissos neque probatos per magistrum et gardianos predictos, quia non credit quod ipsi habent auctoritatem vel potestatem habilitandi sive approbandi ipsos servientes suos quia in illa arte anglice le hatmakyng ipsi magister et gardiani non habent periciam ut dicit'. LMA, DL/C/0206, fol. 301r.

[25] Charlotte Berry, 'Guilds, Immigration, and Immigrant Economic Organization: Alien Goldsmiths in London, 1480–1540', *Journal of British Studies* 60 (2021), 545–49.

mention them. By implication – though not explicit statement – the agreement left the process of ascertaining ability in hatmaking to the hatmakers and their wardens.

Although by the monopolistic logic of English craft regulation all the stranger hatmakers in London and its environs were subject to the 1511 agreement, possibly not all hatmakers in the London area would have recognised or welcomed the Blackfriars fraternity's wardens as their representatives. Before 1511, some stranger hatmakers may have remained unaffiliated with the Fraternity of St James, preferring to work independently: unlike London civic guilds, the Hatmakers' association had had no mechanism to enforce their control of the craft. After the merger, there certainly were some hatmakers, and indeed some haberdashers, who sought to avoid its terms. A few hatmakers continued (or began?) to work in the precinct of the liberty of St Katherine by the Tower, outside the purview of the Haberdashers' guild, and some haberdashers continued to buy hats from them. A citizen haberdasher, John Atkynson, complained to the chancellor that in 1515–16 the London mayor and the master and wardens of the Haberdashers' company had shut down his shop because he was illegally buying hats from those St Katherine's hatmakers.[26] It is worth noting that in his petition Atkynson contended that the directives of the Haberdashers' Company forbidding its members from acquiring hats made in the liberty of St Katherine was 'agayne the comen profett of the peaple and againste the comen weall', using the same language of public utility that the Company itself used in its legal arguments.[27] Haberdashers, in other words, themselves by no means formed a united front, some finding more benefit in working with stranger hatmakers with shops in the liberties, presumably because the price or quality (or both) of the hats made 'illegally' was advantageous for the consumer as well as profitable for the rebel haberdashers.

HATMAKERS AND HABERDASHERS IN FOLLOWING DECADES

The adjustment period following the 1511 agreement between the Haberdashers and the hatmakers was rough, but there is also evidence that the two decades that followed the amalgamation of the hatmakers into the Haberdashers' Company saw substantial expansion of the hatmaking industry in the metropolitan area. The clearest evidence of this is a 1531 document, now in the Archives of Parliament, comprising a petition

---

26   TNA, C 1/462/38. A previous altercation in 1514 between Atkynson and three other haberdashers on the one hand and the master of the Haberdashers' Company on the other, which had resulted in the former's imprisonment, was likely related. TNA, C 1/277/12. Atkynson's disputes with the wardens of the Haberdashers continued until 1517, resulting in the temporary stripping of his citizen status in 1516 before he abjectly and publicly submitted himself in humility to the wardens in 1517. LMA, COL/CA/01/01/003, Repertory 3, folios 5v, 32v, 89v, 98r, 112v, 151rv; COL/CC/01/01/011, Journal 11, folios 260v, 269v, 271v. Atkynson was not a lucky man: in 1503 his haberdashery shop on London Bridge – which he said was ideally situated to capture the passing retail trade – burned down. LMA, COL/CC/01/01/010, Journal 10, fol. 301rv.

27   TNA, C 1/642/38; cf. LMA, DL/C/0206, fol. 320v.

evidently organised by the London Haberdashers' Company on behalf of all the craft workers, both citizen and non-citizen, who worked in the production of hats and caps in the City, Southwark, and environs. It lists masters in those trades and the number of people each employed.[28] The petition itself indicates that the Haberdashers' Company was willing to make efforts on behalf of both citizen and non-citizen workers and associates, although one might cynically note that the impetus likely came from citizen cappers whose large-scale domestic manufacture of caps was threatened by imports.

The London document was related to seven other similar petitions from outside London that were submitted to the king and council around the same time. All of them argued that enforcing a 1529 statute banning imports of headgear (similar to the earlier 1512 statute) would be beneficial to the king's subjects and would foster the domestic cap and hat industries.[29] As the petitioners complained, disregard for the 1529 statute was to the detriment of large numbers of 'pore artificers' who made their living from the many crafts involved in the cap and hat industry (carders, knitters, fullers, etc.). The second part of the London document records the action taken by the City's mayor and aldermen in response to the initial complaint: they ordered the gathering of the names of all those who operated workshops as haberdashers, cappers, thickers, and hatmakers in London and Southwark. The list, divided into those four categories, names 82 citizen haberdashers and cappers in the London guild, 35 cappers of Southwark, 34 thickers and dressers of Southwark, and 35 hatmakers. The last three categories were likely all or mostly non-citizens and thus not full members of the Haberdashers' Company; the Southwark cappers and thickers/dressers appear to be a mix of English and non-English names, while the hatmakers' names are, as far as can be determined, all Dutch.

Even more remarkable than this list of names is a record next to most entries of the number of 'persons' in the artisan's employ. The gender-inclusive language there was evidently deliberate, as the petition above had specified that all manner of men, women, and children worked in the industry. The numbers of employed workers suggest very substantial operations, with numerous masters employing workers in the hundreds. At the damaged tail of the document is a total, which is 5,000 and some (it is not entirely legible); of the workshop figures that are visible, the total is more than 4,500 workers.

---

[28] London, Archives of Parliament, HL/PO/JO/10/3/178/4. This document is incorrectly catalogued by the Archives of Parliament as a petition from the cap and hatmakers of the Borough of Southwark: the petition itself indicates that the document came from the London Haberdashers' Company (who, as above, had governance over the cappers and the hatmakers); the petition itself names both London and Southwark craftworkers.

[29] The London petition is bundled now with seven other petitions from master cappers in other capmaking centres in the west of England (London, Archives of Parliament, HL/PO/JO/10/3/178/1 to 3, 5 to 8). Though they are clearly all related, sharing much of the language, the London petition differs in that it is addressed to the Mayor and Aldermen of London rather than to the king and his council. As it ended up in the Archives of Parliament, there may have been a cover document that has since been lost. The 1529 statute is 21 Hen. VIII, c. 9 (SR, III, 290).

The hatmakers' operations were somewhat smaller in scale than those of many of the citizen cappers, but they were still impressive: a total of at least 1,261 people were employed by the master hatmakers in various aspects of the manufacture of hats. The first named hatmaker was Anthony Leveson – signatory of the 1511 merger agreement and defendant in the 1514 Consistory lawsuit – who had clearly prospered in the years that followed the early 1510s. He had one hundred people in his employ. Only one of his colleagues, Roet Langer, had more workers, with 120. John Vandart, who, as we saw in the previous chapter, testified in the 1560s about his long residence in the Blackfriars precinct, had twenty people working for him.

The 1531 petition presents a very different picture of hatmaking in London than do the ordinances of c.1500, the 1511 agreement, or the 1514 lawsuit. Instead of the workshop on the ground floor of the master's house, where he worked with and closely supervised a small number of servants, we see proto-industrial piecework, a labour structure that cappers and tailors had been using since the later fifteenth century. This was certainly not what the ordinances c.1500 or the 1511 agreement envisaged. The ordinances prohibited members of the hatmakers' fraternity from outsourcing work outside their own shops, and the 1511 agreement specified that hatmakers were to have no more than four servants at any one time, a standard clause limiting the size of workshops of both stranger artisans and citizen guild members. There was some testimony both from the strangers and from the representatives of the Haberdashers' Company in the 1514 Consistory litigation about the number of servants the stranger hatmakers hired; at that point Leveson himself said that he had a single journeyman servant, and both the hatmakers and the haberdashers agreed that none of the hatmakers had more than four servants.[30]

These descriptions and regulations accord with a household-based workshop model; presumably the deponents meant that these were the servants who worked in the master's workshop in his dwelling. As Matthew Davies has observed, however, guild records and ordinances, which emphasise the workshop model of craft production, conceal a more complicated structure of urban artisanal production in many trades in England, a situation also true of the Low Countries.[31] The numbers given in the 1531 document do not imply the operation of vast workshops with one hundred or more people working in them; sixteenth-century English cities simply did not have suitable infrastructure for that. Rather, the workers laboured in their own chambers. We know

---

30   LMA, DL/C/0206, folios 293r–294r, 301r–302r, 317r–321v.

31   Davies, 'Tailors of London', pp. 192–213; Wim Blockmans, Bert De Munck, and Peter Stabel, 'Economic Vitality: Urbanisation, Regional Complementarity and European Interaction', in *City and Society in the Low Countries, 1100–1600*, ed. Bruno Blondé, Marc Boone, and Anne-Laure Van Bruaene (Cambridge: Cambridge University Press, 2020), pp. 48–49, 53–54; Bruno Blondé, Frederik Buylaert, Jan Dumolyn, and Peter Stabel, 'Living Together in the City: Social Relationships Between Norm and Practice', in *City and Society in the Low Countries, 1100–1600*, ed. Bruno Blondé, Marc Boone, and Anne-Laure Van Bruaene (Cambridge: Cambridge University Press, 2020), pp. 69–70; Bert De Munck, 'One Counter and Your Own Account: Redefining Illicit Labour in Early Modern Antwerp', *Urban History* 37 (2010), pp. 29–32.

that the late medieval capping and tailoring industries involved workers for the different production stages from raw wool to finished cap or garment.[32] We are less informed about the different production stages of hatmaking, but we can infer from the 1531 petition that discrete tasks were in the hands of workers doing their piece work in their own dwellings, leaving the coordination and the most specialised and skilled aspects (the ones that made hatmaking the preserve of strangers) for the hatmakers themselves.

It is hard to know whether this putting-out system for felt hatmaking had fairly suddenly blossomed between the 1510s and 1531, or whether it simply suited the political agenda of the petition to expand the range and numbers of 'persons' in a craftsman's employ. The petition's object was to argue that protecting the domestic manufacture of headgear ensured the welfare of thousands of the king's subjects, and that expanding it would bring more of the idle poor to useful and productive lives. This made it expedient to emphasise the large numbers this industry employed. Though in other contexts the master-led household workshop as the basic unit of craft work continued to dominate the conceptualisation of the artisanal economy in guild ordinances, civic policy, and even social thought (as, for instance, in Thomas More's *Utopia* [1516]), here it was advantageous for the petitioners to emphasise and perhaps even to exaggerate the more complex reality.

Despite the complaints in the 1531 document about the damage inflicted on 'English workers' by the import of headgear, it is clear from the document itself that many of those it included, both employers and workers, were immigrants. This was especially so for the hatmakers, whose names were all Dutch; their employees and those working for their fellow artisans associated with the Haberdashers almost certainly also included a large number of immigrants. Their substantial operations indicate that the hatmakers of the Fraternity of St James did ultimately benefit from, or at least were not much weakened by, the 1511 merger, however unhappy they might have been with its implementation in the early years.

This is not to say, however, that they benefited to the same extent as the Haberdashers. It is instructive to compare the careers of Anthony Leveson, the hatmaker who appears most frequently in the records during the reign of Henry VIII, and a prominent citizen haberdasher, Nicholas Spakeman, whose business centred on caps. In the 1531 petition Spakeman was labelled one of the four 'chief Capp Makers' in the Haberdashers' Company while Leveson was named first among the hatmakers. Leveson had come to England from Zeeland,[33] though we don't know when. He first appears in the 1511 Agreement as one of the hatmaker wardens and signatories, so by then already he had achieved some prominence in the craft. Spakeman first appears in civic records not long

---

[32] Davies, 'Tailors of London', pp. 192–213; Charles Phythian-Adams, *Desolation of a City: Coventry and the Urban Crisis of the Late Middle Ages* (Cambridge: Cambridge University Press, 1979), p. 44; Heather Swanson, *Medieval Artisans: An Urban Class in Late Medieval England* (Oxford: Basil Blackwell, 1989), pp. 50–52; Donald Leech, 'Stability and Change at the End of the Middle Ages: Coventry, 1450–1525', *Midland History* 34 (March 2009), 19–20.

[33] TNA, C 1/1021/44.

after, in 1514.[34] The two men are named in tax records in 1523, when both were doing well, though not outstandingly: Anthony Leveson was evaluated as having £40 in goods, while Spakeman had £66.[35] In the 1531 petition, Leveson was listed as having 100 employees and Spakeman 160: again, Spakeman's business was larger, but they were still in the same ballpark. By 1541, Leveson's tax assessment had actually decreased somewhat, to £30; he was elderly by that point (he would die the following year) and perhaps his business had fallen off. In comparison, Spakeman's wealth had skyrocketed and he was assessed on £1000 in goods: he had become one of the wealthiest merchants in London.[36] Other haberdashers had also thrived over the decades that followed the mergers of 1502 and 1511: one of the wardens who represented the Company as plaintiffs in the 1514 Consistory suit, Stephen Pecocke, for instance, went on to become Sir Stephen upon his elevation to the mayoralty in 1532–33 and left his widow a very rich woman.[37]

Neither Anthony Leveson nor any other London hatmaker could match the status and wealth of those prominent haberdashers. As immigrants, the hatmakers were structurally barred from the paths to fortune and success open to citizens. Leveson was nonetheless still well-off in relative terms with a £30 assessment in 1541. He died in 1542. The witnesses to his will included a scrivener with a Dutch name, Thomas Fryse, and two citizens of London, William Stones, a merchant tailor, and a haberdasher, William Roo, who had also been among the cappers listed in the 1531 petition.[38] Thus Leveson had forged an important social relationship with a citizen haberdasher despite his early run-ins with the Company. He left as widow his second wife, Elizabeth; her surname at their marriage, Newton, suggests that she was English or that her earlier husband had been an Englishman. Anthony and Elizabeth married in the late 1520s. We do not know the name or origin of Anthony's first wife, though he had children by both marriages, including son John and an unnamed daughter from the first marriage and a daughter, Barbara, from the second.[39] John and his father were evidently estranged at the time of Anthony's death; John was not mentioned in Anthony's will, which notably revoked a previous

---

34   LMA, COL/AD/01/012, Letter Book M, fol. 220rv.

35   R. E. G. Kirk and Ernest F. Kirk, *Returns of Aliens Dwelling in the City and Suburbs of London from the Reign of Henry VIII. to That of James I*, 2 vols, Publications of the Huguenot Society of London 10 (Aberdeen: Aberdeen University Press, 1900), I, 1; TNA E 179/251/15b, fol. 61.

36   R. G. Lang, ed., *Two Tudor Subsidy Rolls for the City of London, 1541 and 1582* (London: London Record Society, 1993), pp. 40, 81.

37   TNA, PROB 11/25/516, Will of Stephen Pecocke, 1536; *Medieval Londoners Database* (New York: Fordham University, 2020) <https://mld.ace.fordham.edu/s/mld/person?id=539>.

38   LMA, DL/C/B/004/MS09171/011, fol. 75v, Will of Anthony Levenson, 1542.

39   LMA, DL/C/B/004/MS09171/011, fol. 75v; TNA, C 1/1021/44; TNA, PROB 11/42B/194. Barbara later married a merchant tailor, Robert Harpenny. The unnamed daughter of the first marriage may be the Elizabeth Grene who received a bequest alongside John Leveson's wife in Elizabeth Leveson's 1558 will. Another daughter named in Elizabeth Leveson's will, with married name Sybil Ellis, might also have been the offspring of Elizabeth's marriage to Anthony, though equally she could have been Elizabeth's daughter by a previous marriage; Sybil was named as the wife of Thomas Ellis, also a merchant tailor.

testament. Following Anthony's death John challenged the probate in Chancery. He implicitly invoked in his petition the custom of London by which children were entitled to a third of their father's estate, even though Anthony was not a citizen of London to whom such customs applied.[40]

It is interesting to note that both Anthony's son and his grandson became hatmakers, the craft handed down the generations. John Leveson identified himself as a hatmaker in the 1540s Chancery submission. By 1565 he was living in Southwark, on Bermondsey Street, leasing a tenement with a garden from Magdalen College, Oxford; his trade was then given as 'feltmaker', increasingly the term used for the hatmaking trade. The Robert Levinson, feltmaker, who succeeded John as tenant in the same Southwark property in 1575 was presumably his son, and thus a third-generation feltmaker.[41]

John and Robert followed Anthony in another way: neither became citizen members of the Haberdashers' Company. Though John was probably born in the realm, there was no path to citizenship for hatmakers, English or stranger, during most of his career, just as there had not been for his father.[42] Even decades beyond the merger in 1511, hatmakers did not become full members of the Haberdashers' Company: the Haberdashers' Freedom Register, which from 1526 onwards records the entry into citizenship of its members, does not name any of the Levesons. Nor do any of the hatmakers in the 1531 petition appear, either as those being sworn into the freedom or as apprentice-masters of new citizens.[43] This accords with the London logic of citizenship: one became a freeman of the City by apprenticing to a citizen guild member and, if no hatmakers were citizens, their trainees were not eligible for the freedom. That vicious cycle of exclusion could continue in perpetuity if no hatmakers were ever admitted as citizen guild members. There was a path through which the cycle could be broken: though almost all London citizens in the sixteenth century entered through apprenticeship, it was possible to enter by redemption – that is, the paying of a substantial fee in place of an apprenticeship. Up to the 1560s, however, there is no evidence in the Haberdashers' register that any hatmakers made the transition to full citizen guild membership through that route, even though at least some of the hatmakers working in the London area mid century were born in England.

It was in the first decade of Elizabeth I's rule that a legislative change forced the Haberdashers to find a way to offer hatmaker apprenticeships to potential citizens. First, the 1563 Statute of Artificers mandated that the practice of artisanal trades was to be regularised, with only those who had served seven-year apprenticeships under a guild master permitted to work. This legislation especially affected industries in which alien and other kinds of non-citizen labour were integral to the enterprises, but it was

40 TNA, C 1/1021/44.

41 TNA, C 1/1021/44; Magdalen College, Oxford, MS EL/6 folios 109, 116, 250, <https://archive-cat.magd.ox.ac.uk/records/EL/INDEX7>.

42 Though the men of the Leveson family were not citizens, Anthony's daughter Barbara married a merchant tailor, Robert Harpenny, so his grandchildren were raised in a citizen household. LMA, DL/C/B/004/MS09171/011, fol. 75v; TNA, PROB 11/42B/194.

43 GL, MS 15857/001, Haberdashers' Freedom Register, 1526–1642.

confusingly worded and variously interpreted in the following decades.[44] Ambiguity regarding hatmaking, however, was removed in 1566 with an 'Acte for true makinge of Hattes and Cappes', which confirmed specifically that henceforth no one could make felt hats without undergoing an official apprenticeship. For London hatmakers, this was to be regulated by the Haberdashers' Company. Aliens and other non-citizens already working in the trade were exempted, but henceforth the training of new artisans in the craft was to be regularised according to the usual London guild rules.[45]

The 1566 Act was no doubt welcomed by the Haberdashers' Company generally but nonetheless created a logistical problem: at the time of the Act's passing, there were no guild members who could supervise hatmaker apprentices. The Company's response was to admit by redemption a group of eight hatmakers the following year, thereby creating a cadre of apprentice masters and a path to full guild membership for the following generations. Several more such groups of hatmakers entered in the 1570s and 1580s, also by redemption, a total of forty-three men between 1567 and 1583; as a sign that these were not the usual processes for swearing in new Haberdasher citizens, their entrances were recorded separately from the other freedom records.[46]

These new hatmaker guild members were, however, not the strangers who had dominated the industry in the first half of the century or apparently their descendants, but men born in the king's realm eligible for the freedom of London. We can only guess how these new hatmaker guild members had been trained: they could well have been unofficially apprenticed to the Dutchmen who still dominated the craft in 1531 and likely for some decades after. Though English-born, such trainees would still not have been able to enter the company before this point as they had not served a guild-authorised apprenticeship. The continued exclusion of aliens is confirmed not only by their English or Welsh names and the general logic of London citizenship in the later sixteenth century, but also by a further list of nine strangers whose names were submitted by the Haberdashers' Company to the mayor in 1583 in response to an enquiry regarding how many strangers had been admitted to each of the London guilds over the previous six years. The Haberdashers were keen to emphasise how strictly they had held the line against aliens:

> The Master and Wardens of the said Companie of Haberdashers haue licensed but onlye ix straungers to vse the trade of making feltes, and haue taken of them but ij s. vj d. a peece for their admission, viz. James Johnson. Bartholomew Aviser. Lewys Valley. James Eves. Andwew [sic] Jacob. Ellyce Berne. Roberte le John, alias Young. John Gibson. Nicholas Iller.[47]

---

44 5 Eliz. c 4, *SR*, IV 414–22; Harry Duckworth, *The Early History of Feltmaking in London 1250–1604*, Research Paper No. 1 (London: Worshipful Company of Feltmakers, 2013), pp. 25–27; Ian W. Archer, *The Pursuit of Stability: Social Relations in Elizabethan London* (Cambridge: Cambridge University Press, 1991), pp. 131–40.

45 8 Eliz c. 11, *SR*, IV, 494–95.

46 GL, MS 15857/1, Haberdashers' Freedom Register, 1526–1642, folios 104v, 117r, 119r, 123r.

47 Kirk and Kirk, *Returns of Aliens*, II, 307.

These men were not named in the Haberdashers' Freedom Register either among the hatmakers admitted by redemption or among the more ordinary entrants; their 'licence' was not admission to full guild membership. It is also clearly not a complete list of stranger hat- or feltmakers working in the metropolitan area; John Levison is not among them, nor his son Robert. In the later sixteenth century there were still hatmakers migrating from the Continent to England, increasingly from northern France rather than the Low Countries; their alien birth continued to disadvantage them.[48] Indeed, the careers of John and Robert Leveson illustrate how, increasingly, alien descent rather than birth disqualified artisans whose roots lay outside the kingdom from full participation in London civic and economic life.[49]

Tensions regarding stranger artisans and the making of hats and caps, and the place of hatmakers in the Haberdashers' Company, thus endured through the sixteenth century and beyond. Though the relationship between the hatmakers and the Haberdashers' guild remains relatively obscure in the middle years of the century, in the 1560s the Haberdashers made considerable strides to bring the hatmakers more firmly under their supervision and into line with the seven-year apprenticeships and workshop supervision that were the norm in English guilds. The hatmakers and feltmakers who entered the guild, even those who did so as citizens, chafed under these circumstances; over the ensuing decades they lobbied the royal council for a charter that would give them status as a separate guild, finally achieving incorporation as the Feltmakers' Company in 1604.[50] Nonetheless, some of the same problems as had affected the Dutch hatmakers of the early sixteenth century continued to plague the Feltmakers, as they were often still not conferred full status as citizens of London even following the formation of their own company in the early seventeenth century. Finally in 1650 the Feltmakers received full recognition and were admitted as freemen of the City of London.[51]

---

[48] Archer, *Haberdashers' Company*, pp. 61–70. Searching 'Hatmakers' and 'Hatters' in the occupation field and London in the place field of *England's Immigrants* online database indicates a shift from overwhelmingly 'Teutonic' (Dutch) immigrants to Norman or French origins in the mid-sixteenth century. The data comes from letters of denization and alien subsidy assessments.

[49] See above, pp. 64–65.

[50] George Unwin, *The Gilds and Companies of London* (London: Methuen, 1908), pp. 304–6; Weinstein, *Worshipful Company*, pp. 4–14; Archer, *Haberdashers' Company*, pp. 61–70, and especially Harry Duckworth's papers: *Early History*, pp. 25–32; *The Feltmakers' Wool Adventure, 1610–24*, Research Paper No. 2 (London: Worshipful Company of Feltmakers, 2015); and *The Struggle for Recognition, 1604–1667*, Research Paper No. 3 (London: Worshipful Company of Feltmakers, 2019).

[51] Duckworth, *Struggle*, pp. 51–55.

CHAPTER 4

The Manuscript

In the preceding chapters we have followed the lives of the Dutch Hatmakers in the broader context of the history of hats and hatmaking and of the political and economic situation of the city where they worked and lived. In this chapter, we take a closer look at the manuscript, its bilingual format, and the dialects of its scribes. The manuscript is unique, for it contains the earliest document to have been drawn up bilingually in English and Dutch, and the Dutch-language text is equally remarkable. Dutch had certainly been written (and not just copied) by migrants in Britain before this Dutch text was written, but not much of it survives: there are only some rare inscription on funeral slabs, bills of obligation, and snatches of poems on flyleaves.[1] To our knowledge, the bilingual ordinances present us with the earliest substantial Dutch text composed in Britain. The manuscript and its texts are therefore matters of intrinsic interest, but they also give us answers to some of the questions raised by this little community of aliens in London. How did the history of the manuscript intersect with the history of their craft organisation? How did they adapt to the English language and to English styles of handwriting? Do the dialects of the texts offer any clues about their origins? Although we focus now on the manuscript and its language, we hope not to lose sight of these broader questions.

The history of the manuscript has to be reconstructed from its present state. According to a note on a flyleaf of the modern guard book that now contains the manuscript, the manuscript was rebound in February 1985. The stitching (using what appear to be the original needle holes), the collation, and the folio numbers are modern too. It is likely that the original manuscript never had a cover, for the outside folios are grubbier and show signs of wear. It was probably a single-quire manuscript of eighteen leaves giving thirty-six pages, for what is now numbered folio 17 was originally folio 18. All that now remains of the original folio 17 is the stub. The loss of this leaf is also evident from the disruption of the original arrangement of the page openings, which conforms to the usual

---

[1] Some of these surviving snatches are discussed in Ad Putter, 'Materials for a Social History of the Dutch Language in Medieval Britain: Three Case Studies from Wales, Scotland, and England', *Dutch Crossing: Journal of Low Countries Studies* 45 (2021), 97–111, and Sjoerd Levelt and Ad Putter, *North Sea Crossings: The Literary Heritage of Anglo-Dutch Relations, 1066–1688* (Oxford: Bodleian Library, 2021).

medieval design:[2] every verso faces a recto from the same side of the parchment skin, that is flesh-side faces flesh-side (1v-2r, 3v-4r, 5v-6r, etc.) and hair-side faces hair-side (2v-3r, 4v-5r, 6v-7r). However, because of the removal of the seventeenth leaf, we now have hair-side facing flesh-side on the last page opening (16v-17r in the modern numbering).

The manuscript contains the following items:

1. Folio 1r. Ordinances of the Hatmakers. Incipit: 'Fyrst, it is established and ordeyned'. Bilingual English-Dutch prose.

2. Folio 15r. Agreement between the Hatmakers and the Haberdashers. Incipit: 'Be it had in perpetuall memory'. English prose.

3. Folio 17v. Oath of the wardens of the Haberdashers. Incipit: '**The oth of the iiij wardeins of haberdasshers.** Ye shal swere that duringe the tyme of your wardenshipp'. English prose.

The three items in the manuscript were not all written at the same time, and its evolution can be deduced from internal and external clues. There is, in the first place, the parchment. This was more expensive than paper, but prices depended on size and quality, and the Hatmakers were economical in their investment. The parchment is thin and, as the image below shows, the lower edges of the folios are curved, leaving the bottom margin very uneven.

All the folios have curved edges comparable to the one shown here. Parchment was normally cut in neat rectangular shapes, but more affordable parchment could be purchased either in the form of 'offcuts' (what was left of the skins after the rectangles had been cut)[3] or in the form of sheets that included the 'offcut zone'.[4] A pragmatic consideration behind the latter form is that, since manuscript leaves typically had generous margins, a page with a curved edge could still accommodate the normal writing space, but at a cheaper price. Our manuscript is an example of this type of cheap parchment book.[5] Its abnormality is confirmed by the irregular dimensions of the pages: because of the convex curve at the lower edge the height varies from 202mm to 184mm, while the width is consistently 170mm. The writing space (ruled in drypoint) is 160mm x 110mm. The width of the

---

2   Raymond Clemens and Timothy Graham, *Introduction to Manuscript Studies* (Ithaca: Cornell University Press, 2007), pp. 14–15.

3   The practice of using offcuts in manuscripts is discussed and illustrated by Daniel Wakelin, *Designing English: Early Literature on the Page* (Oxford: Bodleian Library, 2018), pp. 44–46 and Erik Kwakkel, 'Discarded Parchment as Writing Support in English Manuscript Culture', *English Manuscript Studies 1100–1700* 17 (2012), 238–61.

4   See Stephanie Lahey, 'Offcut Zone Parchment in Manuscript Codices from Later Medieval England', 2 vols (unpublished doctoral dissertation, University of Victoria, 2021), and Kwakkel, 'Discarded Parchment', p. 254.

5   Other examples are Oxford, Bodleian, Douce 6, digitised at <https://digital.bodleian.ox.ac.uk/objects/ed3b2d6e-28ec-49c1-a369-f3087b52e909/>, and London, British Library, Additional, MS 16431, illustrated in Michelle Brown, *A Guide to Western Historical Scripts from Antiquity to 1600* (London: British Library, 1993), plate 45.

Fig. 7   London, Guildhall Library, MS 15838, fol. 1r. © Haberdashers' Company.

pages, 170mm, is standard, but even the maximal height, 202mm, is well below what would be normal for that width. As a rule, the width of the page in later medieval manuscripts was about seventy per cent of the height,[6] so one would expect the leaves to be about 40mm higher than they actually are.

The text of the Ordinances was the work of two scribes, with scribe 1 producing the first 10 folios and scribe 2 taking over from folio 11r onwards.[7] Some omissions made by scribe 1 were supplied by a corrector, who was probably scribe 2. Scribe 2's handwriting can be dated to 1501 on the basis of the year given in article 25 (folio 12v) by scribe 2. Articles 26 and 27, also written by scribe 2, were probably added slightly later. The provision in article 25 of a date and the names of the four masters is in itself an indication that this article had once been envisaged as the final item, and this supposition is supported by the rubrication. In the case of articles 1–25, a rubricator supplied Lombardic capitals in alternating red and blue ink, but the Lombardic capitals were not supplied for the last two articles, which were thus presumably written some time after the preceding text had already been copied and rubricated. Since they were additions to a manuscript that had several empty pages left, these later items were also written by the scribe without any concern for space: instead of being written on pages containing on average 29 lines (scribe 1, folios 1–10) or 23 lines (scribe 2, folios 11–12), articles 26 and 27 were written by scribe 2 across three pages with progressively more empty space: on folio 13r he wrote 12 lines; on folio 13v just 8 lines, and on folio 14r only four. The scribe here placed and spaced his writing to fill up the empty pages at the end of the quire.

The manuscript acquired a new purpose in 1511, when the Hatmakers agreed to join the Haberdashers. The terms of the agreement were then added to the manuscript, which may at this point have come into the possession of the Haberdashers who added some material to it at some later time in the sixteenth century. The agreement is also the work of two scribes: scribe 3 wrote the text of the agreement up to and including the fourth article; scribe 4 wrote articles 5 and 6 of the agreement. There is good reason to think that these two articles were added later: they are written in lighter ink and without consideration for the writing space observed by scribe 3. In terms of content, the additional articles concern themselves not with the duties of the brothers of the Hatmakers' guild, but rather with the obligations of, and fees payable by, journeymen and servants in their employment. It is probably no coincidence that in the consistory court case pursued by the Haberdashers against some alien hatmakers in the years 1514 and 1515, this precise issue was the main bone of contention. According to the Haberdashers' claims in that case, journeymen and apprentices were expected to contribute the same quarterly fee to the Haberdashers as the master hatmakers who employed them, and the latter were liable to pay up if their employees did not; according to the hatmakers' testimony, conversely,

---

6   Erik Kwakkel and Rodney Thomson, 'Codicology', in *The European Book in the Twelfth Century*, ed. Erik Kwakkel and Rodney Thomson (Cambridge: Cambridge University Press, 2018), pp. 9–24 (14).

7   For completeness we should mention that there are a few handwritten notes, in Dutch, in a much later hand. See the notes to our edition.

masters were liable only for themselves, but not for their employees. Articles 5 and 6 of the agreement were probably additions made after the outcome of the court case. The verdict seems to have gone in the favour of the hatmakers, for the added clauses make the servants and not their employers liable for payment.

Just as the Hatmakers were taken over by the Haberdashers, so was the manuscript. This explains why the last item, written by yet another scribe, scribe 5, in what looks like a slightly later, mid-sixteenth-century hand, and beginning with an elaborate cadel-style initial **Y**, consists of an item that was of no relevance to the Hatmakers, namely the oath of office to be sworn by the wardens of the Haberdashers. While the Hatmakers thus lost exclusive ownership of their little book, this misfortune is also the reason why the manuscript survived after the fraternity that originally owned it had disappeared: it was preserved in the archives of the Haberdashers' Company that still exists today, in the custody of the Guildhall Library in London.

THE ORDINANCES OF THE HATMAKERS: THE BILINGUAL FORMAT IN CONTEXT

The item of greatest interest in the manuscript is the bilingual Dutch-English ordinances. As we shall see, the two scribes who wrote the text were almost certainly Dutch speakers. Their Dutch dialects differ, and this can give us some clues about where in the Low Countries they came from. Just as interesting as their Dutch is the nature of their English, which also differs in some details. Migrants, then as now, faced the challenge of communicating in a second language: how well did they manage this? We will take up this question more fully in the next chapter, and deal with it here only insofar as the question includes, in the case of handwritten text, a palaeographical dimension. Handwritten texts of this period obeyed particular orthographic conventions which differed from country to country. Was the writing style of these aliens insular or continental? Did they try to retain the style of their native country, or did they embrace that of their adopted country?

The fact that the Ordinances were drawn up in two languages, English and Dutch, tells its own story about the Hatmakers' attachments to new and old cultural identities, and we should begin by putting the bilingualism of the manuscript in the right perspective. The Statutes contain twenty-seven articles. Except for the last three, which are in English only, they were all drawn up in two languages, with a Dutch version of every article following the English-language version. The organisation is most easily illustrated with an image of the manuscript.

This page shows the last two lines of article 18, in English, followed by the Dutch-language version of this same article. Then comes, in English, article 19, 'Item, it is established and ordeyned', followed by the version in Dutch, 'Item, dat is versament ende geordinert'. The standard use of alternate red and blue Lombardic capitals to mark

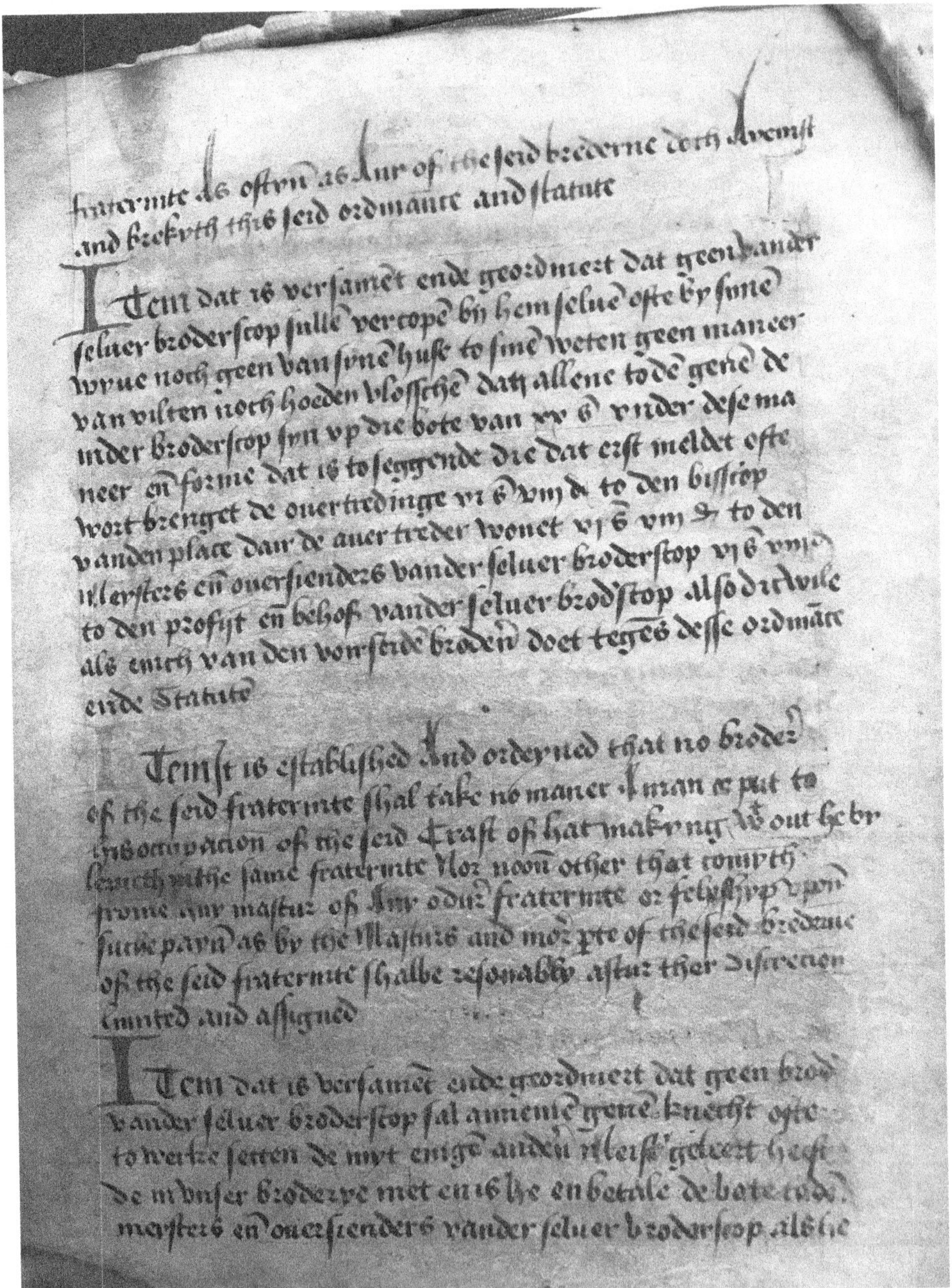

fraternite as often as ony of the seid brederne doth azenst
and brekyth this seid ordinance and statute

Item dat is versamet ende geordinert dat gheen van der
seluer broderscop sulle vercope by hem selue ofte by sine
wyue noch gheen van sine huse to sine weten gheen maneer
van vilten noch hoeden blosschen datt allene to de gene de
inder broderscop syn vp die bote van xx ß vnder dese ma
neer en forme dat is to seggende die dat erst meldet ofte
wort brenget de ouertredinge vi ß viij d to den bisscop
van den place daer de ouer treder wonet vj ß viij d to den
xlersters en ouersienders vander seluer broderscop vj ß viij d
to den profyt en behoff vander seluer broderscop also dicwile
als enich van den vorstade braden doet tegies desse ordinate
ende Statute

Item it is establisshed And ordeyned that no broder
of the seid fraternite shal take no maner of man te put to
inseruicacion of the seid craft of hat makyng with out he br
leneth uthe same fraternite Nor noon other that comyth
fronte any mastur of Any odur fraternite or felyshyp vpon
suche payn as by the Mastirs and most pte of the seid bredeme
of the seid fraternite shalbe resonably aftur ther discrecion
limited and assigned

Item dat is versamet ende geordinert dat gheen brod
vander seluer broderscop sal annemie gheue knecht ofte
to werke setten de myt enige anden xlerss geleert heeft
de in vnser broderye met en is the en betale de bote to de
mastirs en ouersienders vander seluer broderscop als he

Fig. 8 London, Guildhall Library, MS 15838, fol. 10r. © Haberdashers' Company.

textual divisions gives a familiar look to the page, but in fact the phenomenon shown here, Middle English alternating with Middle Dutch, is unique for the period.

The surviving ordinances of English craft and religious associations are, as a rule, monolingual. The earliest ones were written in Latin or French, but from the mid-fourteenth century onwards some crafts had written rules in English.[8] When, in 1388, all guilds were ordered to present information about their organisation to Chancery for inspection, 75% (of 500) were in Latin, 9% in French, and 12% in English (with the remaining 4% being in a combination of languages).[9] By the time the Hatmakers drew up their statutes, however, English had become the norm, as is shown by the fact that a number of crafts took the trouble of having their original ordinances translated into English. Thus in 1509 the Vintners paid 'John Devereux Scryvener' five shillings for 'translatyng of oure Corporacion out of frenshe in to Engllische' plus a further six shillings and eight pence for 'writing of the boke'.[10] It was the custom to read guild ordinances aloud on special days when all members of the guild were assembled, so the written language of the Ordinances was also a spoken one on these occasions.

Where guild ordinances are bilingual, that bilingualism takes a very different form from the one that we find here. Not uncommonly, guild ordinances themselves were in the vernacular but had a preamble and sometimes also a postamble in Latin. For instance, the Rules and Ordinances of the Craft of Shearmen of London from 1452 are written in English, except for a preface and epilogue which state that they were written by the scribe and notary public, Thomas Marvyell, and submitted for approval and registered in the Court of the Commissary of the Bishop of London.[11] The Ordinances of the Fullers of Bristol from 1407 have a similar structure: they begin with a Latin preamble written on behalf of the Mayor of Bristol, then follow the ordinances in the vernacular, though in this case that vernacular is still Anglo-French.[12] Sometimes the Latin preamble contextualises the Statutes, as in case of the Ordinances of the Tailors of Norwich, which explain in Latin that the document was drawn up in response to the order of Parliament in 1388 that all guilds should make returns in writing (*in scriptis*) and that this guild was founded in 1350. Then, under the rubric *Ordinacio,* follow the guild's Statutes, in English.[13] The shift from Latin coincides with a change in hand, probably because the Latin was written by a professional scribe and official, while the English ordinances themselves

---

[8] Caroline M. Barron, *London in the Later Middle Ages: Government and People 1200–1500* (Oxford: Oxford University Press, 2004), p. 207.

[9] Caroline M. Barron and Laura Wright, 'The London Middle English Guild Certificates of 1388–9', *Nottingham Medieval Studies* 39 (1995), 108–45.

[10] Cited by Malcolm Richardson, *Middle-Class Writing in Late Medieval London* (London: Routledge, 2011), p. 48.

[11] Henry Charles Coote and John Robert Daniel-Tyssen, ed., *Ordinances of Some Secular Guilds of London, from 1354 to 1496* (London: Nichols, 1871), pp. 47–56.

[12] Lucy Toulmin Smith, ed., *English Gilds: The Original Ordinances of More than One Hundred Early English Guilds*, EETS, original series 40 (London: Trübner, 1870), pp. 283–86.

[13] Smith, *English Gilds*. pp. 33–36.

were written by a 'craftsman-turned-clerk'. We borrow this term from Matthew Davies, who has discussed the ways in which documents of this type came into being.[14] Many guilds and fraternities, including the Dutch Hatmakers,[15] had a designated clerk among their members, whose duties normally included the writing down of guild regulations.[16] Others outsourced the writing of these documents to professionals *literati*, to notaries and scriveners. Finally, by the late fifteenth century, many craftsmen could also turn their hand to the craft of writing. The multiplicity of scenarios raises issues that anyone interested in the handwritten language of these documents has to confront. Whose writing and whose language are we in fact reading? Were they competent in both languages? Were they writing their own words or copying those of others?

We shall return to these questions in our examination of the language and handwriting of the Ordinances of the Hatmakers shortly, but the question of what language ordinances were composed in is raised with special force by confraternities that consisted wholly or mainly of aliens. Some of the Ordinances of the alien confraternities that were based in London have survived; others, including those of the Dutch-speaking Fraternity of the Holy Trinity, which also met at Blackfriars, have not.[17] As has already been remarked, the Ordinances of alien associations that do survive – those of the Fraternity of the Holy Blood of Wilsnack, the Fraternity of the Immaculate Conception, and the Fraternity of St Katherine – are unlike those of the Dutch Hatmakers in that they are not craft ordinances but, rather, the rules and regulations of religious fraternities. They are also unlike those of the Hatmakers in that they are basically monolingual.

The Fraternity of the Holy Blood of Wilsnack probably catered for German speakers (Wilsnack was a popular pilgrimage destination in Northern Germany), but the statutes were drawn up in English and then officialised by a notary public, John Ecton, who added a Latin preamble and postscript. Because the fraternity changed premises – from the Crossed Friars to Austin Friars – the Statutes were actually drawn up twice, in 1459 and again in 1491. The Latin paratext from the first version, dated 1459, sheds some light on the textual history of this document. For after recording where the document was written (Thames Street, London) and which of the brothers witnessed it, John Ecton goes on to say that the ordinances and founding principles had been read out and shown to the Brotherhood in English (*in vulgari Anglicano*) and form the contents of the paper document (*papyri cedula*) that now follows. The English statutes follow, and in the Latin codicil John Ecton declares that the English document was drawn up by someone else and in a different location, but that he witnessed it and also checked it over, being

---

14   Matthew Davies, '"Writying, making and engrocyng": Clerks, Guilds and Identity in Late Medieval London', in *Medieval Merchants and Money: Essays in Honour of James L. Bolton*, ed. Martin Allen and Matthew Davies (London: Institute of Historical Research, 2016), pp. 21–41.

15   See articles 8, 9, 11, and 14 in the Hatmakers' Guild Ordinances (below in Part II), which mention a 'clerke'.

16   Frances Consitt, *The London Weavers' Company*, 2 vols (Oxford: Clarendon Press, 1933), I, 18.

17   For full discussion and editions of the alien confraternities' ordinances, see Justin Colson, 'Alien Communities and Alien Fraternities in Later Medieval London', *London Journal* 35 (2010).

personally responsible for an emendation in the text: *Et constat michi de Rasura harum dictionum 'and shall pay' in undecima linea a capite* ('The correction "and shall pay" at the erasure of these words, eleven lines from the heading, is mine').[18]

Of the two other alien confraternities of London with surviving ordinances, one that also met, as did the Dutch Hatmakers, at the Dominican church of Blackfriars was the Confraternity of the Immaculate Conception, founded in 1503. The spectacularly beautiful literary remains of this confraternity are now Oxford, Christ Church, MS 179, datable to 1517.[19] The book opens with what is presumably a copy or recreation of the original petition to Henry VII for the foundation of the confraternity, on the initiative of *aucuns voz subiects de la nacion de France habitantz en cestuy votre Royaulme* (fol. 2r). According to the petition, the fraternity had support from an influential insider at Henry's court, the chronicler Bernard André, tutor to Henry VII's son, Arthur, and author of a Latin life of Henry VII. The handwriting exudes quality and privilege, and so do the manuscript illuminations which were executed by a group of Dutch artists known as the 'Masters of the Dark Eyes'.[20] It is a fine example of what Maurits Smeyers called the Ghent-Bruges style, which was now being exported abroad by international artists and scribes commissioned to provide wealthy patrons a touch of Burgundian-Habsburg class and splendour.[21] The language of the Statutes of this order, French and only French, reflects both the nationality of its membership and its exclusivity.

The Ordinances of another alien group, the Fraternity of St Katherine, from 1495, provide a closer parallel to our manuscript.[22] The preamble states that the fraternity was 'founded and ordenyd by Duychmen iiij^{xx} yeres passed [i.e. 1415] in the Crosse Fryers in the City of London'. Thirty-eight members (including the masters) are named and, although the names are anglicised as usual, the Dutch origins of most of them is clear, e.g. 'Gerard Wygarson' (Gerard Wijgartsen), 'John Vansanton' (Jan van Santen), 'Poles Huysman' (Pouwels Huisman), and so on. The whole document is in English, including the preamble and postamble, which name the scribe as 'Richard Bloodywell Doctor of Lawe and Commissary of London', one of the most important diocesan officials. For our purposes, the most interesting thing about the document is the appendix that has not survived but that is mentioned by the Commissary. In addition to the regulations in the English document, the brothers and sisters of the fraternity professed themselves bound to obey 'all other ordenaunces, actis, constitucions and rules made among the

---

[18] The Latin text was edited by Coote and Daniel-Tyssen, *Ordinances*, p. 62; Colson provides a translation.

[19] The manuscript has been digitised. See 'Christ Church MS 179', *Bodleian Library* <https://digital.bodleian.ox.ac.uk/objects/6d9e0fdf-ec06–4d46–952f-e1f1c15198aa/>. Translations from the original are based on our own transcription.

[20] Klara H. Broekhuijsen-Kruijer, *The Masters of the Dark Eyes: Late Medieval Manuscript Painting in Holland* (Turnhout: Brepols, 2009).

[21] Maurits Smeyers, *Flemish Miniatures from the 8th to the Mid-16th Century* (Turnhout: Brepols, 1999), p. 423.

[22] Citations are from Colson, 'Alien Communities', pp. 133–36.

saide Bretherhed by theyre owne free willis and conscensions specyfyed and declared in Dych tong whereof a copy in cedule to these presentis is annexed'. The Statutes of the Fraternity of St Katherine, in other words, were once bilingual, though it is also clear that the Dutch 'cedule' was not a translation of the English ordinances but an appendix to it. Justin Colson assumes that, because they were not translated, the Dutch text had no legal value,[23] but the Commissary thought otherwise, because he goes on to confirm the fines stipulated in the Dutch document ('the paynes therin comprysed and written') and stipulates that half the amount of the fine is for the fraternity's own coffers and the other half for the building work at St Paul's.

The Ordinances of the Dutch Hatmakers are to our knowledge the only extant guild statutes that were drawn up in a bilingual format, and indeed the document appears to be the earliest example of a bilingual English-Dutch text. It is true that there exist, from the late fifteenth century, some official Dutch records that survive in manuscript with English translations. The grant of a house by the town of Antwerp to the English Merchant Venturers from 1474, the Privileges granted to English Merchants by the Lord of Bergen-op-Zoom in 1480, and a few texts of this sort, can be found in a manuscript, now in the archives of the Mercers' Company, that was copied in London around 1485. In this manuscript, copies of the Dutch originals are preceded by translations into Middle English.[24] However, the situation here is quite different. The documents were first issued in Dutch, and only later translated into English. The priority of the Dutch in these cases is apparent from the quality of the translation, which sticks so closely to the Dutch original that the English is at times barely comprehensible without knowledge of Dutch. Compare, for instance, the following Dutch sentence with its translation:

[Wij] doen te wetene ende bekennen bij desen tegenworedigen brieve voir ons, onsen oiren ende nacomelingen, ende allen den ghene dien de zaken onder ghescreuven, nu oft in toecomende tijden, aengaen ende nopen sullen moigen.

[We] doo to wyte and to be knowen by this present lettre for us, our heyres and after-comers, and alle them that the maters underwreton now or in to comyng tyme shall mowe towche or nype.[25]

Here the English, although it comes first in the manuscript, is closely modelled on the Dutch, of which it is a painfully literal translation. Thus the verb 'nip' is only here attested in the sense 'concern': it is a semantic borrowing of Dutch *nopen*, which could mean 'nip, oppress', but also 'touch, concern'. The English 'in to comyng tyme' is calqued on the Dutch *in toecomende tijden*, though the word division in the edition by Sutton and Visser-Fuchs from which we have taken this passage obscures that fact. The adjective 'tocoming'

---

23   Colson, 'Alien Communities', p. 121.

24   Anne F. Sutton and Livia Visser-Fuchs, ed., *The Book of Privileges of the Merchant Adventurers of England, 1296–1483* (London: British Academy, 2009).

25   Sutton and Visser-Fuchs, ed., *Book of Privileges*, pp. 263 and 269.

in the sense of 'future' existed in Old English, but in Middle English it is otherwise found only in William Caxton,[26] whose language shows much interference from Dutch, because he spent some thirty years living in the Low Countries.[27]

The statutes of the Hatmakers present a different case. We are not dealing with a document that was originally written in one language and later translated, but rather with one that seems to have been drawn up bilingually from the start.

THE HANDWRITING OF THE TWO SCRIBES

Given the fact that the Ordinances were drawn up in two languages and copied by two scribes, one might have expected one scribe to write the Dutch and another the English, but this is not what happened. The first scribe wrote the first ten folios, English and Dutch, and then scribe two continued in both languages, although it should be noted that the last three articles written by scribe 2 (article 25, originally intended as the last, plus the two articles that were added later) are exclusively in English. The handwriting of these two scribes is easy to distinguish, and the differences between the two may indicate different levels of acculturation.

Scribe 1 (see fig. 9) writes in a script known as *littera hybrida* because it is a hybrid between the looser cursive script, cursiva, and the formal bookhand known as textura.[28] Characteristic of textura is the careful execution of minims (the downstrokes in **m**, **n**, and **i**), which are separately traced, as in 'instructe' (line 2). From cursiva come the single-compartment **a** and the long **f** and **s**, with descenders extending well below the baseline. In the hand of scribe 1, the long **s** alternates with the round cursiva **s**, which he writes at the end of words (see 'the seid fullers', line 2). There are also two forms of the letter **r**, the two-stroked textura **r** and round **r** (which looks rather like our **z**). The **w** of scribe 1 consists of two open **v**'s. There is a single compartment **g** ('hatmakyng', line 3). The **d** is of the loopless variety, and the **e** has the modern letter shape. Notable decorative features of scribe 1 are the use of elongated ascenders for the top line and the stroking of all majuscules in red ink. However, the most striking thing about scribe 1's handwriting is the absence of any features that we would expect to find in a *littera hybrida* written in England, and this becomes immediately obvious if we compare scribe 1 with scribe 2 (see

---

[26]   See OED s.v. tocoming, adj.

[27]   See Ad Putter, 'Dutch, French and English in Caxton's Recuyell of the Historyes of Troye', in *Medieval Romance, Arthurian Literature: Essays in Honour of Elizabeth Archibald*, ed. A. S. G. Edwards (Cambridge: D. S. Brewer, 2021), pp. 205–26.

[28]   We take our terms and diagnostics for different scripts from Albert Derolez, *The Palaeography of Gothic Manuscript Books from the Twelfth to the Early Sixteenth Century* (Cambridge: Cambridge University Press, 2003).

any odur Artikel br reson wher of ther shald in forme
and instructe The seid fullers weuers Tales and such
other in the seid Crafte of hatmakynge Excepte that
the seid fullers weuers Talke be instructe and lernd
before in the seid Craft of hatmakynge and lafulli
& born and accepte as brederne of the same ffrater
inte. And whosum euer fulfilleth not ne obey th
thre ordinance And statute to fall in to the payn
And multe aftur of the discreon Maysters and bur
deuis of the same fraternite to be limited and w out
any Remission to be paid

Item dat is bevramet ende geordinert dat gheen
vanden broden van d[er] seluer brioderscop sal hebbe
gene wouringe ofte mede mwouringe uut te geuen
andei en laden. Dat is te verstaende fullers weuers
sunders ofte mit engen anderen ambocht te luden
br den welken des sie solden leren ofte ynderwise
den seluen fullers weuers sunders ofte summige and
ren luden vanden ambocht der hoitmakinge. Vt
genomen dat die vorseiden fullers weuers ende
sundes geleert sin gewest vanden seluen ambocht
der hoitmakinge rechtelike ontfangen ende inge
nomen als brodern vander seluer broderscop En
soe wie dat met verunliet noch met horsam enis
to deise ordmanty ende insettinge sal vallen in
ouersienders vand seluer broderscop de daur to
ghel sin ende sunder enige vergiffenisse sullen
betalen;.

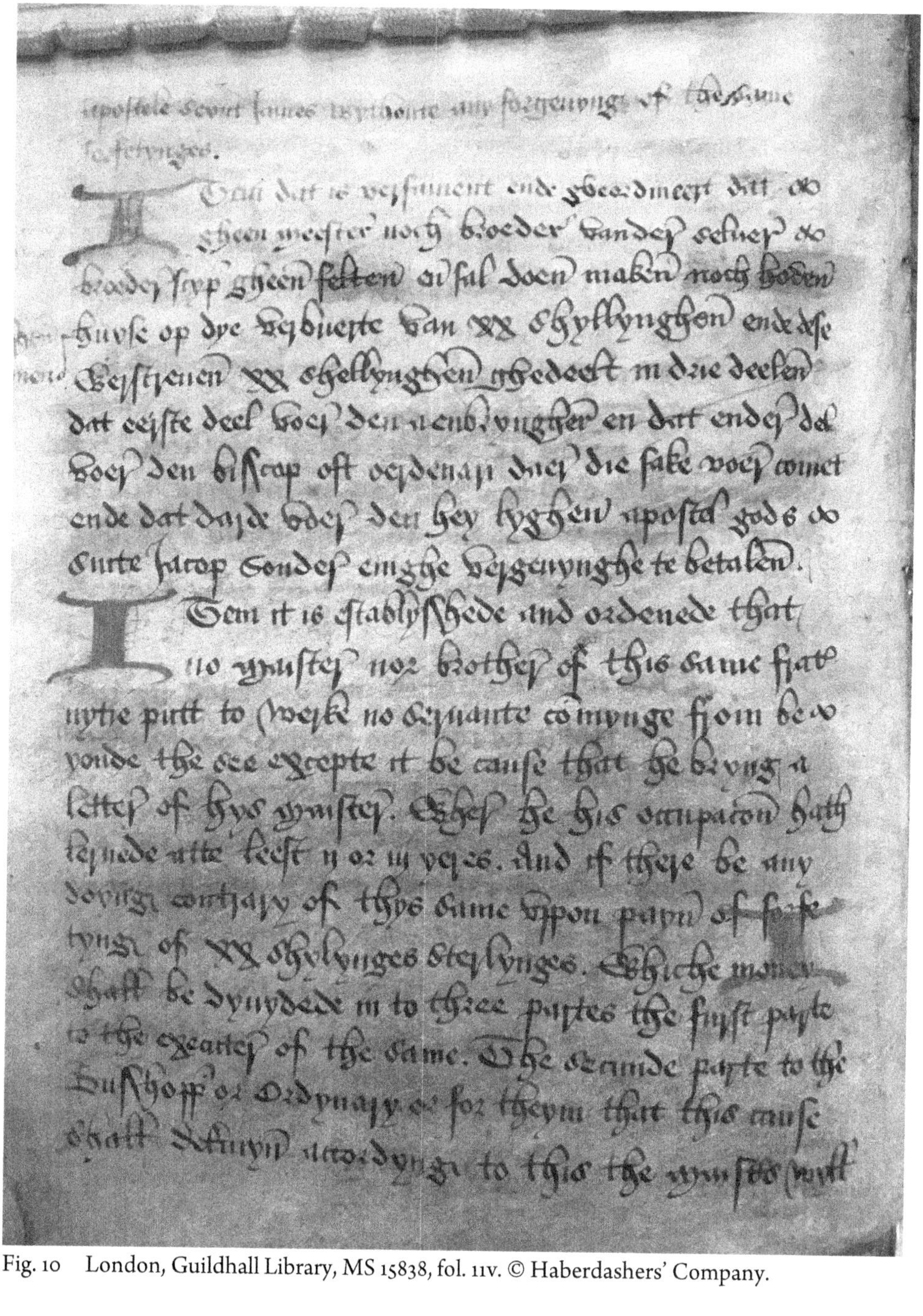

Item dat is vestument ende gheordineert dat . . . gheen meester noch broeder vander selver do broeder scyp gheen setten oi ful doen maken noch . . . huyse op dye verdiente van xx schyllyngthon ende dse Vrystienen xx schellyngthen ghedeelt m drie deelen dat eerste deel voey den aenbrvngher en dat ender del voey den bisscop oft oeydenayr driey die sake voey comet ende dat dayde voey den hey tyghen apostel gods . . . do surte strop sonder enyghe veygenynghe te betalen.

Item it is establysshede and ordenede that no mynyster nor brother of this same hat . . . nythe putt to werke no servante comynge from beyonde the see excepte it be cause that he bryng a letter of hys mynyster. Ther he his occupacion hath termede atte leest ij or iij yeres. And if there be any doyng contrary of thys same upon payn of forfetyng of xx schelynges sterlynges. Whiche money shall be dyvydede in to three partes the first parte to the exsartes of the same. The oramde parte to the Busshoff or Ordynayr or for theym that this muse shall Maynyn acordyng to this the mynster will

Fig. 10   London, Guildhall Library, MS 15838, fol. 11v. © Haberdashers' Company.

fig. 10), whose *littera hybrida* shows many of the features familiar from the cursive script known as Anglicana, because it was typical of England.[29]

Thus scribe 2 alternates between the continental **w** and the one typical of Anglicana, ending in a 3-shaped final stroke. See e.g 'werscreuen' at the beginning of line 7. This word also shows that, apart from the round **r**, scribe 2 writes the tailed Anglicana **r**. Like scribe 1, scribe 2 also uses long **s** and round **s**, but he writes the latter also at the beginning of words (see 'sinte', line 11). This 'most noteworthy feature of Anglicana'[30] is found in scribe 2, but not in scribe 1. Similarly, while both scribes write the loopless **d** and **g**, scribe 2 also employs the Anglicana forms of these letters, that is, the looped **d** (see e.g. 'hoden', line 5) and the 8-shaped **g** (line 5, 'shyllyngen'). A notable feature not found in the handwriting of scribe 1, but present in that of scribe 2 as well as that of the main scribe who penned the 1511 agreement of the Haberdashers, is the use of the infinity sign as a line filler (see e.g. end of lines 3 and 4).

The tentative conclusion to which we are drawn is that scribe 2 acquired his handwriting skills in England while scribe 1 had acquired his writing skills on the continent, though it should be noted that even scribe 1 was familiar enough with English writing to manage standard abbreviations for English words such as **w**ᵗ for 'with' and **eu'ry** for 'euery'. We may be dealing with different generations, with scribe 1 a first-generation migrant, and scribe 2 a second-generation one. Given the confident writing of both scribes, both were probably trained scribes. Scribe 1 could very well be the 'clerke' of the Hatmakers' Fraternity who is repeatedly mentioned in the Ordinances.[31] The English handwriting of scribe 2 could be that of a professional London scrivener of Dutch extraction. (As we shall see below, his Dutch dialect, very different from that of scribe 1, is that of Flanders or Brabant.) Both English and Dutch speakers knew where to find London scribes who knew Dutch. The Mercers, for example, whose trade focused on the Low Countries, needed to have letters and manuscripts written in Dutch, and commissioned expert London scribes to do this,[32] while members of the Dutch immigrant community relied on friars who spoke their language to be their confessors and to record their last testaments.[33]

THE DIALECTS OF THE TWO SCRIBES

Our assumption that the two scribes were Dutch speakers, rather than native English scribes who copied the Dutch without knowing the language, is based not only on the accuracy with which they wrote it but also on the fact that it is not just the handwriting that changes when scribe 2 takes over from scribe 1, but also the dialect. In the case

---

[29]   See M. B. Parkes, *English Cursive Book Hands, 1250–1500* (Oxford: Oxford University Press, 1969).

[30]   Derolez, *Palaeography*, p. 139.

[31]   See n. 15 above.

[32]   Sutton and Visser-Fuchs, ed., *Book of Privileges*, pp. 36–7, and Putter, 'Materials', p. 103.

[33]   See below, p. 106.

of the English written by the two scribes, the differences are very minor and of little or no dialectal significance, though they are nevertheless strikingly consistent. For instance, scribe 1 writes 'them', while scribe 2 writes 'theym'; scribe 1 writes 'established', scribe 2 'establisshed'; scribe 1 writes 'saynt', scribe 2 'seynt'; scribe 1 'fyrst'; scribe 2 'first' and 'furst'. Finally, scribe 1 writes 'fraternite', while scribe 2 writes 'fraternitie'/'fraternytie' or more commonly the native English term *brederhode*, which scribe 1 does not use at all.

However, the differences between the Dutch texts written by the two scribes are much more pronounced and much more revealing. The table below contains features and words that occur in the language of both scribes, but in different forms:

Table 2: Comparison of the Language of the Scribes

Scribe 1	Scribe 2
initial **k**	initial **c**
broder	broeder
an; an-	aen; aen-
voir	voer (voere)
ambocht	ambacht
he; hie	hy
initial and medial **g**	initial and medial **gh**
brengen	brynghen
hilliger	heylyghen
geordinert	gheoerdineert
ander	ender
desse (dese)	dese
to (infinitive marker)	te (infinitive marker)

For a broad-brush localisation of the language of the two scribes we can begin by using the Middle Dutch dialect atlas by Pieter van Reenen and others, where some of these items have been mapped.[34] The local records that form the basis of the Middle Dutch dialect atlas are earlier (pre-1400) than the Ordinances, so where relevant we also refer to the more recent Low German dialect atlas by Robert Peters: this dialect atlas builds on data from the Middle Dutch dialect atlas but has further data on Dutch dialects from the northeast of the present-day Netherlands and northwest Germany,

---

[34] Pieter van Reenen, Matthijs Brouwer, and Evert Wattel, 'Middelnederlands: Vormen en Constructies' <https://www.middelnederlands.nl/>. For methodological discussion, see Evert Wattel and Pieter van Reenen, 'Probabilistic Maps', in *Language and Space: An International Handbook of Linguistic Variation*, ed. by Alfred Lameli, Roland Kehrein, and Stefan Rabanus (Berlin: De Gruyter Mouton, 2011), 2 vols, II, pp. 495–508.

Fig. 11   Dialect map for k/c in *kunnen*, from https://www.middel-nederlands.nl. © Pieter van Reenen.

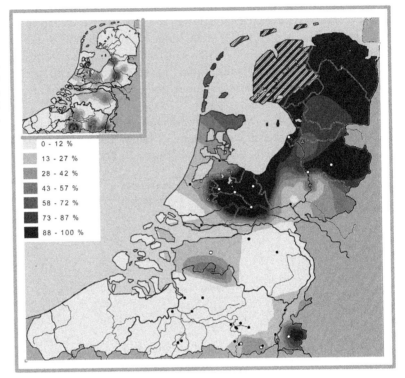

0 - 12 %
13 - 27 %
28 - 42 %
43 - 57 %
58 - 72 %
73 - 87 %
88 - 100 %

and has a broader chronological range, including the fifteenth century.[35] As we shall see, the dialect evidence shows that these Low Countries scribes could hardly be further apart: scribe 1 was from the north-eastern region of what is now the Netherlands while scribe 2 was from the south-western Low Countries, probably the County of Flanders or the Duchy of Brabant.

For the spelling of initial /k/, the Middle Dutch dialect map for spellings of *kunnen* provides useful comparative data (see fig. 11). The dark area is the one where we would expect initial **k**, the light one is where we would expect **c**. The variants of *brengen* (to bring) fit this pattern: the **i/y** forms of scribe 2 are south-western while the **e** forms are generally eastern and northern (see fig. 12).

The distribution of 'desse' ('dese') (scribe 1) and 'dese' (scribe 2) show a comparable distribution. The dialectically marked form is 'desse' is characteristic of the north-eastern parts, bordering on Germany (see fig. 13).[36]

---

[35] Robert Peters, Christian Fischer, and Norbert Nagel, *Atlas spätmittelalterlicher Schreibsprachen des niederdeutschen Altlandes und angrenzender Gebiete*, 3 vols (Berlin: De Gruyter, 2017).

[36] See also the map in Peters et al., *Atlas*, II, 113.

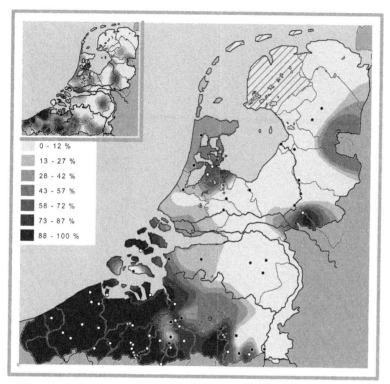

Fig. 12
Dialect map for
e/i variation in
brengen, from
https://middel-
nederlands.nl.
© Pieter van
Reenen.

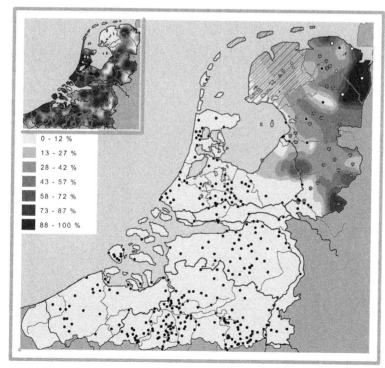

Fig. 13
Dialect map for
'dese'/'desse',
from https://
www.middel-
nederlands.nl.
© Pieter van
Reenen.

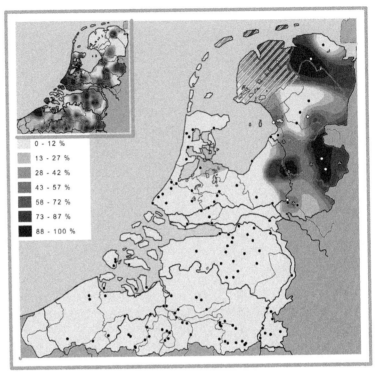

Fig. 14 Dialect map for *heilig*, from https:// www.middel-nederlands.nl. © Pieter van Reenen.

0 - 12 %
13 - 27 %
28 - 42 %
43 - 57 %
58 - 72 %
73 - 87 %
88 - 100 %

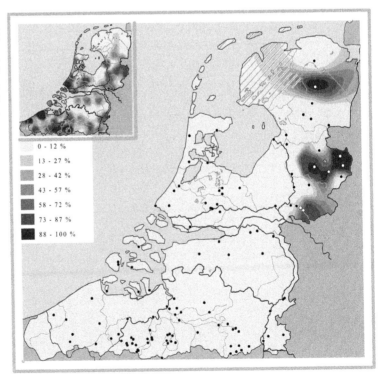

Fig. 15 Dialect map for 'vnt-' in *ontvangen*. Created by Pieter van Reenen. © Pieter van Reenen.

0 - 12 %
13 - 27 %
28 - 42 %
43 - 57 %
58 - 72 %
73 - 87 %
88 - 100 %

The pattern that emerges is that the linguistic habits of scribe 1 fit the north-east of the Netherlands whereas those of scribe 2 fit the south-west of present-day Belgium. The forms 'hillig' (holy) and 'broder' (scribe 1), contrasting with 'heyligh' and 'broeder' (scribe 2), confirm this pattern and help us to pin down the origins of scribe 1 to north-eastern border areas with Germany. The dark areas in the following map indicating forms with <i> in *heilig*, which by and large correspond with the areas where 'broder' was used, show the restricted currency of the forms found in scribe 1 (see fig. 14).[37]

The north-eastern provenance of scribe 1 also explains features of his language that one might otherwise have been tempted to attribute to interference from English. It is striking, for instance, that, unlike scribe 2, who uses 'te' as the infinitive marker, scribe 1 uses 'to', and so writes 'to betalen' in Dutch and in English 'to be paid' (art. 8). And just as in his English he writes 'of olde tyme', so in Dutch he writes not *van ouden tijden*, but 'van olden tijden' (art. 2). Other English-looking spellings are 'holden' for modern Dutch *houden* (art. 10), and 'geholden' for *gehouden* (*passim*). However, although these forms may at first look like anglicisms, they are in fact entirely consistent with the scribe's north-easterly provenance. 'To' or 'toe' are found in eastern Middle Dutch dialects, and spellings of *oud* and *houden* with <l> belong to roughly the same area as *broder* and *hillig*.

A number of other characteristics make it clear that scribe 1 was from the north-east. In the peculiar form of Modern Dutch *volbracht*, 'vullenbracht' (art. 13), the <u> spelling in combination with *-len* points east.[38] 'Gued' for *goed* is also predominantly eastern,[39] as is the unusual pronoun 'he' for *hij*, which is exclusively found in the language of scribe 1.[40] Scribe 1's normal form *vntfangen* (art. 1, 3, etc.) – only once *ontfangen* (art. 2) is also clearly north-eastern, as figure 15 shows.[41]

Can we be more precise? The maps for *hillig* and *broder* place scribe 1 either in the north-eastern tip, in what are now the provinces of Groningen and Drenthe (see fig. 1 for a map showing the provinces), or a little further south, in the eastern parts of the provinces of Overijssel and Gelderland. There are some reasons for thinking the latter was scribe's 1 homeland, for it is to this area (and not the far north-east) that we can assign the following features of his Dutch:

[37] Compare Peters, *Atlas*, II, map 77 (broder) and II, map 139 (hillig).

[38] See MNW, s.v. volbringen, 'vooral in het oost-mnl. vollenbrengen', and on <u> spellings, 'in Gelderland en Overijssel', see Chris de Wulf, *Klankatlas van het veertiende-eeuwse Middelnederlands* (Ghent: Koninklijke Academie voor Nederlandse Taal en Letteren, 2019), p. 318, and Peters, *Atlas*, II, map 52.

[39] See the dialect maps at <https://www.middelnederlands.nl/item/69/480/?text=goed+> and in Peters, *Atlas*, II, map 35.

[40] Scribe 1 uses this alongside the more usual 'hie'; scribe 2 writes 'hy'. The form 'he' is exclusively eastern: see map 90 in de Wulf, *Klankatlas* <https://bouwstoffen.kantl.be/kamnl14/deel2+3. htm>, and in Peters, *Atlas*, II, map 112.

[41] We thank Pieter van Reenen for generating this map for us.

- The forms 'auer' for *over* (art. 3), 'bauen' for *boven* (art. 9). These are typical of the north-eastern provinces of Gelderland and Overijssel, bordering on Germany (*over* is found in Groningen).[42]

- The suffix *-scop*, as in 'geselscop' and 'broderscop' (art. 1). Groningen had *-sc(h)ap*.[43]

- The word 'yegelick' ('every', art. 2, 10, etc.). Groningen had *elk*.[44]

- The form 'maneren' ('manners, art. 13, 17). Groningen had *manieren*.[45]

The provenance of scribe 2 is not quite so easy to determine. We have less Middle Dutch text to go on, and in his writing we do not generally encounter forms restricted to a small area. For instance, while 'desse' (scribe 1) can help us to localise that scribe to a small area, 'dese', the form of scribe 2 (also the minority form of scribe 1) is supragregional, as the dialect map for this item shows (see above, fig. 13).

The raising of *e* to *i* before *n* (e.g. 'brynghet', art. 24) is mentioned as a characteristic of Flanders by Van der Wal,[46] but the dialect map for this item (see above, fig. 12) shows that it had a wider currency in south-western areas, including also Brabant. There are just a few marked forms that might tentatively lead us to Flanders and to the coastal area of that county in particular. 'Darde' (third) in article 23 is unusual. The scribe uses it alongside the normal 'derde'; its use was characteristic of west Flanders and south-west Holland.[47] Also unusual is 'sterlynes' for *sterlynges*: as noted by Van Loey, spellings of <ing> as <in> (e.g. *ghinen* for *ghingen*, *conininnen* for *coninginnen*) are typical of West Flanders.[48]

We have argued so far that the dialects of these two scribes point to opposite ends of the Low Countries, to the north-east, perhaps Gelderland (scribe 1), and to the south-west, perhaps Flanders (scribe 2). Yet against the backdrop of this strongly contrastive pattern some interesting anomalies spring into view. For when scribe 2 begins to write, he initially presents some of the same dialect features of scribe 1, features that later make way for south-western forms. For instance, in the Dutch prepositions *boven* and *over*, forms with **a** are typical of north-eastern Dutch and so it is no surprise that we find them in scribe 1 (see above). We would expect scribe 2, from the southwest, to write them with **o**, and so he does ('ouer', art. 24), and yet when he first takes over from scribe 1 he writes 'bauen gescreuen' (art. 22), adopting both scribe 1's north-eastern vowel and his spelling of the prefix *ge-* (normally *ghe-* in scribe 2). For 'sunte' ('saint'), which again

42   A. van Loey, *Middelnederlandse Spraakkunst. Deel II. Klankleer*, 7th edn (Groningen, Wolters-Noordhoff, 1976), p. 64, De Wulf, *Klankatlas*, p. 64, and Peters, *Atlas*, II, map 61.

43   Peters, *Atlas*, II, map 113.

44   *Ibid.*, map 175.

45   See <https://www.middelnederlands.nl/zoeken/search/?type=simple&prefix=t_lc&text=maneren#tab-documents>.

46   Marijke J. van der Wal, *Geschiedenis van het Nederlands* (Utrecht: Spectrum, 1992), p. 114.

47   van Loey, *Klankleer*, p. 3; and the dialect map at <https://www.middelnederlands.nl/item/146/1073/?text=darde+>.

48   van Loey, *Klankleer*, p. 96.

is predominantly north-eastern and thus predictably scribe 1's form (*passim*),[49] scribe 2 writes 'sinte' (art. 23) and 'sent' (art. 24), but he starts off with 'sunte' (art. 22). For north-eastern 'broder', scribe 1's form, scribe 2 has 'broeder', except in the first article he copies, where he writes 'broderen' and 'broderscop' (art. 22). The suffix 'scop' in 'broderscop' is also north-eastern and characteristic of scribe 1. Scribe 2 writes it only at the start and then goes on to write 'broederscyp' (art. 23) and 'broederscap' (art. 24). Of these later forms, 'broederscyp' is dialectically the most revealing one: it belongs to Flanders.[50]

The curious pattern we find here is consistent with what is known as 'progressive scribal translation': when scribes copy a text written in another dialect they usually begin by adopting the linguistic features of their exemplar but as they warm to the task of writing they progressively resort to forms of their own active repertoire rather than retaining those of the text they are copying.[51] Our analysis of the language thus suggests not only that scribe 1 was from the north-east and scribe 2 from the south-west, but also that scribe 2 was copying a text that had been written in the language of scribe 1 (and presumably by scribe 1) and so began by adopting some of the same north-eastern forms that are the hallmark of scribe 1 before imposing his own linguistic habits.

To conclude, we have seen that the manuscript that contains the Ordinances was put together in different stages: the bilingual Ordinances were copied in 1501, but the last two articles later. The agreement with the Haberdashers was added in 1511, and sometime after the manuscript had come into the possession of the Haberdashers a later hand added the oath of the wardens of the Haberdashers.

The bilingual nature of the Ordinances of the fraternity makes this a unique document: it is the earliest document to have been drawn up bilingually, in Dutch and English. Both scribes were comfortable writing in Dutch and in English, and they were almost certainly Dutch speakers. However, one of them (scribe 1) was from the northeast of the Netherlands, on the border with Germany, while the other (scribe 2) was from the southwest, perhaps Flanders. The first, perhaps to be identified with the clerk of the Hatmakers, wrote in a continental style; the second wrote in a script marked by English features and was probably copying an exemplar written by scribe 1.

---

[49] See the dialect map at <https://www.middelnederlands.nl/item/78/549/?text=sunt+> and Peters, *Atlas*, II, map 101.

[50] See the dialect map for this item at <https://middelnederlands.nl/item/162/1183/?text=schap>.

[51] See M. Benskin et al., 'General Introduction', in *An Electronic Version of A Linguistic Atlas of Late Mediaeval English* (Edinburgh: Angus McIntosh Centre for Historical Linguistics, 2013) <http://www.lel.ed.ac.uk/ihd/elalme/intros/atlas_gen_intro.html>, section 3.3.3, and for discussion of a specific case of progressive scribal translation, see Ad Putter, 'An East Anglian Poem in a London Manuscript? The Date and Dialect of the Court of Love in Cambridge, Trinity College, MS R.3.19', in *Historical Dialectology in the Digital Age*, ed. Rhona Alcorn et al. (Edinburgh: Edinburgh University Press, 2019), pp. 212–43.

CHAPTER 5

The Linguistic Interest of the Bilingual Ordinances

As we have seen in the previous chapter, the Ordinances, devised and written by Dutch-speaking immigrants, are the earliest English-Dutch bilingual document. These exceptional circumstances give this text great curiosity value. In this chapter, we address three questions. The first concerns the exact relationship between the English and the Dutch: is one a translation of the other and, if not, what kind of relationship between the two should we envisage? The second question is: how well did these aliens acquit themselves in English? The third concerns the quality of their Dutch. Emigrants may, with time and disuse, lose some of their grip on their native language, and their second language may start to influence the way they use their first. The linguistic terms for these two processes are 'language attrition' and 'interference' (also known by the less pejorative term 'cross-linguistic influence') respectively.[1] However, to characterise the languages of the Ordinances, it will not do to use only terms that emphasise loss and aberration. In fact, the term we need more than any other to describe their language is semantic and lexical innovation. As we shall see, the document contains various unattested words and spellings as well as several words that appear to occur here for the very first time in the English language.

Such linguistic innovation should not surprise us. As sociolinguists have shown, the movers and shakers of language and the initiators of linguistic change are people with 'loose network ties' – that is, language users who are not tied into a close-knit community but move across and between social networks.[2] Skilled craftsmen in urban environments generally do, and did, have 'loose network ties'. Some aspects of that social mobility are described in the statutes themselves: journeymen and apprentices 'as well beyond the see as on this side' (art. 1) joined workshops; members of the fraternity interacted with

---

[1]   For definitions and analyses of these processes, see Donald Winford, *An Introduction to Contact Linguistics* (Oxford: Blackwell, 2003).

[2]   See James Milroy and Lesley Milroy, 'Linguistic Change, Social Network, and Speaker Innovation', *Journal of Linguistics* 21 (1985), 339–84, and, with specific reference to medieval tradesmen, see the collection *Merchants of Innovation: The Languages of Medieval Traders*, ed. Esther Miriam-Wagner, Bettina Beinhoff and Ben Outhwaite (Berlin: Mouton de Gruyter, 2017).

the Haberdashers, and if they did not sell their wares through them, they must have sold them directly to customers in London. Migrant communities that are plugged into other social networks are not usually backwards or defective in their language use. If anything, they tend to be ahead of the curve. The English text of the Ordinances provides a good test case.

The innovative quality of the Dutch in the Ordinances is harder to quantify. The existence of excellent historical dictionaries in English, the *Oxford English Dictionary* (*OED*) and the *Middle English Dictionary* (*MED*),[3] makes it a worthwhile effort to collect (as we do below) unrecorded spellings and antedatings, and it is safe to draw some conclusions from these data. In Dutch, the historical dictionaries are too patchy to do this. Eelco Verwijs and Jakob Verdam, the original compilers of the Middle Dutch dictionary, *Het Middelnederlandsch Woordenboek* (*MNW*),[4] made no systematic attempt to record spelling variants, and it must be left to experts in Middle Dutch to determine whether unrecorded forms are innovations or not. For instance, while one looks in vain for any other attestation of the spelling 'ender' for Modern Dutch *ander* (art. 23) in the corpus of digitised historical Dutch dictionaries,[5] some digging in other corpora shows that it cannot in fact have been as unusual as this might suggest. The corpus of fourteenth-century local records (Corpus van Reenen-Mulder) documents *enderhalf* in an Antwerp charter of 1392,[6] and a search in the digital library of Dutch literature also finds it in Jan van Ruusbroec's *Vanden Gheesteliken Tabernakel*.[7] Given the rudimentary state of Middle Dutch lexicography, our contribution here must be rudimentary too: we aim to flag up any words or senses that are not in the Middle Dutch dictionary, and we will draw our conclusions about the nature of the language of these Dutch emigrés on that basis.

TRANSLATION OR REFORMULATION?

Perhaps because the English text precedes the Dutch in the manuscript, it has been assumed that the English came first and was 'translated into Dutch',[8] but the rather loose relationship between the wording of the Dutch and the English versions makes it mis-leading to speak of 'translation', at least in the modern sense. Certainly, there is evidence of cross-language influence but, as we shall see in the next chapter, that influence runs in

---

3 We have used the digital versions of MED <https://quod.lib.umich.edu/m/middle-english-dictionary/dictionary> and OED <https://www.oed.com>.

4 Digitised, along with a number of other historical Dutch dictionaries, at <https://gtb.ivdnt.org/search/>.

5 <https://gtb.ivdnt.org/>.

6 <https://middelnederlands.nl/corpora/crm14/>.

7 See *Digital Library for Dutch Literature* <http://www.dbnl.org/>.

8 Ian W. Archer, *The History of the Haberdashers' Company* (Chichester: Phillimore and Co., 1991), p. 61.

both directions, and a comparison of the Dutch text with its English counterpart shows that they are often strikingly independent of each other. Consider, for example, the English and Dutch text (followed in brackets by our translation) of article 19:

> Item, it is established and ordeyned that no broder of the seid fraternite shall take no maner a man or put to his occupacion of the seid craft of hatmakynge without he by lerneth [unless he is instructed] in the same fraternite, nor noon other that comyth frome any mastur of any odur fraternite or felyshyp, vpon suche payne as by the masturs and more parte of the seid brederne of the seid fraternite shal be resonably aftur ther discrecioun limited and assigned.

> Item, dat is versament ende geordinert dat geen broder van derseluer broderscop sal annemen genen knecht ofte to werke setten de myt enigen anderen meister geleert heeft de in vnser broderye niet en is, he en betale de bote to den meysters ende ouersiensiers van derseluer broderscop als he kan corderen mytten iiij meysteren de dair to geset sijn.

> (Item, this is enjoined and ordained that no brother of the same brotherhood shall employ or put to work any servant who has been taught by another master who is not our brotherhood, unless he pay such a fine to the masters and overseers as he can agree with the four masters appointed thereto.)

The English and the Dutch agree on the general sense, but neither version appears to have served as the linguistic model for the other. In fact, they differ on matters of detail. In the English, the penalty is to be decided by the masters and the majority of the membership; in the Dutch the amount is to be decided by mutual agreement between the masters, the supervisors, and the offender.

A revealing detail that shows the relative independence of the Dutch from the English is that the first-person plural pronoun is present only in the Dutch and not in the English. This pattern is remarkably consistent:

Article 3	within this realme of England	*myt vns int konincrik van Engeland*
	the seid craft	*vnse ambocht*
Article 5	of the seid craft	*van vnsen ambocht*
Article 6	the seid craft	*vnsen ambocht*
Article 19	in the same fraternite	*in vnser broderye*

The expression of collective identity (*our* craft, *our* fraternity) apparently felt right in Dutch, but not in English.

There is thus no exact alignment between the wording of the Dutch and the English articles, and the texts in these two languages seem generally to have been drawn up without much cross-checking. They must have been formulated either by two different guild members or by a perfectly bilingual language user who had no need to consult the text in one language to generate its equivalent in the other. Consider, as another example, article 20:

Item, it is established and ordeyned that if any seruant departe fromme his mastur and seruice with licence or without licence asked and obteyned of his mastur, that thenne no broder of the same fraternite shall take or accepte the seid seruant so departyng, without licence of his masturs whome he before serued, vpon payne of iiij li. wex, to be applied and paid to the seyd fraternite without any contradiction or remission.

Item, dat is versament ende geordinert of enich knecht van synen meyster genge myt orlof ofte sunder orlof ende gaet tot enen anderen meister om myt him to werken soe en sal geen broder van derseluer broderscop den knecht to werke setten, hie en vrage ersten sinen meister dair he van gegaen is oft dat sijn wille sy, vp de bote van iiij lb. wasses sunder enige voirgiffenisse te betalen.

(Item, it is enjoined and ordained that if any servant leaves his master with permission or without permission and goes to another master in order to work with him, then no brother of the same brotherhood shall put this servant to work, unless he first asks his master whom he left if it were his will, under penalty of four pounds of wax, to be paid without any remission.)

There is, here and elsewhere in the English text, as indeed in English prose of this period more generally,[9] a fondness for binomial constructions ('asked and obteyned', 'take or accepte', 'to be applied and paid', 'contradiction or remission') that is much less pronounced in the Dutch text, which is consequently shorter. But if the Dutch text had been intended as an abbreviation of the English, we could not explain why it is on occasion much wordier, as in 'hie en vrage ersten sinen meister dair he van gegaen ist of dat sijn wille sy', which bears little lexical and grammatical resemblance to the succinct English formula, 'without license of his masturs whom he before serued'. Nor could we explain why the Dutch occasionally indulges in binomials, as in 'Ende we dit voirsmaet ende ofte dair tegen doet' (And whoever violates this or acts against it), when the English has just one phrase ('And whoseumeuyr attempte the contrary', article 5) or indeed nothing at all. For example, in article 16, de dat versumet ende niet en doet ('who disregards this and does not do it'), has no English equivalent, even as the English has a formula containing a binomial ('to be applied vnder maner and forme before rehersed') that is not in the Dutch.

The hypothesis that explains this variation is that we are dealing with bilingual text formulated either by two speakers or by one bilingual speaker who aimed to say more or less the same thing in both languages. That 'more or less' applies both to the number of words *and* to the content. For another example, compare the last sentence of article 9, where the English and the Dutch again part ways:

And the partie hurt or aggreuyd to be recompensed after the discrecion of the wardens.

9   See David Burnley, 'Curial Prose in England', *Speculum* 61 (1986), 593–614, and Elizabeth Kubaschewski, 'Binomials in Caxton's Ovid (Book I)', in *Binomials in the History of English*, ed. Joanna Kopaczyk and Hans Sauer (Cambridge: Cambridge University Press, 2017), pp. 141-58.

Ande ofte de partien malcanderen beclagen, sullen de meysters nae hour verstandenisse verenigen ende to to vrede stellen. (And if the parties accuse each other, the masters shall, according to their understanding, unite and conciliate [them]).

Unlike the slavish Dutch-English translations that we encountered in *The Book of Privileges* (see above, p. 78), the prose here is perfectly idiomatic in both languages, and neither sentence 'translates' the other. What is striking, in fact, is the difference between the English sentence and the Dutch one, and precise minds will have noticed the procedural discrepancy. In the English text, it is the wardens who must settle the dispute and specify the compensation due to the aggrieved party. In the Dutch, the masters are responsible for reconciling the parties: payment of compensation may have been understood, but it is not explicitly mentioned.

We conclude that the English and the Dutch versions give expression to the same basic idea, but that most of the text was formulated without any 'translation' being involved.

THE ENGLISH LANGUAGE OF THE ORDINANCES

Since the English text and the Dutch are not translations of each other, it makes sense to look at the prose in the two languages separately. We shall begin with some observations about the English language in the Hatmakers' ordinances, focusing on spelling and lexis.

English orthography was not easy for foreigners and some of the mistakes which they were prone to making can be seen in the writing of a Dutch scribe who was active in England in the second half of the fifteenth century, Theodoric Werken.[10] Born in Abbenbroek, near Rotterdam, he mostly copied Latin texts, which caused him no trouble, but in one of the manuscripts (San Marino, CA, Huntington Library, MS HM 142, fol. 60v) he wrote, in addition to a set of Latin prayers, a colophon in English. This colophon immediately reveals his Dutch origin: at one point he wrote **d** instead of **th** or thorn (perhaps a reflection also of how this Dutchman pronounced a sound alien to Dutch), and instead of 'he' Werken wrote the equivalent Dutch pronoun 'hi'.[11] Such spelling errors due to interference from Dutch are absent in the English ordinances. There is one possible case of **d/th** confusion, this time not <d> for <th>, but <th> for <d>, and that is in article 19: 'without he by lerneth in the same fraternite'. It is clear from the context that this means 'unless he is instructed in the same fraternity', and so 'lerneth' is *lerned*. However, this is more probably to be explained as a dialect feature than as a mistake: <th> for <d> is known to be a regional characteristic associated with Middle

[10] On this scribe, see David Rundle, *The Renaissance Reform of the Book and Britain* (Cambridge: Cambridge University Press, 2019), pp. 124–42.

[11] The colophon is reproduced and discussed in Sjoerd Levelt and Ad Putter, *North Sea Crossings: The Literary Heritage of Anglo-Dutch Relations, 1066–1688* (Oxford: Bodleian Library, 2021), p. 99.

English texts written in and around Surrey.[12] The spelling could well reflect the scribe's local dialect.

The various anomalous spellings in this document do not suggest foreignness either. Below is a list of notable spellings:

- 'cownandes' (covenants), art. 1. Not recorded in *MED*, which does, however, record 'cownant' (s.v. *covenaunt*) But see *OED* s.v. 'covenant': 'every prentes … that trewly servethe his cownand' (guild statute from Exeter, 1481).

- 'shabbe', art. 2. This contraction of 'shal be' is neither in *MED* nor *OED*.

- 'whichsumeuer', art 3; 'whichsumeuyr', art. 5. Not recorded as a form of 'whichsever' in either *MED* or *OED*. The pronoun 'whichsoever' appears to be a late starter (the only attestation in *MED* is dated c. 1475).

- 'artifer', art. 4. Neither in *MED* nor *OED*. Perhaps an error for 'artificer', influenced by 'artifex'.

- 'talors' [taylors]. Neither in *MED* nor *OED*. It is clearly not an error (the spelling is repeated), but rather a reflection of the falling together of *ai* and long *a* 'in the popular stratum of speech'.[13]

- 'brodrun' [brothers], art. 8. Not in *MED* or *OED*, but entirely plausible. Compare the spellings 'broderyn', 'brodurne' and 'brodyrn' in *OED*.

- 'whomsumeuyr', art. 9. Neither *MED* nor *OED* have forms with initial 'whom' (but see *MED*, s.v. 'whomever', for variation between 'whoever' and 'whomever', and compare 'whichsumeuer' above).

- 'ouyer', art. 12. Unattested as a spelling of 'over' in *MED* and *OED*. Did the scribe waver between <y> and <e> and end up writing both?

- 'iniurioseis' ('injuries'), art. 12. *MED* records the plural 'iniurious'. It looks as if the scribe wrote a plural inflection twice.

With the exceptions of 'artifer', 'iniurioseis' and 'ouyer', which look like scribal mistakes, there is nothing here that could not pass as plausible Late Middle English.

From spellings, we move to lexis, and what is striking here is the precocious modernity of the diction. A number of words occur in the Ordinances before the earliest attestations recorded in *MED* and *OED*. 'Reception' is recorded in *OED* in a technical astrological sense, but not in the sense 'admittance' until 1525. That, however, is clearly the sense in which the word is used in the Ordinances – 'before ther admission and

---

[12] See M. Benskin et al., *An Electronic Version of A Linguistic Atlas of Late Mediaeval English* (Edinburgh: Angus McIntosh Centre for Historical Linguistics, 2013), dot map for item 399.

[13] Richard Jordan, *Handbook of Middle English Grammar: Phonology* (The Hague: Mouton, 1974), p. 242.

recepcion' (art. 1).[14] The adverb 'inobediently' (art. 6) is also novel. *OED* gives the earliest attestation as 1536, while *MED* (s.v. 'inobedientlie') has only one attestation, from the Chester Plays, extant in a very late copy (1607). But 'inobediently' occurs twice in article 6 of the Ordinances and once more in article 11, this time in the otherwise unrecorded spelling 'inobedientli'.

The noun 'hat-making' is not recorded in *MED* and the earliest attestation in *OED* is from 1547 ('*Act 1 Edward VI* c. 6 §3 in *Statutes of Realm* (1963) IV. i. 12: Yarne ... wrought in hattes or employed to hatte-making'). It is, however, frequently used in our Ordinances, once in an article that is only in English (art. 25), but otherwise as the equivalent of Dutch *hoed(en)making*, as in 'the seid crafte of hatmakynge' (art. 21), corresponding with Dutch 'denseluen ambocht van hoitmakyng'. Perhaps the English word was calqued on the Dutch, but in Dutch the word appears to be even more precocious: the historical Dutch dictionaries do not record it, and we have not found any trace of it before the 1800s.[15]

Another word that occurs in the Ordinances before the earliest dictionary attestations is the noun 'multe' (art. 4), Modern English 'mulct' (penalty, fine). This is not in *MED*, while *OED* gives the earliest attestation as 1586. The word is ultimately derived from Latin *mulcta*, but the Dutch hatmakers would have known it from their mother tongue, where it had been in use since at least the fifteenth century.[16] Also new in English is 'draw' in the sense of 'to draw a weapon'. *OED* (s.v. draw, sense 33b) credits the first usage to Shakespeare (1599), 'Draw if you be men' (*Romeo & Juliet*, I.i.59), but the absolute use is already present in the Ordinances: 'And he that drawith ... shall pay to the seid fraternite iiij lb. of wexe' (art. 12).

A couple of English words are not in the dictionaries at all, though they look plausible enough. 'Finiall' (art. 8) is nowhere else found as an adverb, but it was common enough as an adjective (see *OED* s.v. finial), and there is the mystery verb *flosh*. Article 23 stipulates 'that no maister nor brother of this same fraternitie shall put no hattes for to be flosshede, nor cause no hattes to be flosshede, nor put no feltes to be made withoute his house'. What 'floshing a hat' means is obscure. Neither *MED* nor *OED* has this word, and while the Dutch says something very similar – 'dat gheen meester noch broeder van derseluer broederscyp gheen felten en sal doen maken noch hoden doen floschen buten synen huyse' – the problem is that 'floschen' is not attested in Dutch either. It is true that the verb 'vloschen' can be found as a technical term in salt production (see *MNW*), but this particular verb, modern Dutch *vlossen* (also *flossen, florsen*), perhaps related to 'vlos' (an implement for scooping solid substances out of water),

---

[14] There is an even earlier attestation in Caxton's Blanchardyn and Eglantine (c. 1489): 'the fayr welcome and honourable recepcion'. See William Caxton, *Blanchardyn and Eglantine*, ed. Leon Kellner, EETS, extra series 58 (London: Trübner, 1890), p. 194.

[15] 'Hoedenmaking' is in S. J. M. van Moock, *Nieuw Fransch-Nederduitsch en Nederduitsch-Fransch Woordenboek* (Gouda: G. B. van Goor, 1849), and 'hoedmaking' in *Arnhemsche Courant* (Arnhem, 20 November 1821).

[16] K. Stallaert, *Glossarium van verouderde rechtstermen, kunstwoorden en andere uitdrukkingen uit Vlaamsche, Brabantsche en Limburgsche oorkonden*, 2 vols (Leiden: Brill, 1886–1891), II, s.v. 'mulcte'.

is unlikely to be relevant here. The word is probably related to the French *floche* (tuft, tassel), attested in Anglo-Norman as a past participle *floché* (tassled, fringed), with reference to textiles. The so-called 'thrum hats' of this period were adorned with ends of yarn or silk,[17] and 'floshing' a hat may be the same as what was later called 'thrumming' (see *OED* under the verb 'thrum', with the first attestation of 1525, 'Hattes thrommyd with silke of diuerse collours').

We have mentioned apropos of 'multe' the possibility of Dutch influence and there are some other cases where this seems likely. Middle English guild ordinances use the term *prentis* for 'apprentice', but the Hatmakers called a trainee a 'lerner', perhaps influenced by the Dutch word *leerknecht* (art. 21). Another example of possible Dutch influence is the expression 'fall into the payne' (art. 4), meaning 'to incur a penalty'. The normal Middle English idiom, a loan translation of Latin *incurrere*, was to *renne in the pain*,[18] but the expression in the Ordinances follows the Dutch idiom *in de boete vallen* ('vallen in de bote', art. 4) and appears to be Dutch-inspired.

THE DUTCH LANGUAGE OF THE ORDINANCES

The Dutch text also contains various words and forms that have not previously been recorded by lexicographers, and there is strong evidence of interference from their second language.

The Dutch word *menigmaal* (often), though very well attested in early modern Dutch, is not attested until very late in Middle Dutch. *MNW*, s.v. *menichmael*, gives as the only attestation a legal record of 1558, and points out that the Middle Dutch word was *menichwerf*. However, the new word *menigmaal* was already in use in the language of scribe 1. He spells it 'menichmael' (art. 5), but also 'mannichmal' (art. 11), a spelling reflecting his original dialect on the German border. The word 'broderye' (brotherhood) is not to be found in any Dutch dictionary, though it sounds entirely idiomatic and can be found in German.[19] Again, the fact that we find it in the north-eastern Dutch language of scribe 1 (art. 19) seems relevant. *Oversiener* ('supervisor') has no entry in *MNW*, but the word was well established in Dutch. The earliest attestation we have found is in Ordinances of the Orphanage of Kortrijk in 1411 (*oversienre ende scepenen*).[20] Here and in

---

[17]   See John S. Lee, 'Thrums', in *Encyclopedia of Medieval Dress and Textiles*, online edition, ed. Gale Owen-Crocker, Elizabeth Coatsworth, and Maria Hayward (Leiden, 2021), <http://dx.doi.org/10.1163/2213-2139_emdt_SIM_001171>.

[18]   See MED, s.v. peine, 1b, rennen in the peine, and 'The Statutes of the Craft of Dyers (1439)', from *The Little Red Book of Bristol*, ed. Francis B. Bickley, 2 vols (Bristol: W. C. Hemmons, 1900), II, pp. 170–76 (172), and see *Little Red Book of Bristol*, p. 181.

[19]   Wilhelm Deecke, *Die Deutsche Verwandtschaftsnamen: eine sprichwissenschaftliche Untersuchung* (Weimar: Böhlau, 1870), p. 106.

[20]   'Ordinances of the Orphanage of Kortrijk' <http://www.diachronie.nl/corpora/chna/document/kortrijk_1411_1>. See also Stallaert, *Glossarium*, II, s.v. oversiener.

the Ordinances of the Hatmakers the word designates an official charged with ensuring that rules are observed: a 'supervisor'.

More so than in the case of their English, however, we can tell that the Dutch of the Hatmakers interacted with the other language that was hardwired into their brains, for there are some striking cases of interference. 'Stedfastelick' (art. 3) is peculiar, because Dutch *steeevast* is already an adverb and so does not take and never took the adverbial suffix *-lijk* (see *MNW*, s.v. *stedevaste*). However, the suffix makes sense in a Middle English context, which had *stedefast* as the adjective and *stedefastli* as the adverb. The curious use of 'versament' in the repeated formula 'dat is versament ende geordynert' ('it is decreed and ordained') may also reflect interference from English. Middle Dutch *versamenen* is well attested, but only in the sense 'unite, to join'. Middle English (and French) *enjoinen*, however, did cover both these senses, and perhaps we are dealing here with a semantic extension influenced by the English word.

More obvious cases of interference are those where the English text contains the model on which Dutch words or phrases were calqued. 'Meer ouer' (art. 5) in the sense of 'moreover' is more English than Dutch, and the possibility that it is due to linguistic interference is confirmed by the English text, which reads 'Moreouer' at this point. 'Soe dat' in the sense of 'so long as, on condition that' in article 22 is another anglicism. In Middle Dutch, the basic sense of *so dat* was 'with the result that', but the provisional sense was perfectly normal in Middle English (see *MED* s.v. *that*, 3a) and is exemplified by the English *so that* in article 22. The alternative for 'soe dat' in the Ordinances, 'angesien dat', is equally curious. The normal sense of this phrase is 'because' (*MNW* s.v. *aengesien*II), but in the Ordinances it is used as an equivalent of *provided that* (art. 8 and 17). The underlying metaphor (Middle Dutch *sien* and Latin *videre* both mean 'see') is the same. 'In dat behalue', meaning 'on that point', is another anglicism.[21] In Middle Dutch *behalue* is a preposition ('except for, apart from'), and the whole phrase seems to be based on the Middle English phrase 'in that behalfe' (see art. 8).

A couple of spellings also point to interference. The Dutch word for 'dagger' was *dagge*, and the reason why it is spelt with a final **r** in article 12 must be that the English is *dagger* (here spelt 'daggar'). The Middle Dutch spelling of 'space' is *spacie* or *spatie*, but scribe 1 slips into the English spelling 'space' (art. 17).

The influence of the English text is naturally a factor here, but the impact of English goes deeper than that. Influence from Middle English *stedfastli* and *enjoinen* may explain 'stedfastelick' and 'versament', but these English words do not appear in the text. The interference was from a language which the Hatmakers had in their heads as well in this written document. And while 'Moreouer' in the English text may have triggered the first 'Meer ouer' in article 5, it is noticeable that it occurs again in article 12 where the English text has no equivalent. In short, the anglicisms are not the result of the Hatmakers' lazy translation but the by-product of their bilingualism. The close genetic relation between the two West-Germanic languages they spoke, Dutch and English, would have made

---

[21] See WNT for a later seventeenth-century example of this anglicism: 'ick ben beladen Mijn Heer in U behalf' (I am weighed down, my Lord, on your behalf).

such interference all the more likely, for close genetic relationships between languages and the perception of such closeness by bilingual speakers of such languages have been shown both to motivate and to facilitate cross-language transfer.[22]

Two other conclusions can be drawn from the data presented here. While interference from Dutch is not absent from the English written by these two scribes, most of the cross-language influence is from English to Dutch. For many bilingual speakers one language tends to be more dominant than the other. In the case of the two scribes who devised and wrote the Ordinances, the dominant language must have been English, a language which they managed to write with native-like competence. Of course, such competence may not have been characteristic of the Dutch-speaking hatmakers as a whole. However, these two writers at least had adapted very well to their new surroundings. We have mentioned the contrasting case of Theoderic Werken, who betrays his Dutch origins in his written English, but to give a balanced perspective we should point out that there are also contemporary examples of successful linguistic integration. Edmund Hermanson, a Dutch beer brewer who emigrated to Colchester around 1460 and died there in 1502, was responsible for a set of churchwarden accounts which are almost certainly written in his own hand. In terms of both his handwriting (a *cursiva* with a blend of Anglicana with secretary features) and language, there is nothing to suggest that he was not a native speaker and writer.[23] In the case of Edmund Hermanson, his linguistic integration was matched by his successful social integration more broadly. He became a burgess of Colchester in 1466; was married twice, both times to English women; and was elected churchwarden at a time when such a position was still deemed desirable and prestigious. The lives of the two scribes who write the Ordinances cannot be documented, but there seems no reason to doubt that their linguistic assimilation reflected a measure of wider cultural assimilation also. The above-mentioned case of Anthony Levison, who signed the 1511 agreement with the Haberdashers, married an Englishwoman (Elizabeth Newton) and headed the 1531 petition against the import of headgear from abroad, tells a similar story.

Finally, the Ordinances of the Hatmakers are linguistically innovative in their Dutch as well as their English: some words and spellings are otherwise unrecorded, and others (such as English *mulct* and Dutch *menigmaal*) appear here for the first time. The Ordinances thus testify to the dynamism of this speech community and to the fertile interaction between the two languages in which they expressed themselves. They are a valuable source for the history of both languages, English and Dutch, and confirm the premise of modern sociolinguistics that linguistic innovation was driven by speakers who moved between different social networks and navigated different linguistic communities.

---

22   See Patience Epps, John Huehnergard, and Na'ama Pat-El, ed., 'Contact Among Genetically Related Languages', *The Journal of Language Contact* 6 (2013), 209–19.

23   Bart Lambert, '"I, Edmund": A Microhistory of an Immigrant Churchwarden in Fifteenth-Century Colchester', in *People, Power and Identity in the Late Middle Ages: Essays in Memory of W. Mark Ormrod*, ed. Gwilym Dodd, Helen Lacey, and Anthony Musson (London: Routledge, 2021), pp. 92–114.

Conclusion

Our research began with a scruffy parchment booklet, for centuries kept among the archives of the Haberdashers' Company and now in the London Guildhall Library. A group of Dutch-speaking hatmakers originally bought it, blank, in the years around 1500. They had established in the London Blackfriars' priory a craft association, the Hatmakers' Fraternity of St James the Less, and needed a book in which to record their ordinances. Though made from parchment, not paper, this booklet was nonetheless a bargain purchase, constructed from cheaper fragments of parchment with curved and irregular margins rather than squared-off and even edges. The small group of immigrant artisans from the Low Countries used the book to record regulations that organised their occupation of hatmaking and the social and religious functions of their fraternity. The ordinances were composed in both English and Dutch, making this booklet the earliest bilingual English-Dutch document we know of.[1]

The felt hats these craftsmen made were one of the essential consumer commodities fundamental to the post-plague economy in Europe. Craftsmen in Europe developed new processes for making a high-quality felt from the fur of certain mammals – beavers were best, but some kinds of sheep wool also worked. These felts could be moulded into brimmed hats that kept their shape in all weathers; by the end of the fourteenth century, 'bever hats' had become fashionable. The skills for making this kind of felt were unknown in England in the decades following the Black Death; caps were made in England, but so far as we were able to find hats made from felt or straw were imported from abroad, from the Low Countries, France, and Italy. In the fifteenth century we see the first evidence of felt hatmaking in England, but those hats were made by immigrants, not by English craft workers. By the 1480s and 1490s, there was a sizeable number of felt hatmakers in London, all, as far as we can tell, immigrants from the Low Countries. They kept a careful guard on the skills by which they produced their felt and, for decades to come, it was Dutch migrants who retained a monopoly on the knowledge of this artisanal process in England.

Though advantaged by their unique ability to make this popular form of headgear, the hatmakers settling in London in the later fifteenth century arrived at a turbulent moment for labour and craft organisations in London. The turn of the sixteenth century

---

[1]   See chapter 4.

saw aggressive manoeuvring among the London citizen guilds, as larger crafts swallowed smaller ones and engaged in intense competition to control workers outside their memberships. Among those workers outside the London guilds were stranger artisans; anyone born outside the realm, as the Dutch hatmakers were, was barred by civic ordinance from full membership in the London craft guilds. Those guilds nonetheless wanted to control alien labour, ideally bringing skilled stranger artisans under the supervision of citizen guild masters.[2]

It was in that context that, around the year 1500, the Dutch hatmakers met in the Dominican priory to establish their fraternity. They undoubtedly chose Blackfriars because it was a liberty, outside City jurisdiction; some may have lived and worked within the precinct, while others certainly lived nearby in the parish of St Andrew by the Wardrobe. The hatmakers formed their association to resist incorporation as subordinate members of a London guild, a strategy that seems to have worked for about a decade. In 1511, however, the king's council ordered the Hatmakers' Fraternity of St James to be amalgamated into the much larger London Haberdashers' Company. The terms of this merger were also written into the booklet with the ordinances, along with some modifications to that agreement probably written several years later following a court case about its terms.[3]

Prising open this unassuming document makes us pose new questions about language, writing, translation, labour, migration, and culture in London and across the North Sea at the threshold between the medieval and early modern ages. The way the ordinances were written reveals much about the linguistic reality of immigrants from the Low Countries in London in these years. Two scribes successively wrote the ordinances, the first around 1501, the second continuing in the decade following. They may have been the clerks of the Fraternity mentioned in the Ordinances or Dutch priests or friars hired for the occasion. The first scribe's Dutch dialect shows origins in the north-eastern Netherlands and the handwriting reflects Dutch scripts; the second scribe, by contrast, wrote in a script with both English and continental features and in a dialect of Dutch spoken in the southwestern Low Countries. Perhaps in their places of origin, the two scribes would each have regarded the other as a stranger but, in London, linguistic commonality rather than dialectal difference brought them together. The scribes were also very much at home in English, showing a high level of bilingualism. The ordinances were not composed in one language and then translated into the other: the scribes drew up each version independently, conveying the same meaning but with different phrasing. If anything, the scribes were more comfortable in English than in Dutch, with the Dutch showing influence of anglicisms in some of its ordinary vocabulary: the Dutch ordinances, for instance, use 'meer ouer' when an English speaker would say 'moreouer [moreover]': a useful phrase but not a Dutch one. It is probable, then, that both scribes were immigrants from the Low Countries who often spoke both English and Dutch; the fact that the second scribe seems to have been trained to write in England could suggest

[2]   See chapter 1.
[3]   See chapter 3.

that he was a second-generation Dutch speaker. As their language shows, they lived in a bicultural world, a common feature of immigrant life.[4]

The work life of the hatmakers also straddled the North Sea. The artisanal cultures in London and the Low Countries had much in common with one another, as we might expect given the close economic and cultural ties. They had some striking differences, too. English artisanal training was lengthy and more formalised than was the norm in the Low Countries and elsewhere on the European continent. For continental artisans, movement from city to city for work or for training was straightforward, allowing for easier responses to market conditions and facilitating a culture of artisanal exchange between cities. In London, by contrast, labour migration of skilled craftsmen was inhibited by the tight control of entry into citizen guilds: not only were aliens and strangers generally barred but so also were those who undertook apprenticeships anywhere else in England. The restriction of London guild membership to those who completed their training under those guilds' aegis inhibited both geographical and social mobility: save for a few wealthy and well-connected exceptions, only boys with parents or guardians able to arrange London apprenticeships could become London guildsmen. Though the path to master citizen artisan in London was narrow, for those able to take the prescribed route the benefits were clear. The economic structures of the metropolis were configured as much as possible to favour citizens' production and sale of goods at the expense of those outside the freedom of London.[5]

These differences meant that the culture of artisanal labour to which the Dutch hatmakers were accustomed when they came to London was substantially different from what English Londoners expected. The Dutch craftsmen were presumably baffled by the restrictiveness of London's guild membership, not to mention insulted by the nativist rules that excluded anyone born outside the realm. To English guildsmen, the short continental apprenticeships must have appeared laughably inadequate, while the Dutch craftsmen themselves probably rightly regarded their artisanal skills as no less developed than those of their English counterparts, though acquired differently. In the case of the hatmakers, the quality of continental artisanal training was even more obvious, as no English artisans had the skills to make the fashionable felt hats. When they established their ordinances in the Blackfriars' priory around the year 1500, the Dutch Hatmakers adhered closely to continental norms in the structure of their craft: 'learners' (the word they used in English instead of 'apprentice') trained for two years, not seven to ten; artisans trained in other crafts or in other cities were welcome to join their association simply by demonstrating their skills; procedures for establishing the credentials of those migrating from elsewhere (letters of attestation) were written into the rules. The 'Dutchness' of the ordinances of the Hatmakers' Fraternity suggests an implicit rejection of the English way of organising artisanal labour: to the Hatmakers, their own way of doing things seemed right.[6]

---

4   See chapters 4 and 5.

5   See chapter 1.

6   See chapter 2.

The Dutchmen who formed the Fraternity of St James the Less in the London Blackfriars priory did so not simply or even primarily because they wanted to organise their craft as suited them, but because they needed to act collectively to resist absorption as subordinate members of one of the London citizen guilds. Though they were able to avert a takeover for about a decade, in 1511 they were forced by order of the royal council to put themselves under the supervision of the London Haberdashers' Company. As legal wrangles in the following years show, this was not a friendly union: in at least some cases, hatmakers agreed to swear an oath to the Haberdashers only after all their goods had been seized by civic authorities. Testimony in litigation in the 1510s shows mutual disdain between the English haberdasher merchants and the Dutch hatmaker artisans: the former decried the stranger artisans' unwillingness to subordinate themselves to the company wardens' authority, while the latter complained that the haberdashers knew nothing of hatmaking and should leave them to regulate themselves.[7]

Though hostility may have prevailed in the initial years after the forced merger in 1511, in subsequent years both citizen haberdashers and stranger hatmakers prospered in an expanding market for consumer goods. We can see this especially in a parliamentary petition which the London Haberdashers' Company organised in 1531 on behalf of many different artisans who made headgear, including citizen haberdashers who made caps and non-citizen artisans who participated in various parts of the industry, including the Dutch hatmakers. As the petition shows, the stranger artisans shared interests with the citizen guild members and benefited from collective representation. Two decades after the Hatmakers' merger with the Haberdashers, thirty-five hatmaker masters employed over a thousand workers. The small workshop-based hatmaking craft had become part of a larger development in textile production in London and other parts of Europe in the early sixteenth century: chains of production with pieceworkers performing different stages of the process of making a hat in their own homes. The hatmaker masters – still overwhelmingly Dutch, judging by their names – oversaw these production sequences, presumably performing the most recondite aspects of fabrication of hats in their own shops. As tax records show, at least some of these hatmakers were doing well.[8]

Yet as the 1510s court cases and the Haberdashers' records of later decades make clear, neither the haberdashers nor the hatmakers themselves regarded the Dutch artisans as full members of the London Haberdashers' Company. As strangers born outside the realm they were ineligible for citizenship. Because only those alien-born artisans knew the craft of hatmaking, however, the nativist logic of London guild membership meant that no hatmakers, regardless of where they were born, became citizen guild members over the first half of the sixteenth century. Only citizen guild members could be apprentice masters, but no hatmakers could be citizens, as they were strangers; that, in turn, meant there could be no future hatmaker citizens, as only those who had served an officially registered guild apprenticeship could become freemen of London and guild members. It was only in the 1560s following parliamentary legislation mandating

---

7   See chapters 2 and 3

8   See chapter 3.

seven-year apprenticeships for all artisanal trades that this vicious circle was interrupted: following the statute, the Haberdashers were forced to make special grants of citizenship and guild membership to several cohorts of hatmakers so they could serve as apprentice-masters for new generations of English-born apprentices. These new hatmaker citizen haberdashers were English or Welsh, judging by their names. We can guess that they had trained with the stranger hatmakers who had dominated the craft in the London area over the previous three generations; up to 1567, however, they, like their alien hatmaker masters, were excluded from London citizenship despite their English birth because they had not undertaken a formal apprenticeship. Though immigrant hatmakers, increasingly from northern France rather than the Low Countries, continued to move to the London area in the second half of the sixteenth century, the craft was no longer entirely confined to stranger artisans. Hatmaking grew, of course, to be an even more significant industry in England over the early modern centuries.[9]

The exclusion of the stranger hatmakers from the London guilds affected them economically, socially, and culturally. We can trace the outline of the career of Anthony Levison, one of the four Hatmaker wardens in 1511, a defendant in a 1514 lawsuit between the Haberdashers' company and several hatmakers, and the chief hatmaker master in the 1531 parliamentary petition. He certainly prospered over the decades, but not nearly as much as citizen cappers and haberdashers whose careers coincided with his: inability to retail his own goods and significantly higher tax rates were structural disadvantages that affected him and every other immigrant artisan working in London. The strangers were also excluded socially and culturally from most aspects of guild life, the often-elaborate feasts, processions, and other ceremonies that have been much studied as occasions for the building of conviviality and solidarity among London's artisans. Such ceremonial demonstrated who was in and who was not. Yet if excluded from the company feasts, hatmakers nonetheless developed social relationships with their English neighbours and business associates: they married English women, they gossiped with their English neighbours, they stood as guarantors for work colleagues in legal disputes. Strangers in London, even those who had lived in the City for decades, experienced that liminal status of both belonging and not-belonging: vital to the labour and production of the City's economy and tied by close relationships with the English-born, yet vulnerable to xenophobic resentments that at times turned violent, as during the Evil May Day anti-immigrant riot in 1517.

The Dutch artisans in London in the early to mid-sixteenth century thus straddled a line between inclusion and exclusion in the City's life – but, of course, they themselves were sometimes ambivalent about or resistant to assimilation. The reasons for these artisans' leaving the Low Countries in the first place are unclear. The usual push and pull factors were no doubt pertinent: intermittent political turmoil in Dutch cities and poor employment prospects on the one hand; economic opportunity, higher wages, new horizons, and personal ties in London on the other. The evidence of the Dutch hatmakers' lives in London, fragmentary as it is, suggests, however, that by no means did they seek

---

[9]   See chapter 3.

to abandon their culture in their move across the North Sea. It is no surprise that Dutch immigrants had close relationships to one another. The will of one of the hatmakers, Gerard Rowst, who together with Anthony Levison signed the 1511 agreement, shows those ties: he, like so many other Dutchmen, made his last confession to the subprior of the Crossed Friars, Brother Godfrey Borken, who, together with other Dutch-speaking confessors, Bartholomew Lanselott of Antwerp and Brother John Hellinck, looked after the spiritual needs of the 'strangers' in their mother tongue in the early sixteenth century.[10] And just as they cleaved closely to the underlying structures of Dutch artisanal life when they wrote the ordinances for their fraternity at the turn of the sixteenth century, so also did they stick to other aspects of Dutch life. The ordinances, for instance, provided for situations of interpersonal violence between the fraternity's members, including even the possibility of homicide; the hatmakers who drew up these ordinances imagined that the usual Dutch arrangement for such conflicts, private settlement between the parties, would prevail, though the very different English legal context mandated that serious crimes be prosecuted in the royal courts. The Dutch hatmakers may simply have been unaware of the usual English way of doing things – or they may have preferred the more direct Dutch way of resolving conflicts.[11]

The Dutch hatmakers who came together in Blackfriars in the late fifteenth century to make the Fraternity of St James carried with them a host of assumptions, understandings, and practices from their formation as artisans in the Low Countries. Their lives as Dutch-speaking immigrants in an English-speaking city were marked by linguistic and cultural cross-currents. Though limited by the structures that constrained their labour as alien-born artisans, they established a new industry in their adopted country. Over the ensuing centuries the making of hats became an ever more central sector in the English economy, growing from the small seed planted by several dozen immigrants from the Low Countries in the fifteenth century.

---

[10]   LMA, DL/C/B/004/MS09171/9, fol 94rv, will of Gerard Roest, 1518; cf. other Dutch wills in the same register at folios 46r, 87r–88r, 113rv, 126v.

[11]   See chapters 2, 3, and 5.

PART II

Texts

Editorial Conventions

Part II consists of editions of the three texts contained in London, Guildhall Library, MS 15838: (1) The Bilingual Ordinances of the Fraternity of St James; (2) The Agreement with the Haberdashers; (3) The oath of the Wardens of the Haberdashers. The following editorial conventions have been adopted. We have added punctuation and modernised capitalisations. Titles are editorial. Only obvious errors have been emended; emendations have been flagged up in notes and/or square brackets (otherwise only used for folio numbers). Scribal abbreviations have been expanded and are marked in italics. Difficult words or constructions are glossed after every item in Middle Dutch and Middle English.

The Bilingual Ordinances of the Hatmakers

ARTICLE 1

Fyrst, it is established and ordeyned that all and singuler brederne, whatsomeuer nacion they be, of the feliship and ffraternite of Saynt Jamys, begonne and kepte in the church of the frirys prechoures of the Cyte of London by the hatmakers dwellinge within and nighe the seid Cite of London, in tyme folowing to ben electe and chosyn brederne of the same fraternite shal be of good name and fame. And namely such as before ther admission and recepcion into the seid fraternite shalle fulfille their cownandes, as well beyonde the see as on this side, with ther masturs with which they lerned ther craft and science of, if they before the tyme of their admission haue serued any mastur.

frirys prechoures: friars preacher, Dominicans
in tyme folowing: from now on
cownandes: covenants, agreements

Item, dat is versament ende geordynert dat alle ende eenyegelick broderen, van wat lande ofte nacion dat sye siin, van den geselscop ende broderscop van Sunte Jacobs, begunnen ende geholden in de kerke der prediker orden in de stat van London by den hoitmakers wonende in London ofte omtrent London, in nacomende tijden sullen vntfangen ende ingenomen broders van derseluer broderscop wesen sullen van gueden name ende van gueden geruchte sijn, ende namelike voer hoer incomynge ende vntfangynge in dese selue broderscop sullen hebben wuldaen als truwe dienres tobehoert also well begeenzide de see als an deser zide der see myt horen meyster daer sie hoer ambocht ende kunst mede geleert hebben ende of sie voir der tijd hoere incomynge hebben gedient enigen meyster.

versament: enjoined, agreed
eenyegelick: every
geruchte: repute
wuldaen: fulfilled
begeenzide: on the other side

[f. 1v]

ARTICLE 2

Item, it is established and ordeyned that all and singuler brederne of the seid fraternite at ther fyrst entering into the same fraternite shall pai or do to be paid to the maisturs and kepers of the same fraternite xx d. sterling and singuler termes aftur, that is to sey, eueri quarter immediatly folowyng such a summe as of olde tyme haue byn vsed and obserued and as by the maisturs and wardens of the same fraternite shabbe reasonabli limyted and assigned.

d.: pence
singuler termes aftur: each and every period thereafter
shabbe: shall be
limyted: prescribed

Item, dat is versament ende geordinert dat alle ende eenyegelicken broderen van der voirseide broderscop tot hoer eerste incomynge sullen betalen ofte doen betalen tot den meysters ende ouersienders van derseluer broderscop xx d. sterling ende woert to sunderliken terminen, dat is to voirstaen, to elken quaten dage dairna comende al sulken summe als van olden tijden geusyert ende geholden gewest is bi den meysters ende ouersienders van der suluer broderscop de daer to geset sijn.

woert: continuing on
to voirstaen: to wit
geset: appointed

ARTICLE 3

Item, it is established and ordeyned that no maystur ne bredur of the seid fraternite shall take, occupi, or accept ani man that commith from beyonde the see wishyng or intendyng to occupy and vse the seid craft of hatmakyng within this realme of England but if the seid seruaunt haue continuelli been a lerner of the seid occupacion with a maistur of the seid crafte by the space of ij yere at the leist, and he at hys fyrste entrynge pay, or do to be payed, to the maisturs and wardeins of the same fraternite which- [f. 2r] sumeuer, for the tyme being, viij d. sterling, or els his maistur whomme he is to serue to answere and pay the seid viij d. undur payn of vi s. viij d. at euery such defaute without any remission, to be payd to the seid maisturs and wardens to the use of the seid craft and feliship of Saynt Iamys before rehersed.

but if: unless
whichsumeuer: whichever
answere: assume liability
payn: fine
s.: shilling

Item, dat is versament ende geordinert dat geen meyster noch broder van derseluer broderscop sal genen knecht tot him nemen ofte to werken setten de dair van auer geen zide der zee comet om vnse ambocht te done ende to vseren myt vns int koninck-rik van Engeland – dat en sij sake dat die selue knecht stedfastelick heeft gewest een leerknecht myt enen meyster van denseluen ambocht den termyn van ij iaren ten alre mynsten. Ende hie to sijn erste incomynge sal betalen ofte doen betalen den meysters ende ouersienders van derseluer broderscop to elken tijden enigen knecht so komende viii d. sterlinges, ofte anders sijn meyster to verantworden ende betalen voir denseluen knecht viij d. vp een bote van vi s. viij d. to elker sulker wirsumenisse sal betalen sunder enige voirgeuynge to denseluen meysters ende ouersienders van denseluen ambocht ende geselschop van Sunte Iacobs voirgesproken.

auer geen zide: from over the other side
dat en sij sake: unless it be the case
den enigen knecht so komende: for every apprentice thus arriving
to elker sulker wirsumenisse: for every such infringement

ARTICLE 4

Item, it is established and ordeyned that nown of the brederne of the seid fraternite shall haue any mansion or inhabbite within nown othyr man, that is to sey, within any fuller, weuer, taylor, or [f. 2v] any odur artifer, by reson wherof they schuld informe and instructe the seid fullers, weuers, talors, and such other in the seid crafte of hat-makynge, excepte that the seid fullers, weuers, talors be instructe and lernid before in the seid craft of hatmakynge and lafulli chosin and accepte as brederne of the same fraternite. And whosumeuyr fulfilleth not ne obeyth this ordinaunce and statute to fall into the payn and multe aftur, of the discrecion maysters and wardene of the same fraternite to be limited, and without any remissioun to be payd.

nown: none
inhabbite: lodge
artifer: craftsman
excepte that: unless
instructe and lernid: educated and trained
lafulli: lawfully
accepte: accepted
fall into the payn and multe aftur: subsequently incur the penalty and fine
limited: determined

Item, dat is versament ende geordinert dat geen van den broderen van derseluer broderscop sal hebbe gene wonynge ofte mede-inwonynge myt genen anderen luden, dat
is te voirstaen de fullers, weuers, snyders ofte mit enigen anderen ambochtsluden by
den welken dat sie solden leren ofte vnderwise denseluen fullers, weuers, snyders,
ofte summige anderen luden van den ambocht der hoitmakynge, vtgenomen dat die
voirseiden fullers, weuers, ende snyders geleert sijn gewest van denseluen ambocht
der hoitmakynge, rechtelike ontfangen ende ingenomen als broderen van derseluer
broderscop. Ende soe wie dat niet veruullet noch niet horsam en is tot desse ordinancy
ende insettinge sal vallen in de bote ende to den seggen van den meysters ende ouersienders van derseluer broderscop de dairto geset sijn, ende sunder enige vergifenisse
sullen betalen.

vtgenomen dat: unless
horsam: obedient
insettinge: statute

[f. 3r]

ARTICLE 5

Item, it is established and ordeyned that no maistur ne brodur of the seid craft of
hatmakynge schall take or accept any man to be instructe and informed in the crafte,
but he within vi wekes aftur and immediatly folowyng the tyme of his admission pre-
sente the seid seruaunte to iiij maisturs of the same fraternite whichsumeuyer, for the
tyme beyng. Moreouer, no brodur of the seid fraternite shall take passing oun seruant
to lerne the seid craft within the space of ij yere, but if it fortune his seid seruante by
the visitacion of god to dye or absente hymsilf continuelly from his seid maistur and
seruice. The seid seruaunt at his fyrst entring to pay, or his maistur which he is to serue,
i lb. of wex. And whosumeuyr attempte the contrary to pay xx s. at eur such tyme. The
seid xx s. to be deuided into ii partis: the fyrst to the bishop or ordinary before whom
the seid cause shal be discussed or moued; the secunde to the maysturs and wardence
of the seid fraternite.

but: unless
passing oun: more than one
lb.: pound (in weight)
eur: every
ordinary: ecclesiastical official with jurisdiction appointed by the bishop

Item, dat is versament ende geordinieert dat geen meyster noch broder van vnsen
ambocht van hoitmakyng sal vntfangen ofte annemen genen leerknecht om te lerne
hem dat selue ambocht meer bynnen vi weken sal presenteren denseluen knecht voir
de iiij meysters van derseluer broderscap ende laten hem inscriuen. Meer ouer dat

geen broder van derseluer broderscap en sal tot ij iaren meer enen knecht an setten dat en weer sake dat die knecht ouermits bij [f. 3v] visitatien uns here storue ofte en wech liepe van synen meyster dair he mede diende. Deselue knecht tot synre ersten inscriuinge sal betalen, ofte sijn meyster dair he mede wonet, i lb. wasses. Ende we dit voirsmaet ofte dair tegen doet sal verboren xx s. also menichmael als hie dat voirboirt. Welke xx s. sullen gedelt werden in twen delen: dat eerste deel to ten biscop ofte ordinary dar de saken sullen voirkomen; dat ander deel sal gaen to den meysters ende ouersienders van derseluer broderscap ende gilde.

meer ouer: moreover
dat een weer sake: unless it were the case
overmits bij: on account of
storue: were to die
wasses: of wax
voirsmaet: disregards
verboren: incur a fine of
voirboirt: offends

ARTICLE 6

Item, it is established and ordeyned that if any seruaunt of the seid craft be a rebell or inobediently with his free will, without licence asked and obteyned of his maistur, departe and go awey from his seid maistur and seruice, that than no maistur ne broder of the same fraternite shall take or accepte the seid seruante so inobediently departing without licence of his fyrst maistur whom he before serued, vndyr payn of vi s. viii d. sterling to the forseid fraternite as oftin tymes as he shall contrary this statute, to be assigned and payd without any remission.

Item, dat is versament ende geordinert ofte dair enich knecht van vnsen ambocht weer unhorsam ende ende myt synen vrien willen sunder orlof en wech liepe van synen meyster dair he mede dent, dat dan geen meyster noch broder van der seluen broderscop sal annemen noch vntfangen denseluen knecht, het en sij by willen van synen ersten meyster dair he to voren mede diende, [f. 4r] vp de bote van vi s. ende viij. d sterling to derseluen broderscap also dicwile als hie doet tegen de artikelen sal betalen als is voirseid sunder enige voirgiffenisse.

ofte: if
weer unhorsam: were disobedient

ARTICLE 7

Item it is established and ordeyned that if it fortune any seruaunte of the same fraternite inobediently, as is before rehersed, to departe from his maistur and seruice and aftyr by repentaunce to be reconsiled and gladde to serue his seid maistur, that thenne the seid seruant so conuerted and comyng agayn shal pay or do to be payed to the vse and profet of the same fraternite vi s. viiij d. And the maystur keping and accepting the seid seruant shall answore the seid vi s. viiij d. and pay.[1]

Item dat is versamet ende geordinert dat est dat soe queme ouermits enige fortune dat een leerknecht van derseluer broderscap vnhorsamlike als is voirgescreuen en wech liepe van sijnen meysters dienste ende dan ouermits verbeteringe ende der versanynge weder quame ende gueden willen hebbende synen meister weder te denende, dat dair die selue knecht so bekert ende weder comende sal betalen oft doen betalen to den behof ende profijt van derseluer broderscop vj s. viiij d. Ende deselue meyster de den knecht to werke set sall verantworden voir de vj s. ende viiij d. ende betalen.

est dat soe queme: should it come about
ouermits: because of
versanyge: reconciliation

ARTICLE 8

Item, it is established and ordeyned that if any brodrun of the seid fraternite fall into any contra- [f. 4v] versie or variaunce and can not aggre bi themesilfe, that then ij masturs of the seid fraternite with assistence of ther clerke lafully deputed to the same shall examen and finiall determe and ende the said cause of discorde, prouided allwey that the seid cause of discorde nethor twich the kynges highnes, ne liberte and right of the church. And whosumeuyr attempeth the contrary of this forseid statute in word or deed, pryvely or opynli, to forfet at eury suche tyme and defaute vi s. viij d., to be applied to the vse and profeit of the same fraternite, without contradicion or remission to be paid.

variaunce: discord
deputed: assigned
finiall determe: conclusively resolve
twich: touch, affect

Item dat is versament ende geordinert ofte dair enich van den brederen van der broderscap de een den anderen voircoim mit gramscop ofte mit anderen saken, ende en kunne gene vrede tusschen malcanderen hebben, dat dan ij van den meysteren van derseluer broderscop myt bystandicheit van horen clerke dairto

---

[1]   pay] MS payed.

rechtwerdelick sullen examineren ende voirenigen de selue sake der twidracht, alle wege angesien dat die selue sake ende twidracht niet an en gaet des koninges maieste, noch vridom ende recht van der hilliger kerken. Ende we dat dair doet contrary desen voirseiden artikell in worden ofte in dade, hemelick ofte openbaerlic, de sal voirboren tot allen tijden als hie dair in is gewonden vj s. viiij d. sterling to den behof ende profijt van der broderscop sunder enige wederseggynge noch voirgiffenisse to betalen.

rechtwerdelick: fairly
angesien dat: provided that
voirenigen: arbitrate

[f. 5r]

ARTICLE 9

Item, it is established and ordeyned that non of the seid fraternite shall arreste or cause to be arrested or imprison any other broder of the same fraternite for any summe which extendith not aboue xx s. but ii maisturs or wardens of the same fraternite whit th'assistence of ther seid clerke shall resonabli aggre, accorde, and make pease betwix the seid parties, assignyng the tyme of payment aftur ther discrecion. And whomsumeuyr douth ayenst this ordinaunce and statute, to be condemned in iiij li. of wex at euery such defaute, to be applied to the vse of the seid fraternite. And the partie hurt or aggreuyd to be recompensed aftur the discrecion of the wardens.

douth ayenst: contravenes

Item dat is versament ende geordinert dat geen broder van derseluer broderscop sal reisteren ofte doen reisteren ofte in wangenisse leggen enigen broder van derseluer broderscop voir enige summe van gelde dat niet en draget bauen xx s. sterling. Meer ii meysters ende ouersienders myt bystandicheid van horen clerke sullen redeliken corderen ende vrede make tusschen de partien ende setten een certeyn tijd der betalinge na horen voirstandenisse. Ende we tegens dessen ordinanci ofte artikell doet sal voirboren iiij lb. wasses to allen tijden als hie schuldich is gewunden, ende dat sal gaen to den behof der broderscop. Ende ofte de partien malcanderen beclagen, sullen de meysters nae hour verstandenisse verenigen ende to vrede stellen.

reisteren: arrest
in wangenisse leggen: put in prison
bauen: above, exceeding

[f. 5v]

ARTICLE 10

Item it is established and ordeyned that all and singuler brederne of the said fraternyte shall kepe and obserue vnite and pease, and no broder of the same fraternite shall bring forth or sey to, or of, any broder of the seid fraternite any maliciouse, iniurose, or wordes of dispite. And whosumeuyr douth or attemptit the contrary shall pay or do to be payd to the masturs and wardens of the seid fraternite ij li. of wex. And the partie in that behalfe aggreued or hurt ayenst and of whome the seid maliciose or iniurose wordis were spokyn to be rewarded and recompensed aftur the discrecion of the maisturs and wardens of the seid ffraternite or by any other juge competente before whome[2] the seid cause shall fortune to be mouued and finally determenyd.

bring forth: utter
iniurose: offensive (words)
in that behalfe: in this matter

Item dat is versament ende geordinert dat alle ende yegelike broderen van derseluer broderscop sullen holden ende bewaren endrechticheid ende vrede ende geen van den broderen van derseluer broderscop sall voirt brengen ofte seggen tot synen broder[3] enige quade ofte vnrechtwerdighe worde van spite. Ende we dair tegens doet sal betalen ofte doen betalen to den meysters ende ouerseinders van derseluer broderscop ij lb. wasses, ende in dat behalue dat de partien to den welken dur de quade ende spityge worde togesecht sijn sullen hebben verberteringe na den voirtstandenisse van den meysters ende ouersiendes derseluer broderscop ofte to enigen anderen rechtere voir ween de saken geopenbaert mogen werden ende voireniget.

spite: contempt
in dat behalue: on this point
voirstandenisse: judgement, discretion
voireniget: arbitrated

[f. 6r]

ARTICLE 11

Item, it is established and ordeyned that if any seruaunte or iurneyman of the iseid fraternite, without license asked of his mastur and obteyned of the same, inobedientli or with his good wyll departe and goo awey as is before rehersed, being in his

---

2   Written above the line, with caret mark after 'before', in different hand (scribe 2?).
3   'tot syne broder' written above line, preceded by caret mark, in different hand (scribe 2?).

mastur his deit or owyng hym any seruice, that than no broder of the same fraternite shal take, accepte, or occupy the seid seruant. And if the mastur from whome the seid seruant or iourneyman so departed send for his seid seruant or iourneyman by the clerke of the felischyp or the same fraternite vnto the broder that so shall occupy hym contrary to this statute, the same broder doyng so contrary to this statute shall, immediatly aftur that the clerke shall warne hym, put that seruant or iourneyman owt of his howse and not to kepe hym, vndyr payn of vi s. viii d., as oftyn as the iseid[4] clerke shall so warne hym, to the seid fraternite to be applyed, and the mastur so agrreuyd in that behalfe to be recompensed aftur the discrecion of the masturs and wardence of the same fraternite.

mastur his deit: master's debt

Item, dat is versament ende geordinert ofte enige knecht van synen meyster gaet myt orlof ofte sunder orlof, wesende in sijns meysters schult, denst, ofte gelt, ende werket myt enigen anderen broder ofte meyster ofte him dan syn meyster den he so schuldich is sijn werck doet verbeiden myt den clerke soe sal syn meyster dair he mede werket hem siin werck doen laten liggen ende laten hem gaen vt synen huse ende corderen mit sinen meister de he schuldich is, vp de bote van vi s. viii d. [f. 6v] sterling also mannichmal als hem de clerck warning gift, te voirboren tot den profit ende behof der gilden voirscreuene, ende de broder to vrede geset de hem beclaget naden verstande van den meysters ende ouersienders van derseluer broderscop.

te voirboren: to pay

ARTICLE 12

Item, it is established and ordeyned that if any broder of the same fraternitte maliciousli drawe owt his daggar, sword, or knyf, or any other instrument defensive to hurt or wronge any man of the same fraternite, that he shall pay to the masturs and wardence at euery suche defaut ii s. iiij d. And he that drawith or castith, hurt or wronge any man of the same fraternite with stonys, lovis, pottis, dishis, candilstickis, or any other thing aboue rehersed, all though ther folow no blode-scheding of the seid hurtys or iniurioseis, shall pay to the seid fraternite iiij lb. of wexe. And if he drawe blodde, all though ther folow no maymme therof, he shall pay vi s. viii d. And if it be a mayme, he shall pay x s. ouyer and byside that he so hurtith and wrongyth shall compownde with hym that is so hurte and wronged and recompense and satisfy him for his hurtis and wrongis aftur the discrecion of the maisturs and wardens of the same fraternite

---

4   isied] MS idseid.

or any other iuge before whome it shall fortune hym to be callid for the same trespasse. And if any broder of the seid fraternite wilfully sle any man of the same fraternite, that thenne he shal be put owt and vtturly excludet from the seid fraternite to be.

drawith: draws a weapon
castith: aims blows
hurt or wronge: should he hurt or wrong
lovis: loaves of bread
iniurioseis: injuries
he so hurtith and wrongyth: he who so hurts and wrongs someone
compownde: come to a settlement with

[f. 7r]

Item, dat is versament ende geordinert dat of enich broder van der broderscop ut trecket synen dagger, mes, ofte swert, ofte enigherhande ander wapen in gramschap om synen broder mede te krenken, he sal verboren iii s. iiij d. also mennich- mael als hie dat doet. Ende hie dat slaet ofte werpet synen medebroder myt enigerhande dinge, als myt stenen ofte myt brode, myt potten, scotelen, candelers ofte enigerhande ander dinck, al reyst hie geen bloet, sal betalen totter broderscop iiij lb. wasses. Ende ofte dat so weer dat hie bloet reisede de sal betalen totter broderscop vi s. viiij d. Ende ofte hie enige broder lam sloge ofte vermencte, hie sal voirboren x s. Meer ouer, de den anderen so mysdoet de sal beteringe doen van der mysdaet totten seggen van den meysters ende ouersienders van der broderscop ofte enigen anderen rechter voir ween de sake mochten komen. Ende ofte enich broder myt voirrade enigen broder van der broderscap doet sloge, den sal men vtdoen ende niet meer voir enen broder nemen.

gramschap: anger
reyst bloet: draws blood
vtdoen: expel
voirrade: premeditation

ARTICLE 13

Item, it is stablished and ordeyned that if it fortune any broder of the seid fraternite to be lame, blinde, febill, brokyn with age, or visited with any other sekenesse so that he may not labour ne gete his clothinge and foode, ne otherwyse help hymsilfe, if so be that he before that same sekenesse haue stonde a broder of the same fraternite by the space of vij yerys and haue done and paid duly, ryghtfully, and feithfully all his dewtyes to the seid ffraternite [f. 7v] and haue fulfilled, obserued, and kept all maner of ordin- aunces and statuteys of the seid ffraternite, that thenne he that is so visited shall retene wekeli durynge his lif x d. of the seid wardence and fraternite, prouided alwey that the seid seke and febill man haue not good sufficiente to finde himsilfe.

haue stonde: has continued to be
find himsilfe: provide for himself

Item, dat is versament ende geordinert dat it queme dat dair enich broderen van der broderscap lam worde, blind, amechtich, ouerkomen myt older, ouermits enige ander sekenisse so dat hie niet mochte arbeiden noch wynnen syne kost noch cleding, ofte in geenre maneren hemseluen helpen, is dat sake dat hie voir derseluer sekenesse heeft gewest een broder van derseluer broderscap den termyn van vij jaren ende heuet wuldaen ende betalt rechtuerdelick al dat hie schuldig was to derseluer broderscop ende heeft geholden ende vullenbracht al maner van der ordinanci ende artikel van der voirseiden broderscap, dat dan de is so geuisitiert van gode sal vntfangen elke weke nacocomende so lange als hie leuet x d. van den voirseiden meysteren ende ouersienders van der broderscop, alle tijd angesien dat dieselue man en heuet niet guedes ghenoch hemseluen mede to wynden tot sijnre notdruft.

it qeme: should it befall
amechtig: disabled
is dat sake: if it is the case that
to wynden tot sijnre notdruft: to provide for his need

ARTICLE 14

Item, it is established and ordeyned that all the brederne of the seid fraternite shal come and appere togedur iiij tymes in the yere, that is to sey, euery quaterday in a conuenyent place to be lymyted and assigned by the masturs and wardene of the seid fraternite for the tyme [f. 8r] beyyng. And not onli in the iiij seid quater days but as oft as they be warned by the seid maisturs and wardene or any of them be monyshed to appere for any conuocacion to be had the which concernith any poynt of the statuteis or ordinawnces of the seid fraternite or craft, vpon payn of i lb of wexe to be applied to the seid fraternite as oft as they fayle.

monyshed: admonished, instructed

Item, dat is versament ende geordinert dat alle de broderen van derseluer broderscop sullen comen te gader ende openbaeren hem to samen to iiij tijden inden jaer, dat is te voirstaende, to elken quaterdage in een stede die dair to geordinert wort by den meysters ende ouersienders van derseluer broderscop ende wort tot allen tijden als sie gewarnt werden by horen clerke ouermits den meysters ende ouersienders om enige poynten ofte om enige saken de angaen derseluer broderscop, vp ene bote van i lb. wasses.

wort tot allen tijden: further at all times
overmits: on behalf of

ARTICLE 15

Item, it is established and ordeyned that all the brederne of the seid fraternite in the fest of Saint Jamys shal be at the high masse of the seid Saint Jamys weryng suche liuery as shal be though beste by the wardence of the seid fraternite. And euery broder shall offer at the same masse i d., and euery wyf of the seid brederne shall offer ob. And the same brederne next in the morow next and immediatly folwyng the same feste shal be at the masse of requiem weryng also ther seid lyuereys. And euery broder shall offer ther ob., vpon payn of ij li of wexe to be payd to the masturs and brederne [f. 8v] of the seid fraternite without any remission by eueri broder that obseruyth not ne kepith this ordinaunce without a lafull excuse, to þe vse and profyt of the same fraternite as oft as they fayle.

though: thought
ob.: halfpenny

Item, dat is versament ende geordinert dat alle de broderen van derseluer broder-scop inder hochtijt van Sunte Iacobs sullen comen[5] in der hogen myssen van Sunte Iacobs dragende al sulke leuerye als hem alle gued dancket te wesen. Ende elke broder sal offeren to derseluen missen i d. ende ellick wyf van derseluer broderscop sal offeren enen half pennyng. Ende deselue broderen des naesten dages des morgens dairna comende to seluer hochtijd sullen wesen to der missen van requiem ende dragende hoer leuery. Ende elke broder sal offeren i d. vp de bote of ij lb. wasses to betalen to de meysters ende ouersienders van derseluer broderscop sunder enige vergiffenisse. Ende ellick broder de dat niet en doet ende holt desse ordinanci, vtgenomen een redelick excusacie, de sal verboren totter seluer broderscop also dicwill als hie dat versumet.

ARTICLE 16

Item, it is established and ordeyned that if any broder or broderis wyf of the ffraternite decesse, that thenne all the brederne of the same fraternite shal goo to the burying and sepulture, ther abydyng vnto the tyme that the body be buried. Also, the seid brederne shal be at the masse of requiem to be sange or to be seid for the sowle of the seyd deed man or woman, and eche of them shall offer aftur ther deuocioun vppon payne [f. 9r] of i li. wexe at euery suche tyme, to be applied vnder maner and forme before rehersed.

Item, dat is versament ende geordinert dat dair enich broder ofte broders wijf van der-seluer broderscop storue dat dan alle die broderen van den broderscop sullen comen to de begrauinge myt hoere leuerye als dairto geordinert is ende dair bliuende to der tijd dat de licham is begrauen. Ende alle de broderen sullen wesen to der missen van

---

5   Written above the line and preceded by caret mark (scribe 2?).

requie*m* de men sal singen ofte lesen voir de ziele des doden ma*n*nes ofte vrouwen. Ende ellick brod*er* van derseluer broderscop sullen offere*n* i d., vp de bote van i lb. wasses de dat versumet en*de* niet en doet.

ARTICLE 17

Item, it is established and ordeyned, if it fortune any broder of the seid fraternite to be impoue*ry*sshid be the visitacyoun of god or otherwise of any other sekenesse, and be so febill and seke that he may not labour for his leuing, and haue byn in the same debylite and sekenesse by the space of vj days, that then the same febyll and seke man shall receue wekeli during his infirmite or sekenesse of the maysturs and wardence of the same fraternyte viiij d., prouided alwey that the same broder so being seke that he is compelled to kepe his beed, and all the tyme that he hath bin a broder of the same fraternite before his infirmite, pouerte, and sekenesse haue obse*r*ued and kepte all maner of ordinaunc*es* and laudable custum*m*es and statutes of the same frayernite as odire brederne of the seid fraternite haue obserued and⁶ fulfilld and [f. 9v] kepte.

he hath bin: he who has been

Item, dat is versame*nt* ende geordinert dat of enich broder van derseluer broderscop comende in sekenesse ouermits der visiteringe ons here*n* ofte in ander manere*n* van siecknesse, end so sieck wesende dat hie mach niet arbeiden voir de noetdruft synes liues, ende dat hie heeft gewest in der sekenesse ende kra*n*cheid ouermits de space van vj dage, dat dan deselue krancke ende sieck man sal vntfange*n* elke weke nacomende, so lange⁷ als hie sieck is, van den meyste*r*s en*de* ouersienders van derseluer broderscop viiij d. sterling, alle tijd angesien dat die selue broder soe sieck wesende dat hie te bedde licht ende alle die tijd dat hie heuet geweset een broder van der broderscop voir sine sieckenesse ende krancheid heuet vuldaen ende geholden al maner van ordinanci en*de* erlike custume en*de* articule*n* van derseluer broderscop als ander brod*er*en hebben vuldaen ende geholden.

noetdruft: essential needs
angesien dat: provided that

ARTICLE 18

Item, it is established and ordeyned that no broder of the seid fraternite shal bey by himsilf or by his wyf nor seru*a*unt to his knowlege no maner of felt*es*, flossche noon hattis, to any man but only to them that be of the same fraternite vnder payn of xx s., to be applied vndur maner and forme folowyng: that is to sey, vi s. and viii d. to hym that detectith him that so trespassith, vi s. viii d. to the bishop of the place where the

---

⁶ Illegible. MS reading conjectural.
⁷ Written above line, with caret mark after 'so'.

trespasser dwelleth, vi s. viij d. to the masturs and wardence of the same fraternite to the behof and profete of the seid [f. 10r] fraternite, as often as any of the seid brederne doth ayenist and brekyth this seyd ordinaunce and statute.

bey: the sense must be 'sell'.
flossche: adorn with thrums? (see above, p. 98)

Item, dat is versament ende geordineert dat geen van derseluer broderscop sullen vercopen bii hem seluen ofte by synen wyue noch geen van synen huse to sinen weten geen maneer van vilten, noch hoeden vlosschen, dan allene to dengenen de inder broderscop syn, vp die bote van xx s. vnder dese maneer ende forme: dat is to seggende, die dat erst meldet ofte wort brenget de ouertredinge vi s., viij d. to den bisscop van den place dair de auertreder wonet, vi s viij d to den meysters ende ouersienders van derseluer broderscop, vi s. viii d. to den profijt ende behof van derseluer broderscop, also dicwile als enich van den voirseiden broderen doet tegens desse ordinance ende statute.

vlosschen: adorn with thrums? (see above, p. 98)
auertreder: trespasser

ARTICLE 19

Item, it is established and ordeyned that no broder of the seid fraternite shall take no maner a man or put to his occupacion of the seid craft of hatmakynge without he by lerneth in the same fraternite, nor noon other that comyth frome any mastur of any odur fraternite or felyshyp, vpon suche payne as by the masturs and more parte of the seid brederne of the seid fraternite shal be resonably aftur ther discrecioun limited and assigned.

without he by lerneth: unless he has learned his trade

Item, dat is versament ende geordinert dat geen broder van derseluer broderscop sal annemen genen knecht ofte to werke setten de myt enigen anderen meister geleert heeft de in vnser broderye niet en is, he en betale de bote to den meysters ende ouersienders van derseluer broderscop als he [f. 10v] kan corderen mytten iiij meysteren de dair to geset sijn.

he en betale: and if he does not, he must pay

ARTICLE 20

Item, it is established and ordeyned that if any seruant departe fromme his mastur and seruice with licence or without licence asked and obteyned of his mastur, that thenne no broder of the same fraternite shall take or accepte the seid seruant so departyng without licence of his masturs whome he before serued, vpon payne of iiij li. wex, to be applied and paid to the seyd fraternite without any contradiction or remission.

Item, dat is versament ende geordinert of enich knecht van synen meyster genge myt orlof ofte sunder orlof ende gaet tot enen anderen meister om myt him to werken soe en sal geen broder van derseluer broderscop den knecht to werke setten, hie en vrage ersten sinen meister dair he van gegaen is oft dat sijn wille sy, vp de bote van iiij lb. wasses sunder enige voirgiffenisse te betalen.

hie en vrage: unless he asks

ARTICLE 21

Item, it is established and ordeyned that euery lerner [of] the seid crafte of hatmakynge in the ende of his termys, bifore he be admitted and accepte als a felow and iorneyman of the same fraternite, shall pay to the seid fraternite i lb. of wex.

Item dat is voirsament ende geordinert dat elke leerknecht van denseluen ambocht van hoitmakyng in dat eende van synen termyne, eer hie togelaten is ende ingenomen als een geselle, sal betalen to derseluer broderscop i lb. wasses.

[f. 11r]

ARTICLE 22

Item, it is establisshed and ordeyned that it shal be lefull to the maisters and brederne of the saide fraternitie of Seynt James before rehersede to amende and correcte alle the articles, statutes, and ordynaunces aboue rehersed and yche of theym, so that the saide correcion be not repugnaunt to the lawes of god and the kyng.

lefull: permissible
so that: provided that, as long as
repugnaunt: contrary

Item dat is togelaten ende geordinert dat sie machtich sullen wesen rechtuerdelike de meisters end de broderen van derseluer broderscop van Sunte Jacobs als is voirgheseid to verbeteren en corrigeren alle die articulen, statuten ende ordinancien bauen gescreuen ende ellick van hem soe dat dieselue correctie sij niet tegen godes recht noch des konynges maieste.

soe dat: provided that

ARTICLE 23

Item, it is establisshed and ordeyned by the hole fraternitie that no maister nor brother of this same fraternitie shall put no hattes for to be flosshede, nor cause no hattes to be flosshede, nor put no feltes to be made withoute his house, vp payne of forfetyng of xx shyllynges, which xx s. to be dyuydede into three partes, that is to say: the furste part to th'accuser; the secunde part to the buschoppe or ordynarie for hym afore whom any such cause shal be discussede; and the thred parte therof to the holy [f. 11v] apostele Seynt James, wythoute any forgeuyng of the same forfetynges.

flosshede: ?
put: arrange for
withoute his house: out of house (the outsourcing of work is prohibited: see above, p. 46).

Item, dat is versament ende gheordineert dat gheen meester noch broeder van der-seluer broederscyp gheen felten en sal doen maken noch hoden doen floschen buten synen[8] huyse op dye verbuerte van xx shyllynghen ende dese werscreuen xx schellyn-ghen ghedeelt in drie deelen: dat eerste deel voer den aenbryngher, en dat ender del voer den bisscop oft oerdenari daer die sake voer comet, ende dat darde voere den heylyghen apostel Gods Sinte Jacop sonder enighe vergeuynghe te betalen.

floschen: ?

ARTICLE 24

Item, it is establysshede and ordenede that no maister nor brother of this same frater-nytie putt to werke no seruante commynge from beyonde the see, excepte it be cause that he bryng a letter of hys maister where he his occupacon hath lernede atte leest ij or iij yeres. And if there be any doynge contrary of thys same, vppon payne of forfetynge of xx shylynges sterlynges, whiche money shall be dyvydede into three partes: the furst parte to the executer of the same; the secunde parte to the busshoppe or ordinary, or for theym that this cause shall determyne accordyng to this, the maisters wyll [f. 12r] and dede; and the thredde parte therof to the holy apostell Seynt James, wythoute forgevynge any of the same forfetynges.

except it be cause: unless it be the case

Item, dat is versament ende gheoerdineert dat gheen meester noch broeder van derseluer broederscap en sall gheen knecht to werke setten die daer comet van ouer see ofte aen dese side van der se oft en si sake dat hy eenen leerbrief brynghet van sinen meester daer hy syn ambacht ofte const mede gheleert heeft ten alder minsten ij ofte

---

8   'doen floschen buten synen' supplied in margin.

iij jaren. Ende so wye hyer teghe doet vp dye boete van xx shellynghen sterlynes, ende dese voerscreuen xx shellynghen ghedeelt in drien deelen: dat eerste del voer den aenbryngher, ende dat ender deel voer den bisscop ofte oerdenari daer die sake voer comet, dat derde deel voer den heylyghen apostell Gods Sent Jacop, ende dat sonder enyghe vergeuynghe te betalen.

oft en si sake: unless it were the case

ARTICLE 25

It is establisshed and ordeyned by the .iiij. maisters, Andrewe Morter, James Lese, Bartylmewe Brynke, Herry Gram, and also by the hole brederhode of Seynt James in London of the freers prechours there in the yere of oure lord God mlccccc and one that euery seruaunt of that occupacion [f. 12v] of hatmakynge that makyth and flosshyth hattes shall wassh theym and make theym clene, redy to the sale. Yf any such seruaunt refuse so to doo, nor wyll not, and therfore depart from his maister, then after that if any brother sett hym on werke shall forfete xx s., to be dyuydede into two partes: the one part therof to the busshopp or ordynary afore whome any such matter shall be examyned and discussed, and the tother parte thereof to the said bretherhode of Seynt James.

[f. 13r]

ARTICLE 26

[I]t⁹ is establysshed and ordeynede that any of the breder of the fraternytie of Seynt James by the hole brotherhode therof chosen warden doo disobey the good ordre of the said brederhode and specially the maisters of the same, and so vtterly refuse to be warden of the same fraternytye and will be no warden whan he is chosen so to be, therfore shall forfete xx shellynges, the one halfe thereof to the busshop or ordenarie afore whome any suche cause shall be examyned and discussede, and the tother halfe thereof to the said brederhode of Seynt James, wythoute forgeuyng of any parte of such forfetynges.

---

9   Space left for a decorated Lombardic capital that was never supplied.

[f. 13v]

ARTICLE 27

[I]t[10] is establysshede and ordeyened that if any of the said brederhode of Seynt James will not com to the maisters of the same fraternytie whan they be sent fore, and so inordynatly disobey there wardens agaynste the order of the said brederhode, wherefore any such offender shall forfete for euery such trespasse xx s., the one halfe thereof to the busshopp or ordinary afore whom any [f. 14r] such cause shall be examynede and discussed, and the tother half to the said brederhode of Seynt James, wythoute any forgeyuyng of the said forfetynges.

[f. 14v blank]

[10]   As above.

The Agreement with
the Haberdashers

Be it had in perpetuall memory that the viiijth day of September in the yere of our lord God m^lv^cxi and in the thirde yere of the reigne of Kyng Henry the VIIIth is condescended, accorded and fully aggreed bitwene Robert Aldernes maister of the crafte or mystery of haberdasshers of the citye of London, John Ever, Henry Hille, Edward Bellowe, and John Hasilfote, wardyens of the said craft and the hole clothyng of the same, and Gerard Rowst, Antony de Wyne, Antony Levyson, and James Lees, wardyens and gouernoures of the crafte & facultie of hatmakers of the said citye and suburbes of the same and other, the most honeste persones of hatmakers aforsaid, that thise articles ensuyng for the comon weale as well of the said crafte of haberdasshers as of hatmakerys be ratifyed and establisshed in maner and fourme folowyng, that is to wite:

Fyrst, that the said hatmakers from hensfurth shall haue liberte euery yere at the day of Seynt James the appostill, their patrone, to elect and chose amonges their feliship ij honest persones hatmakers to be maisters & wardyens of their feliship, for good order & rule to be kepte and had amonges theym herafter. And that euery brother and suster of the same shall pay their dueties at their dayes of recreacon whether they be present or absent.

Also that euery persone of the said crafte of hatmakers from hensfurth that begynneth to kepe houshold and occupyeing the crafte and feates of the same at his first entre into the same shall pay and content to the maisters and wardeyns of the crafte of haberdasshers aforsaid xiii s. iiij d. sterlinges, the oon half therof to the comon box of the said haberdasshers and the other half to the box of hatmakers, and that euery person from henssfurth commyng from beyonde the see or owte of any other contre, entendyng to vse the occupacion of hatmakers or kepyng any habitacion within the citye of London or the suburbes of the same, shall pay at euery of their fyrst entre into the same xxvi s. viiij d. to be devided in maner and fourme as is aforsaid. Also all such persones as haue lerned the occupacion of hatmakers within the said citie and suburbes of the same shal be sett to werk before any other *person* straungere co*m*myng owt of any other coun-trey so that he an able werkman, trew and feithfull.

Also that eu*er*y *per*sone from hensfurth occupyeng the facultie of hatmakers shall haue to werk w*ith* hym or theym the nombre of iiij *per*sones werkmen and lerners werkyng at his or their boorde and not above, vpon peyn of forfaiture vi s. viii d. sterling*es* [f. 16r], as often as he or they shal be therwith fownd doyng the contrary, to be devided in maner and forme aforerehersid.

And that also eu*er*y suche *per*sone, hatmaker, seruyngman co*m*myng and repaireng from the p*ar*ties of beyond the see or owt of any other countrey from hensfurth att their furst entre into their seruice shall pay iij s. and iiij d. to be devidede in man*er* and fourme aforsaid.

Also if any iurneyman of the same facultie of hatmakers happen herafter to be in seruice w*ith* any broder of the fraternite of Seynt James w*ith*in London or w*ith*in iij myles nere aboute the citie of London, & woll not pay his duties as other of his brod-erne of the same company and felishippe of Seynt James doo, shall at eu*er*y tyme he doth the contrary pay iij s. iiij d. sterlyng*es* to be levied, deuyded, and paide in maner and fourme forsaid and to the same vse of the said crafte & facultie.

Also, if any yong *per*sone herafter entende and bynde hymselff seruaunt allowes, and be covenant w*ith* any such *per*sone that is or shal be wilfull or obstinat, and [f. 16v] pay not his duties accordyng as other of his saide brotherne done, that than the saide *per*-sone so beyng couenaunt seruaunt, at suche tyme and whan as his yeris be expired and ended, to pay to the said vse of the haberdasshers and hatmakers vi s. viiij d. sterlyng*es* if he worke and be a broder of the said facultie of hatmakers, or els not to be sett on worke among the craft of hatmakes aforsaid in no wise.

mystery: guild
condescended: granted
hole clothyng: all the liverymen
dayes of recreacon: feast days
content: pay
feates: professional pursuits
person straungere: person born outside the realm
so that: provided that, on condition that
facultie: craft
repaireng: arriving
parties of: regions from
seruaunt allowes: a hired servant
covenant with: contracted to
couenaunt: contractual

[f. 17r blank]

[f. 17v]

The Oath of the Wardens of the Haberdashers

The oth of the iiij wardeins of haber*dasshers*

Ye shal swere that duringe the tyme of your wardenshipp, in that [in]¹ you is, ye shall obserue, mainteine, and kepe all the goode rewlys & ordening now made and to be made concerninge the wele & politik gou*er*nanuce of oure fellowshippe, and also ye shal be egall and indifferent betwene partie and party of suche matters as shal be deposed and ministred tofore you; & to th'encrease of the fellowshipe ye shall do your parte nothinge concele nor enbesile by the which our saide fellowship may be hurte, defamed or sclaundered, but ye shall doo due administracon & execucion as wele vppon the riche as vpon the poore, soo healpe you god and holydom.²

in that in you is: to the best of your abilities
enbesile: embezzle
holydom: all things sacred

---

¹ The emendation restores sense and brings the wording in line with that of other later Middle English oaths, such as the heralds': 'Item ye shall be servisable […] in that in you is, so helpe you God and holy dom'. Travers Twiss, *Monumenta Juridica: The Black Book of the Admiralty*, 4 vols (London: Longman, 1871–1876), I, p. 297.

² Two partly erased lines, written in different hand, immediately below the text block remain partly visible: it is ordeyn [….] not to be sett on werke vntyll conceite'.

Bibliography

MANUSCRIPT SOURCES

Antwerp, Municipal Archives, FelixArchief
Regesten van de schepenregisters, SR#50

Kew, National Archives (TNA)
C 1, Early Chancery Proceedings
CP 40, Court of Common Pleas, Plea Rolls
E 179, King's Remembrancer, Lay and Clerical Taxation Accounts
PROB 11, Prerogative Court of Canterbury: Will Registers

London, Archives of Parliament
HL/PO/JO/10/3/178/1 through 8, Petitions of the cap and hat makers of Shrewsbury,
   Bridgenorth, Bristol, Southwark [*recte* London and Southwark], Gloucester,
   Bewdley, Stafford, and Lichfield, 1531.

London, British Library
Additional, MS 16431

London, Goldsmiths' Hall
Wardens Accounts and Court Minutes [WACM]

London, London Metropolitan Archives, Guildhall Library (GL)
CLC/L/BF/D/001/MS05442/2, Brewers' Company Wardens' Account, 1508–1541
CLC/L/CI/C/009/MS05614A, Coopers' Quarterage Books, 1439–1517
CLC/L/HA/A/009/MS15838, Guild Ordinances of the Hatmakers, 1501, & Agreement
   between them and the Haberdashers' Company, 1511
CLC/L/HA/C/007/MS15857/001, Haberdashers' Freedom Register, 1526–1642
CLC/L/SE/C/005/MS30719/001, Skinners' Apprentice Binding Book, 1496–1603
CLC/L/SE/D/007/MS30727/002, Skinners' Company Receipts and Payments Book,
   1510–1535

London, London Metropolitan Archives (LMA)
COL/AD/01, Letter Books, City of London
COL/CA/01/01, Repertory Books of the Court of Aldermen, City of London
COL/CC/01/01, Journals of the Court of Common Council, City of London
DL/A/A/005/MS09531/009, Register of R. Fitzjames, Bishop of London
DL/C/B/004/MS09171, Will Registers of the London Commissary Court
DL/C/B/043/MS09064/011, Act Book of the Commissary Court of the Diocese of
    London, vol. 11, 1511–1516
DL/C/0206 and /0207, Deposition Books of the Consistory Court of the Diocese of
    London, 1511–1516, 1521–1524

London, Mercers' Company Archives
Book of Privileges (no shelfmark)

Oxford, Bodleian Library
MS Douce d. 6

Oxford, Christ Church
MS 179, Ordinances of the Confraternity of the Immaculate Conception <https://digi-
    tal.bodleian.ox.ac.uk/objects/6d9e0fdf-ec06-4d46-952f-e1f1c15198aa/>

Oxford, Magdalen College
MS EL/6, Estate Ledgers (accessed through <https://archive-cat.magd.ox.ac.uk/
    records/EL/INDEX7>)

San Marino, CA, Henry E. Huntington Library
MS HM 142
MS EL 2652
MS EL 2654
MS EL 2655
MS EL 2768

Washington D.C., Folger Shakespeare Library
MSS L.b., Papers of the More family of Loseley Park, Surrey, <https://findingaids.
    folger.edu/dfoloseley.xml>

PUBLISHED SOURCES

Primary Sources

Armstrong, Clement, 'A Treatise Concerning the Staple and the Commodities of
    This Realme', in *Tudor Economic Documents, Being Select Documents Illustrating the
    Economic History of Tudor England*, ed. R. H. Tawney and Eileen Edna Power, 3 vols
    (New York: Barnes & Noble, 1965), III, pp. 90–114

Arnold, Morris S., ed., *Select Cases of Trespass from the King's Courts, 1307–1399*, 2 vols, Selden Society 100 (London: Quaritch, 1985)

Arnhemsche Courant (Arnhem, 20 November 1821)

Battistini, Mario, ed., *La Confrérie de Sainte-Barbe des Flamands à Florence. Documents relatifs aux tisserands et aux tapissiers* (Brussels: Commission royale d'histoire, 1931)

Bickley, Francis B., ed., 'The Statutes of the Craft of Dyers (1439)', in *The Little Red Book of Bristol*, 2 vols (Bristol: W. C. Hemmons, 1900), II, pp. 170–76

Bolton, J. L, ed., *The Alien Communities of London in the Fifteenth Century: The Subsidy Rolls of 1440 & 1483–4* (Stamford: Paul Watkins, Richard III & Yorkist History Trust, 1998)

Brewer, J. S., James Gairdner, and R. H. Brodie, ed., *Letters and Papers, Foreign and Domestic, of the Reign of Henry VIII*, 21 vols (London: Longman, Green, Longman & Roberts, 1862–1932)

Calendar of the Patent Rolls Preserved in the Public Record Office, 1232–1509. 53 vols (London: HMSO, 1891–1961)

Cam, Helen M., ed., *The Eyre of London, Pt. 2: 14 Edward II (1321)*, Selden Society 85 (London: Quaritch, 1968)

Caxton, William, *Blanchardyn and Eglantine*, ed. Leon Kellner, EETS, extra series 58 (London: Trübner, 1890)

Chaucer, Geoffrey, *The Canterbury Tales*, ed. Larry D. Benson, *The Riverside Chaucer* (Boston: Houghton Mifflin, 1987)

Coote, Henry Charles, and John Robert Daniel-Tyssen, ed., *Ordinances of Some Secular Guilds of London, from 1354 to 1496* (London: Nichols, 1871)

Davies, Matthew P., ed., *The Merchant Taylors' Company of London: Court Minutes 1486–1493* (Stamford: Richard III and Yorkist History Trust in assoc. with Paul Watkins, 2000)

Davis, Norman, ed., *The Paston Letters and Papers of the Fifteenth Century*, 2 vols (Oxford: Clarendon Press, 1971)

De Beatis, Antonio, *Voyage du Cardinal d'Aragon*, ed. & trans. by Madeleine Havard de la Montagne (Paris: Perrin, 1913)

De Beatis, Antonio, *The Travel Journals of Antonio de Beatis*, trans. J. T. Hale and J. M. A. Lindon (London: Hakluyt Society, 1976)

De Damhouder, Joost, *La practique et enchiridion des causes criminelles* (Louvain: Jehan Bathen, 1555) <https://gallica.bnf.fr/ark:/12148/bpt6k536727>

England's Immigrants 1330–1550: Resident Aliens in the Late Middle Ages <http://england-simmigrants.com>

Fitch, Marc, ed., *Index to Testamentary Records in the Commissary Court of London, 1374–1570*, Historical Manuscripts Commission, JP 12–13, 2 vols (London: HMSO, 1969)

Hall, Edward, *Hall's Chronicle*, ed. Henry Ellis (London: J. Johnson, 1809)

Howes, Edmund, *The Annales, or a Generall Chronicle of England, Begun First by Maister John Stow* (London: Thomas Dawson for Thomas Adams, 1615)

Jenks, Stuart, ed., *The London Customs Accounts*, Hansischer Geschichtsverein, 74 (Cologne: Böhlau, 2018) <https://www.hansischergeschichtsverein.de/london-customs-accounts>

Lang, R. G., ed., *Two Tudor Subsidy Rolls for the City of London, 1541 and 1582* (London: London Record Society, 1993)

'London Lickpenny', in *Medieval English Political Writings*, ed. James M. Dean, TEAMS Middle English Texts (Kalamazoo: Medieval Institute Publications, 1996)

Mackman, Jonathan, and Matthew Stevens, 'Court of Common Pleas: The National Archives, CP40, 1399–1500', (*British History Online*, 2010) <http://www.british-history.ac.uk/no-series/common-pleas/1399-1500>

Nederlandse Familienamenbank <https://www.cbgfamilienamen.nl/nfb/>

'Ordinances of the Orphanage of Kortrijk' <http://www.diachronie.nl/corpora/chna/document/kortrijk_1411_1>

Palmer, Robert, ed., 'Anglo-American Legal Tradition', *Anglo-American Legal Tradition*, 2011 <http://aalt.law.uh.edu/>

Pepys, Samuel. *The Diary of Samuel Pepys*, ed. Henry B. Wheatley and Phil Gyford (New York: Brainard, 1893) <https://www.pepysdiary.com/>

Schayes, A. G. B., ed., 'Inventaire des joyaux et curiosités du Duc de Brabant, Jean IV, en 1419', *Annales de l'Académie royale d'archéologie de Belgique* 9 (1852), 156–58

Stamp, A. E., et al., eds *Calendar of Close Rolls*. 47 vols (London: HMSO, 1900–63)

The Statutes of the Realm, 11 vols (London: G. Eyre and A. Strahan, 1810–28)

Stow, John, *A Survey of London*, ed. Charles Lethbridge Kingsford, 2 vols (Oxford: Clarendon Press, 1908)

Sutton, Anne F., and Livia Visser-Fuchs, ed., *The Book of Privileges of the Merchant Adventurers of England, 1296–1483* (London: British Academy, 2009)

Twiss, Travers, *Monumenta Juridica: The Black Book of the Admiralty*, 4 vols (London: Longman, 1871–76)

Welch, Charles, ed., *Register of Freemen in the City of London in the reigns of Henry VIII and Edward VI* (London: London and Middlesex Archaeological Society, 1908)

Secondary sources

Adams, Joseph Quincy, 'The Conventual Buildings of Blackfriars, London, and the Playhouses Constructed Therein', *Studies in Philology* 14 (1917), 64–87

Anstruther, Godfrey, 'The Last Days of the London Blackfriars', *Archivum Fratrum Praedicatorum* 45 (1975), 213–36

Archer, Ian W., *The History of the Haberdashers' Company* (Chichester: Phillimore and Co., 1991)

Archer, Ian W., *The Pursuit of Stability: Social Relations in Elizabethan London* (Cambridge: Cambridge University Press, 1991)

Baker, Sir John, *Oxford History of the Laws of England*, VI, 1483–1558 (Oxford: Oxford University Press, 2003)

Barron, Caroline M., *London in the Later Middle Ages: Government and People 1200–1500* (Oxford: Oxford University Press, 2004)

Barron, Caroline M., and Matthew Davies, ed., *The Religious Houses of London and Middlesex* (London: Institute of Historical Research, 2007)

Barron, Caroline M., and Laura Wright, 'The London Middle English Guild Certificates of 1388–9', *Nottingham Medieval Studies* 39 (1995), 108–45

Bedford, Richard P., *St. James the Less: A Study in Christian Iconography* (London: Quaritch, 1911)

Bellamy, John G., *The Criminal Trial in Later Medieval England: Felony Before the Courts from Edward I to the Sixteenth Century* (Toronto: University of Toronto Press, 1998)

Benskin, Michael, Margaret Laing, M. L. Samuels, Angus McIntosh, Vasilis Karaiskos, and Keith Williamson, ed., 'General Introduction', in *An Electronic Version of A Linguistic Atlas of Late Mediaeval English* (Edinburgh: Angus McIntosh Centre for Historical Linguistics, University of Edinburgh, 2013) <http://www.lel.ed.ac.uk/ihd/elalme/intros/atlas_gen_intro.html>

Berry, Charlotte, 'Guilds, Immigration, and Immigrant Economic Organization: Alien Goldsmiths in London, 1480–1540', *Journal of British Studies* 60 (2021), 534–62

Blockmans, Wim, Bert De Munck, and Peter Stabel, 'Economic Vitality: Urbanisation, Regional Complementarity and European Interaction', in *City and Society in the Low Countries, 1100–1600*, ed. Bruno Blondé, Marc Boone, and Anne-Laure Van Bruaene (Cambridge: Cambridge University Press, 2020), pp. 22–58

Blondé, Bruno, Marc Boone, and Anne-Laure Van Bruaene, ed., *City and Society in the Low Countries, 1100–1600* (Cambridge: Cambridge University Press, 2020)

Blondé, Bruno, Frederik Buylaert, Jan Dumolyn, and Peter Stabel, 'Living Together in the City: Social Relationships Between Norm and Practice', in *City and Society in the Low Countries, 1100–1600*, ed. Bruno Blondé, Marc Boone, and Anne-Laure Van Bruaene (Cambridge: Cambridge University Press, 2020), pp. 59–92

Boone, Marc, and Peter Stabel, 'New Burghers in the Late Medieval Towns of Flanders and Brabant: Conditions of Entry, Rules and Reality', in *Neubürger im späten Mittelalter: Migration und Austausch in der Städtelandschaft des Alten Reiches (1250–1550)*, ed. Rainer Christoph Schwinges and Roland Gerber (Berlin: Duncker & Humblot, 2002), pp. 317–32

Bratchel, M. E., 'Regulation and Group-Consciousness in the Later History of London's Italian Merchant Colonies', *Journal of European Economic History* 9 (1980), 585–610

Broekhuijsen-Kruijer, Klara H., *The Masters of the Dark Eyes: Late Medieval Manuscript Painting in Holland* (Turnhout: Brepols, 2009)

Brown, Andrew, and Jan Dumolyn, ed., *Medieval Bruges, c.850–1550* (Cambridge: Cambridge University Press, 2018)

Brown, Michelle, *A Guide to Western Historical Scripts from Antiquity to 1600* (London: British Library, 1993)

Buckland, Kirstie, 'Cappers', in *Encyclopedia of Medieval Dress and Textiles*, ed. Gale Owen-Crocker, Elizabeth Coatsworth, and Maria Hayward (Leiden: Brill, 2016), 110–12

Burnley, David, 'Curial Prose in England', *Speculum* 61 (1986), 593–614

Caldicott, J. W., *The Values of Old English Silver and Sheffield Plate from the XVth to the XIXth Centuries* (London: Bemrose, 1906)

Carlin, Martha, *Medieval Southwark* (London: Hambledon Press, 1996)

Cartlidge, Neil, 'Medieval Romance Mischief', in *Romance Rewritten: The Evolution of Middle English Romance*, ed. Elizabeth Archibald, Megan G. Leitch, and Corinne J. Saunders (Cambridge: D. S. Brewer, 2018), pp. 27–48

Carus-Wilson, E. M., *Medieval Merchant Venturers: Collected Studies*, 2d edn (London: Methuen, 1967)

Cheney, C. R, *A Handbook of Dates for Students of British History* (Cambridge: Cambridge University Press, 1997)

Clemens, Raymond, and Timothy Graham, *Introduction to Manuscript Studies* (Ithaca: Cornell University Press, 2007)

Coatsworth, Elizabeth, 'Hurers', in *Encyclopedia of Medieval Dress and Textiles*, ed. Gale Owen-Crocker, Elizabeth Coatsworth, and Maria Hayward (Leiden: Brill, 2016), 284

Coatsworth, Elizabeth, and Gale Owen-Crocker, *Clothing the Past: Surviving Garments from Early Medieval to Early Modern Western Europe* (Leiden: Brill, 2018)

Colson, Justin, 'Negotiating Merchant Identities: The Stockfishmongers and London's Companies Merging and Dividing, c.1450–1550', in *Medieval Merchants and Money: Essays in Honour of James L. Bolton*, ed. M. Allen and M. Davies (Institute of Historical Research, 2016), pp. 3–20

Colson, Justin, 'Alien Communities and Alien Fraternities in Later Medieval London', *London Journal* 35 (2010), 111–43

Consitt, Frances, *The London Weavers' Company*, 2 vols (Oxford: Clarendon Press, 1933)

Crean, J. F., 'Hats and the Fur Trade', *Canadian Journal of Economics and Political Science* 28 (1963), 373–86

Crowfoot, Elisabeth, Frances Pritchard, and Kay Staniland, *Textiles and Clothing c.1150–c.1450: Finds from Excavations in London, c.1150–c.1450*, Museum of London: Medieval Finds from Excavations in London (London: HMSO, 1992)

Database of Dutch Family Names, <https://www.cbgfamiliennamen.nl/nfb>

Dauven, Bernard, 'Composition et rémission au XVe siècle: confusion, concurrence ou complémentarité? Le cas du Brabant', in *Préférant miséricorde à rigueur de justice: pratiques de la grâce (XIIIe-XVIIIe siècles)*, ed. Bernard Dauven and Xavier Rousseaux (Louvain-la-Neuve: Presses Universitaires de Louvain, 2017), pp. 31–52 <http://books.openedition.org/pucl/3365>

Davids, Karel, 'Apprenticeship and Guild Control in the Netherlands, c.1450–1800', in *Learning on the Shop Floor: Historical Perspectives on Apprenticeship*, ed. Bert de Munck, Steven L. Kaplan, and Hugo Soly (New York: Berghahn, 2007), pp. 65–84

Davies, Matthew P., 'The Tailors of London and Their Guild, c.1300–1500' (unpublished doctoral dissertation, University of Oxford, 1994) <https://ora.ox.ac.uk/objects/uuid:577c6a65-92cb-4f30-b4fd-e123096dbf43>

Davies, Matthew P., and Ann Saunders, *The History of the Merchant Taylors' Company* (Leeds: Maney, 2004)

Davies, Matthew, "'Writing, Making and Engrocyng": Clerks, Guilds and Identity in Late Medieval London', in *Medieval Merchants and Money: Essays in Honour of James L. Bolton*, ed. Martin Allen and Matthew Davies (London: Institute of Historical Research, 2016), pp. 21–41

Davies, Matthew, 'Aliens, Crafts and Guilds in Late Medieval London', in *Medieval Londoners: Essays to Mark the Eightieth Birthday of Caroline M. Barron*, ed. Elizabeth A. New and Christian Steer (London: University of London Press, 2019), pp. 119–48

Davies, Matthew, 'Citizens and "Foreyns": Crafts, Guilds and Regulation in Late Medieval London', in *Between Regulation and Freedom: Work and Manufactures in European Cities, 14th–18th Centuries*, ed. A. Caracausi, Matthew Davies, and L. Mocarelli (Newcastle: Cambridge Scholars, 2018), pp. 1–21

Davies, Matthew, 'Crown, City and Guild in Late Medieval London', in *London and Beyond: Essays in Honour of Derek Keene*, ed. Matthew Davies and James A. Galloway (London: Institute of Historical Research, 2012), pp. 247–68

Davies, Matthew, 'Lobbying Parliament: The London Companies in the Fifteenth Century', *Parliamentary History*, 23 (2004), 136–48

De Marez, Guillame, *Le Compagnonnages des chapelliers Bruxellois* (Brussels: Lamertin, 1909)

De Munck, Bert, 'One Counter and Your Own Account: Redefining Illicit Labour in Early Modern Antwerp', *Urban History*, 37 (2010), 26–44

De Munck, Bert, *Technologies of Learning: Apprenticeship in Antwerp Guilds from the 15th Century to the End of the Ancien Régime* (Turnhout: Brepols Publishers, 2007)

De Munck, Bert, and Hilde de Ridder-Symoens, 'Education and Knowledge: Theory and Practice in an Urban Context', in *City and Society in the Low Countries, 1100–1600*, ed. Bruno Blondé, Marc Boone, and Anne-Laure Van Bruaene (Cambridge: Cambridge University Press, 2020), pp. 220–54

De Munck, Bert, Steven L. Kaplan, and Hugo Soly, ed., *Learning on the Shop Floor: Historical Perspectives on Apprenticeship* (New York: Berghahn, 2007)

De Munck, Bert, Raoul De Kerf, and Annelies De Bie, 'Apprenticeships in the Southern Netherlands, c.1400-c.1800', in *Apprenticeship in Early Modern Europe*, ed. Maarten Roy Prak and Patrick Wallis (Cambridge: Cambridge University Press, 2020), pp. 217–46

De Wulf, Chris, *Klankatlas van Het Veertiende-Eeuwse Middelnederlands* (Ghent: Koninklijke Academie voor Nederlandse Taal en Letteren, 2019) <https://bouwstoffen.kantl.be/>

Deecke, Wilhelm, *Die Deutsche Verwandtschaftsnamen: Eine Sprichwissenschaftliche Untersuchung* (Weimar: Böhlau, 1870)

Derolez, Albert, *The Palaeography of Gothic Manuscript Books from the Twelfth to the Early Sixteenth Century* (Cambridge: Cambridge University Press, 2003)

Digital Library for Dutch Literature <http://www.dbnl.org/>

Duckworth, Harry, *The Early History of Feltmaking in London 1250–1604*, Research Paper No. 1 (London: Worshipful Company of Feltmakers, 2013)

Duckworth, Harry, *The Feltmakers' Wool Adventure, 1610–24*, Research Paper No. 2 (London: Worshipful Company of Feltmakers, 2015)

Duckworth, Harry, *The Struggle for Recognition, 1604–1667*, Research Paper No. 3 (London: Worshipful Company of Feltmakers, 2019)

Dugdale, William, *Monasticon Anglicanum: A History of the Abbies and Other Monasteries, Hospitals, Frieries, and Cathedral and Collegiate Churches, with Their Dependencies, in England and Wales*, ed. Henry Ellis, 6 vols (London: Longman, Hurst, Rees, Orme & Brown, 1817)

Dupont, Guy, 'Le temps des compositions: Pratiques judiciaires à Bruges et à Gand du XIVe au XVIe siècle', in *Préférant miséricorde à rigueur de justice: Pratiques de la grâce (XIIIe–XVIIe siècles)*, ed. Bernard Dauven and Xavier Rousseaux (Louvain-la-Neuve: Presses Universitaires de Louvain, 2017), pp. 55–61 <http://books.openedition.org/pucl/3365>

Dyer, Christopher, *An Age of Transition: Economy and Society in England in the Later Middle Ages* (Oxford: Oxford University Press, 2005)

Epps, Patience, John Huehnergard, and Na'ama Pat-El, ed., 'Contact Among Genetically Related Languages', *The Journal of Language Contact* 6 (2013), 209–19

Epstein, Stephan R., 'Labour Mobility, Journeymen Organisations and Markets in Skilled Labour in Europe, 14th–18th Centuries', in *Le technicien dans la cité en Europe occidentale, 1250–1650*, ed. Mathieu Arnoux and Piere Monnet, Collection de l'Ećole française de Rome, 325 (Rome: Ećole française de Rome, 2004), pp. 251–69

Epstein, Stephan R., and Maarten Roy Prak, *Guilds, Innovation, and the European Economy, 1400–1800* (Cambridge: Cambridge University Press, 2008)

French, Katherine L., *Household Goods and Good Households in Late Medieval London: Consumption and Domesticity After the Plague* (Philadelphia: Pennsylvania University Press, 2021)

Gowler, James, *James Through the Centuries* (Chichester: Wiley, 2014)

Gross, Charles, 'Modes of Trial in the Mediæval Boroughs of England', *Harvard Law Review*, 15av (1902), 691–706

Guidi-Bruscoli, Francesco, and Jessica Lutkin, 'Perception, Identity and Culture: The Italian Communities in Fifteenth-Century London and Southampton Revisited', in *Resident Aliens in Later Medieval England*, ed. Nicola McDonald, W. Mark Ormrod, and Craig Taylor (Turnhout: Brepols, 2017), pp. 89–104

Heal, Chris, *Felt-Hatting in Bristol & South Gloucestershire. I: The Rise*, ALHA Books, 5 (Bristol: David Harrison Printing for Avon Local History & Archaeology, 2013)

Heal, Christopher John, 'The Felt Hat Industry of Bristol and South Gloucestershire, 1530–1909' (unpublished doctoral dissertation, University of Bristol, 2012) <https://research-information.bris.ac.uk/en/studentTheses/4db07a69-269c-456c-9687-e9cfb63ce929>

Highley, Christopher. *Blackfriars in Early Modern London: Theater, Church, and Neighborhood* (Oxford: Oxford University Press, 2022)

Holder, Nick, *The Friaries of Medieval London: From Foundation to Dissolution* (Woodbridge: Boydell, 2017)

House, Anthony Paul, 'The City of London and the Problem of the Liberties, c1540–c1640' (unpublished doctoral dissertation, Oxford University, 2006)

Hovland, Stephanie R., 'Apprenticeship in Later Medieval London (c.1300–c.1530)' (unpublished doctoral dissertation, University of London, 2006)

Hsy, Jonathan, 'City', in *A Handbook of Middle English Studies*, ed. Marion Turner, (Hoboken, New Jersey: Wiley, 2013), pp. 315–29

Johnson, A. H., *The History of the Worshipful Company of the Drapers of London*, 5 vols (Oxford: Clarendon Press, 1914)

Jordan, Richard, *Handbook of Middle English Grammar: Phonology* (The Hague: Mouton, 1974)

Kilburn-Toppin, Jasmine. *Crafting Identities: Artisan Culture in London, c.1550–1640* (Manchester: Manchester University Press, 2021)

Kim, Ki-ch'ang, *Aliens in Medieval Law: The Origins of Modern Citizenship* (Cambridge: Cambridge University Press, 2000)

Kirk, R. E. G., and Ernest F. Kirk, *Returns of Aliens Dwelling in the City and Suburbs of London from the Reign of Henry VIII. to That of James I*, Publications of the Huguenot Society of London, 10, 2 vols (Aberdeen: Aberdeen University Press, 1900)

Kubaschewski, Elizabeth, 'Binomials in Caxton's Ovid (Book I)', in *Binomials in the History of English*, ed. Joanna Kopaczyk and Hans Sauer (Cambridge: Cambridge University Press, 2017), pp. 141–58

Kwakkel, Erik, 'Discarded Parchment as Writing Support in English Manuscript Culture', *English Manuscript Studies 1100–1700*, 17 (2012), 238–61

Kwakkel, Erik, and Rodney Thomson, 'Codicology', in *The European Book in the Twelfth Century*, ed. Erik Kwakkel and Rodney Thomson (Cambridge: Cambridge University Press, 2018), pp. 9–24

Lahey, Stephanie, 'Offcut Zone Parchment in Manuscript Codices from Later Medieval England' (unpublished doctoral dissertation, University of Victoria, 2021)

Lambert, Bart, '"I, Edmund": A Microhistory of an Immigrant Churchwarden in Fifteenth-Century Colchester', in *People, Power and Identity in the Late Middle Ages: Essays in Memory of W. Mark Ormrod*, ed. Gwilym Dodd, Helen Lacey, and Anthony Musson (London: Routledge, 2021), pp. 92–114

Lambert, Bart, 'Citizenry and Nationality: The Participation of Immigrants in Urban Politics in Later Medieval England', *History Workshop Journal* 90 (2020), 52–73

Lambert, Bart, and Milan Pajic, 'Immigration and the Common Profit: Native Cloth Workers, Flemish Exiles, and Royal Policy in Fourteenth-Century London', *Journal of British Studies* 55 (2016), 633–57

Lee, John S., 'Thrums', in *Encyclopedia of Medieval Dress and Textiles*, online edition, ed. Gale Owen-Crocker, Elizabeth Coatsworth, and Maria Hayward (Leiden, 2021), <http://dx.doi.org/10.1163/2213-2139_emdt_SIM_001171>

Leech, Donald, 'Stability and Change at the End of the Middle Ages: Coventry, 1450–1525', *Midland History* 34 (2009), 1–21

Levelt, Sjoerd, and Ad Putter, *North Sea Crossings: The Literary Heritage of Anglo-Dutch Relations, 1066–1688* (Oxford: Bodleian Library, 2021)

Liddy, Christian D., *Contesting the City: The Politics of Citizenship in English Towns, 1250–1530* (Oxford: Oxford University Press, 2017)

Liddy, Christian D., and Jelle Haemers, 'Popular Politics in the Late Medieval City: York and Bruges', *The English Historical Review*, 128 (2013), 771–805

Lis, Catharina, and Hugo Soly, 'Craft Guilds in Comparative Perspective: The Northern and Southern Netherlands, a Survey', in *Craft Guilds in the Early Modern Low Countries: Work, Power, and Representation*, ed. Maarten Prak, Catharina Lis, Jan Lucassen, and Hugo Soly (London: Routledge, 2006), pp. 1–31

Lis, Catharina, and Hugo Soly, 'De Macht van "Vrije Arbeiders": Collectieve Acties van Hoedenmakersgezellen in de Zuidelijke Nederlanden (Zestiende-Negentiende Eeuw)', in *Werken volgens de Regels. Ambachten in Brabant en Vlaanderen, 1500–1800*, ed. Catharina Lis and Hugo Soly (Brussels, 1994), pp. 15–50

Luu, Lien Bich, 'Aliens and Their Impact on the Goldsmiths' Craft in London in the Sixteenth Century', in *Goldsmiths, Silversmiths, and Bankers: Innovation and the Transfer of Skill, 1550 to 1750*, ed. David Mitchell (Stroud, Gloucestershire: Alan Sutton, 1995), pp. 43–52

Luu, Lien Bich, 'Alien Communities in Transition, 1570–1640', in *Immigrants in Tudor and Early Stuart England*, ed. Nigel Goose and Lien Bich Luu (Brighton: Sussex Academic Press, 2005), pp. 192–210

Luu, Lien Bich, *Immigrants and the Industries of London, 1500–1700* (Aldershot, Ashgate, 2005)

Luu, Lien Bich, 'Natural-Born versus Stranger-Born Subjects: Aliens and Their Status in Elizabethan London', in *Immigrants in Tudor and Early Stuart England*, ed. Nigel Goose and Lien Bich Luu (Brighton: Sussex Academic Press, 2005), pp. 57–75

Maes, Louis, *Vijf Eeuwen Stedelijk Strafrecht. Bijdragen tot de Rechts- en Cultuurgeschiedenis der Nederlanden* (Antwerp: De Sikkel, 1974)

Marnef, Guido, and Anne-Laure Van Bruaene, 'Civic Religion: Community, Identity, and Religious Transformation', in *City and Society in the Low Countries, 1100–1600*, ed. Bruno Blondé, Marc Boone, and Anne-Laure Van Bruaene (Cambridge: Cambridge University Press, 2020), pp. 128–61

McSheffrey, Shannon, 'Research: Residents of St Martin Le Grand' <https://shannon-mcsheffrey.wordpress.com/research/>

McSheffrey, Shannon, 'Stranger Artisans and the London Sanctuary of St Martin Le Grand in the Reign of Henry VIII', *Journal of Medieval and Early Modern Studies* 43 (2013), 545–71

McSheffrey, Shannon, *Seeking Sanctuary: Crime, Mercy, and Politics in English Courts, 1400–1550* (Oxford: Oxford University Press, 2017)

McSheffrey, Shannon, 'Liberties of London: Social Networks, Sexual Disorder, and Peculiar Jurisdictions in the Late Medieval English Metropolis', in *Crossing Borders: Boundaries and Margins in Medieval and Early Modern Britain*, ed. Krista J. Kesselring and Sara M. Butler (Leiden: Brill, 2018), pp. 216–36

McSheffrey, Shannon, 'Quarrel over a "Frowe"', *Sanctuary Seekers in England, 1394–1557* (2020) <https://sanctuaryseekers.ca/2020/07/06/frowe/>

Medieval Londoners Database (New York: Fordham University, 2020) <https://mld.ace.fordham.edu>

Milroy, James, and Lesley Milroy, 'Linguistic Change, Social Network, and Speaker Innovation', *Journal of Linguistics* 21 (1985), 339–84

Miriam-Wagner, Esther, Bettina Beinhoff, and Ben Outhwaite, ed., *Merchants of Innovation: The Languages of Medieval Traders* (Berlin: Mouton de Gruyter, 2017)

Müller, Miriam, 'Social Control and the Hue and Cry in Two Fourteenth-Century Villages', *Journal of Medieval History* 31 (2005), 29–53

Nightingale, Pamela, *A Medieval Mercantile Community: The Grocers' Company and the Politics and Trade of London, 1000–1485* (New Haven, Connecticut: Yale University Press, 1995)

Ormrod, W. Mark, 'England's Immigrants, 1330–1550: Aliens in Later Medieval and Early Tudor England', *Journal of British Studies* 59 (2020), 245–63

Ormrod, W. Mark, Bart Lambert, and Jonathan Mackman, *Immigrant England, 1300–1550* (Manchester: Manchester University Press, 2019)

Ormrod, W. Mark, and Jonathan Mackman, 'Resident Aliens in Later Medieval England: Sources, Contexts, Debates', in *Resident Aliens in Later Medieval England*, ed. Nicola McDonald, W. Mark Ormrod, and Craig Taylor (Turnhout: Brepols, 2017), pp. 1–32

Owen-Crocker, Gale, Elizabeth Coatsworth, and Maria Hayward, ed., *Encyclopedia of Medieval Dress and Textiles* (Leiden: Brill, 2016)

Palmer, Raymund, 'The Black Friars of London', *Merry England* 12 and 13 (1889), 12, 428–42; and 13, 33–43, 116–32, 191–205, 266–88, 354–66

Parkes, M. B., *English Cursive Book Hands, 1250–1500* (Oxford: Oxford University Press, 1969)

Peters, Robert, Christian Fischer, and Norbert Nagel, *Atlas Spätmittelalterlicher Schreibsprachen des Niederdeutschen Altlandes und angrenzender Gebiete*, 3 vols (Berlin: De Gruyter, 2017)

Pettegree, Andrew, *Foreign Protestant Communities in Sixteenth-Century London* (Oxford: Clarendon Press, 1986)

Phythian-Adams, Charles, *Desolation of a City: Coventry and the Urban Crisis of the Late Middle Ages* (Cambridge: Cambridge University Press, 1979)

Powell, Edward, 'Settlement of Disputes by Arbitration in Fifteenth-Century England', *Law and History Review* 2 (1984), 21–43

Prak, Maarten, *Citizens without Nations: Urban Citizenship in Europe and the World, c.1000–1789* (Cambridge: Cambridge University Press, 2018)

Prak, Maarten, and Patrick Wallis, ed., *Apprenticeship in Early Modern Europe* (Cambridge: Cambridge University Press, 2020)

Putter, Ad, 'An East Anglian Poem in a London Manuscript? The Date and Dialect of the Court of Love in Cambridge, Trinity College, MS R.3.19', in *Historical Dialectology in the Digital Age*, ed. Rhona Alcorn et al. (Edinburgh: Edinburgh University Press, 2019), pp. 212–43

Putter, Ad, 'Dutch, French and English in Caxton's Recuyell of the Historyes of Troye', in *Medieval Romance, Arthurian Literature: Essays in Honour of Elizabeth Archibald*, ed. A. S. G. Edwards (Cambridge: D. S. Brewer, 2021), pp. 205–26

Putter, Ad, 'Materials for a Social History of the Dutch Language in Medieval Britain: Three Case Studies from Wales, Scotland, and England', *Dutch Crossing: Journal of Low Countries Studies* 45 (2021), 97–111

Rappaport, Steve, *Worlds Within Worlds: Structures of Life in Sixteenth-Century London* (Cambridge: Cambridge University Press, 1989)

Ravenhill, Joshua, 'The Earliest Recorded Spectacle Makers in Late Medieval England: Immigration and Foreign Expertise', *Notes and Queries* 65 (2018), 11–13

Raye, Lee, 'The Early Extinction Date of the Beaver (Castor Fiber) in Britain', *Historical Biology* 27 (2015), 1029–41

Reddan, Minnie, and Jens Röhrkasten, 'The Black Friars', in *The Religious Houses of London and Middlesex*, ed. Caroline M. Barron and Matthew Davies (London: Institute of Historical Research, 2007), pp. 116–21

Reith, Reinhold, 'Circulation of Skilled Labour in Late Medieval and Early Modern Central Europe', in *Guilds, Innovation, and the European Economy, 1400–1800*, ed. Stephan R. Epstein and Maarten Roy Prak (Cambridge: Cambridge University Press, 2008), pp. 114–42

Richardson, Malcolm, *Middle-Class Writing in Late Medieval London* (London: Routledge, 2011)

Richter, Michael, *Sprache und Gesellschaft im Mittelalter* (Stuttgart: Hiersemann, 1979)

Rigby, S. H., *English Society in the Later Middle Ages: Class, Status, and Gender* (New York: St Martin's Press, 1995)

Rodes, Michael, 'A Pair of Fifteenth-Century Spectacles Frames from the City of London', *The Antiquaries Journal* 62 (1982), 57–73

Röhrkasten, Jens, *The Mendicant Houses of Medieval London, 1221–1539* (London: Münster, 2004)

Rosser, Gervase, 'Crafts, Guilds and the Negotiation of Work in the Medieval Town', *Past & Present* 154 (1997), 3–31

Rosser, Gervase, 'Going to the Fraternity Feast: Commensality and Social Relations in Late Medieval England', *Journal of British Studies* 33 (1994), 430–46

Rosser, Gervase, *The Art of Solidarity in the Middle Ages: Guilds in England 1250–1550* (Oxford: Oxford University Press, 2015)

Rubin, Miri, *Cities of Strangers: Making Lives in Medieval Europe* (Cambridge: Cambridge University Press, 2020)

Rundle, David, *The Renaissance Reform of the Book and Britain* (Cambridge: Cambridge University Press, 2019)

Sandy, Rhiannon, 'Apprenticeship Indentures and Apprentices in Medieval England, 1250–1500' (unpublished doctoral dissertation, University of Swansea, 2021)

Schulz, Knut, 'Handwerkerwanderungen und Neuburger Im Spätmittelalter', in *Neuburger im Späten Mittelalter: Migration und Austausch in der Städtelandschaft des alten Reiches (1250–1550)*, ed. Rainer Christoph Schwinges (Berlin: Duncker & Humblot, 2002), pp. 445–78

Selwood, Jacob, *Diversity and Difference in Early Modern London* (Farnham: Ashgate, 2010)

Simons, Rosemary, and Vance Mead, 'CP40 Indices', in *Anglo-American Legal Tradition*, ed. Robert C. Palmer <http://aalt.law.uh.edu/Indices/CP40Indices/CP40_Indices.html>

Smeyers, Maurits, *Flemish Miniatures from the 8th to the Mid-16th Century* (Turnhout: Brepols, 1999)

Smit, H. J., *Bronnen tot de Geschiedenis van den Handel met Engeland, Schotland en Ierland 1150–1585* (The Hague: Nijhoff, 1942)

Smith, Lucy Toulmin, ed., *English Gilds: The Original Ordinances of More than One Hundred Early English Guilds*, EETS, original series 40 (London: Trubner, 1870)

Stabel, Peter, 'Social Mobility and Apprenticeship in Late Medieval Flanders', in *Learning on the Shop Floor: Historical Perspectives on Apprenticeship*, ed. Bert De Munck, Steven L. Kaplan, and Hugo Soly (New York: Berghahn, 2007), pp. 158–78

Stallaert, K., *Glossarium van verouderde rechtstermen, kunstwoorden en andere uitdrukkingen uit Vlaamsche, Brabantsche en Limburgsche oorkonden*, 2 vols (Leiden: Brill: 1886–91)

Sutton, Anne F., *The Mercery of London: Trade, Goods and People, 1130–1578* (Aldershot: Ashgate, 2005)

Swanson, Heather, *Medieval Artisans: An Urban Class in Late Medieval England* (Oxford: Basil Blackwell, 1989)

Thielemans, Marie-Rose, *Bourgogne et Angleterre: Relations politiques et économiques entre les Pays-Bas et l'Angleterre, 1435–1467* (Brussels: Presses Universitaires de Bruxelles, 1966)

Thompson, John, *A Treatise on Hat-Making and Felting* (Philadelphia: Henry Carey Baird, 1868)

Twycross, Meg, 'Some Aliens in York and Their Overseas Connections: Up to c.1470', *Leeds Studies in English* 29 (1998), 359–80

Unwin, George, *Industrial Organization in the Sixteenth and Seventeenth Centuries* (Oxford: Clarendon Press, 1904)

Unwin, George, *The Gilds and Companies of London* (London: Methuen, 1908)

Van der Wal, Marijke J., *Geschiedenis van het Nederlands* (Utrecht: Spectrum, 1992)

Van Loey, A., *Middelnederlandse Spraakkunst. Deel II. Klankleer* (Groningen: Wolters-Noordhoff, 1976)

Van Moock, S. J. M, *Nieuw Fransch-Nederduitsch en Nederduitsch-Fransch Woordenboek* (Gouda: G. B. van Goor, 1849)

Van Reenen, Pieter, Matthijs Brouwer, and Evert Wattel, 'Middelnederlands: Vormen en Constructies' <https://www.middelnederlands.nl/>

Vanhemelryck, Fernand, *De Criminaliteit in de Ammanie van Brussel van de Late Middeleeuwen tot het Einde van het Ancien Regime (1404–1798)* (Brussels: Koninklijke Academie voor Wetenschappen, Letteren en Schone Kunsten van België, 1961)

Veale, Elspeth M., *The English Fur Trade in the Later Middle Ages*, London Record Society 38 (London: London Record Society, 2003) <https://www.british-history.ac.uk/london-record-soc/vol38>

Viaene, Antoon, 'Hoedenvlechters uit Gelderland Werkzaam in Brugge Omstreeks 1440', *Biekorf* 70 (1969), 163–68

Wakelin, Daniel, *Designing English: Early Literature on the Page* (Oxford: Bodleian Library, 2018)

Walker-Meikle, Kathleen, 'Felt-and Hat-Making Workshop (School of Historical Dress)', *Renaissance Skin*, 2018 <https://renaissanceskin.ac.uk/news/felt-and-hat-making-workshop-school-historical-dress/>

Wattel, Evert, and Pieter van Reenen, 'Probabilistic Maps', in *Language and Space: An International Handbook of Linguistic Variation*, ed. Alfred Lameli, Roland Kehrein, and Stefan Rabanus (Berlin: De Gruyter, 2011), 2 vols, II, pp. 495–508

Weinstein, Rosemary, *The History of the Worshipful Company of Feltmakers, 1604–2004* (Chichester: Phillimore, 2004)

Winford, Donald, *An Introduction to Contact Linguistics* (Oxford: Blackwell, 2003)

Yungblut, Laura Hunt, *Strangers Settled Here amongst Us: Policies, Perceptions, and the Presence of Aliens in Elizabethan England* (London: Routledge, 1996)

Index

The index covers the main text and notes but excludes the transcribed texts. Page numbers in *italics* indicate an illustration or map, and the suffix *t* indicates a table. References to footnotes are in the form 12n.34.

MEDIEVAL AND RENAISSANCE CLOTHING AND TEXTILES

Previous volumes in this series:

Printed in the United States
by Baker & Taylor Publisher Services